Patronage Copy No.386

This book was made possible by
the support of Patrons who pre-paid for their
copies. This copy was subscribed for by

KING ALFRED'S
COLLEGE, WINCHESTER

to whom sincere thanks are expressed

Lou Warwick

Lou Warwick

8 November 1978

DRAMA THAT SMELLED

Or "Early Drama in Northampton and Hereabouts"

Written and published
by
LOU WARWICK

Obtainable from the Publisher at 54 St. George's Avenue,
Northampton, and from
R. HARRIS & SON, LTD, 6 Bridge Street, Northampton.
KINGSTHORPE BOOKSHOP, 6-8 Harborough Road, Northampton.
J. W. McKENZIE, 12 Stoneleigh Park Road, Ewell, Epsom, Surrey.
F. A. MOORE, 33 Montagu Street, Kettering.
MOTLEY BOOKS, Mottisfont Abbey, Romsey, Hampshire.
BASIL SAVAGE, 46 Brookfield, Highgate West Hill, London N6 6AT.

Dedicated to the late Bernard Holloway

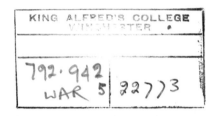
"If one half of the people enjoy any particular form of amusement or sport the other half endeavours to get a Bill through the Legislature prohibiting it"

—*Philadelphia Ledger, 1913*

RUNNING ORDER

OVERTURE—Thanks . . . & Un-Thanks   9

ROYAL CURTAIN RAISER—Deity in Drama   13

ACT THE FIRST: THE EARLY YEARS   31
    Scene One: Drama in the News   33
    Scene Two: The Drumless Durravans   53
    Scene Three: Garrick—The Greatest?   79

INTERLUDE—The Pariah Profession   87

ACT THE SECOND: KEMBLE & WHITLEY   141
    Scene One: Sans Sarah—The Kembles   143
    Scene Two: Strolling with Shatford   153
    Scene Three: Sans Jemmy—Nottingham and Derby   163

ACT THE THIRD: CUPBOARD DRAMA   185
    Scene One: Enter the Lincoln   187
    Scene Two: Theatre Un-Royal   199

PATRONS   205

NEXT PRODUCTION (and Positively Final and Farewell
    Appearance)   217

INDEX   221

By particular Defire of feveral Gentlemen *and* Ladies.
For the B E N E F I T of Mr. *William Dillon.*
Being pofitively the laft Night of Playing in Town.

On *Monday* Evening, being the 18th of *September*, *N. S.* will be Acted a T R A G E D Y, call'd,

THEODOSIUS:
O R, T H E
FORCE of LOVE.
C O N T A I N I N G,

A View of the Manner of Worfhip us'd by the primitive *Chriftians* under *Atticus* the High Prieft, Succeffor of Saint *Chryfoftom* ; alfo, a Magnificent Reprefentation of the Infide of the Temple, in which will be exhibited a curious tranfparent Scene, which difplays the Vifion of *Conftantine* the Great, which with the High Altar will be illuminated with upwards of *One Hundred* Wax Lights. The Scenery, Machinery, Decorations and Cloaths to be entirely New ; and the Characters of the Play to be drefs'd after the Ancient Manner of the *Romans* and *Perfians.*-------The Play-houfe will be left open all Day on *Monday*, for the Infpection of the Curious, and for the better Accommadion of thofe *Ladies* and *Gentlemen*, &c. who propofe favouring Mr. *Dillon* with their Company. ----- *The Doors will be open'd at Half an Hour after Five, and the Curtain go up at Half an Hour after* Six *to a Minute.*

The Part of Theodofius,		Mr. *W. Dillon.*	*The Part of*		Mrs. *Burt.*
Atticus,		Mr. *Dillon.*	Pulcheria,		
Leontine,	by	Mr. *Edwards.*	Maria,	by	Mrs. *Quelch.*
Marcian,		Mr. *Howell.*	Flavilla,		Mifs *Burt.*
Aranthes,		Mr. *Neal.*	*And the Part of*		Mrs. *Campbell.*
And the Part of Varanes,		Mr. *Quelch.*	Athenais,		

With Entertainments *of* SINGING *and* DANCING, *between the* ACTS, *particularly between the* 2d *and* 3d Mafk-all. 3d *and* 4th, *A favourite Song by Mrs.* Campbell, *call'd The* New Flown Birds. 4th *and* 5th, *A* Scaramouch Dance, *by Mr.* Quelch.

To which will be added, A *P A N T O M I M E* Entertainment, call'd,

HARLEQUIN MILLER:
O R, T H E
Art of Grinding Old Men and Women young.

The Whole to conclude with a Grand *Dance*, by Mr. and Mrs. *Quelch*, Mr. *Dillon*, Mrs. *Campbell*, Mr. *Edwards*, Mrs. *Burt*, &c. &c.

N. B. *Tickets* to be had at Mr. *Dillon's* Lodgings at the *White-Lion* in *Abington*-Street.
Pit 2 *s.* Gallery 1 *s.*

THE ONLY surviving eighteenth-century Northampton playbill is this one, apparently of 1752, the year when "New Style" was introduced and twelve days missed from September to bring the English calendar into line with the Continent. (*Northamptonshire County Library at Northampton*)

THE VISUAL REPRESENTATIONS

MAP OF NORTHAMPTON DISTRICT, 1774   14

ANNE OF DENMARK   25

ALTHORP—1669 drawing   26

ABINGTON ABBEY—17th Century drawing   26

PAGEANT AT ALTHORP in the 1930s   27

THE BEGGAR'S OPERA by Northampton Theatre Guild   28

OLD TOWN HALL in Abington Street, Northampton   32

ABINGTON STREET PLAYHOUSE, 1743 Advertisement   40

RIDING HOUSE THEATRE—1742 Advertisement   41

MAPS BEFORE AND AFTER the Dreadful Fire of 1675   42

WARWICK COMPANY, 1756 Advertisements   48

DURRAVANS 1768 Advertisements   52 and 58

RATE BOOK of St. Giles Parish, 1803   62

DURRAVANS 1768 and 1771 Advertisements   63, 69 and 75

THEATRE MAPS of Street and Town   64 and 65

BRIXWORTH 1769 Advertisement   68

CARLETONS 1772 Advertisement   75

SHAKESPEARE'S LAST DESCENDANT, A Memorial   78

WILLIAM CHARLES MACREADY   88

ALL SAINTS STATUE of Charles II drawn by R. C. Chatburn   95

ACT AGAINST THE DRAMA, 1737   109

NEW THEATRE, a dressing room warning   129

"A PHRENZY FOR SPOUTING", Scene from "All The World's a Stage"   130

ROGER KEMBLE   142

KEMBLES 1778 Advertisement   144

ARRIVING AT THE RIDING SCHOOL, drawing by R. C. Chatburn 152

SHATFORD PLAYBILLS, Towcester and Wellingborough 156 and 157

WHITLEY & HERBERT PLAYBILL, Lincoln 1775 162

BEYNON PLAYBILL, Stratford-upon-Avon, 1795 170

STAMFORD THEATRE 173

BLACK LION INN, St. Giles Street, Northampton 174

NEW THEATRE, in 20th Century Northampton 174

JOHN DRYDEN, statue in Abington Street, Northampton 174

HENRY COMPTON (alias Mackenzie) 174

ISABEL BATEMAN, Actress turned Nun 175

PROFESSOR ALLARDYCE NICOLL in his garden 176

BEYNON Advertisement, 1796 181

GRANTHAM THEATRE 186

LINCOLN COMPANY, 1802 and 1804 Advertisements 189

THEATRE, MAREFAIR, 1804 Appeal to Build 189

LETTER from Thomas Shaftoe Robertson to James Winston, 1804 197

LINCOLN PLAYBILL of "Castle Spectre", 1798 198

THEATRE, MAREFAIR, Advertisement of First Night, 1806 203

OVERTURE

THANKS...
AND UN-THANKS

*Explaining how this book is the first (yet the third)
in a series of four and how it came out despite the
worst efforts of British Governments in general and
the Post Office for what the land of the Penny Black
is currently suffering. And soliciting support for the
Last Lap...*

THANKS...
AND
UN-THANKS

This is the place in the two previous books in the Northampton Theatre History series where I thanked people who helped to make publication possible. This time I depart somewhat from that procedure. The third book has emerged despite the worst efforts of British Governments in general and the British Post Office in particular to make such publications impossible to print, and if you do manage to print them, prohibitively expensive to circulate. As if hell-bent on killing the Printed Word altogether.

By an attitude of complacency on the part of United Kingdom governments at both national and local level Inflation has been allowed to rage, at least until mid-summer, 1975, so that, as the Sunday Telegraph gave timely warning in October, 1974: "The civilised pleasures of dining in restaurants or buying books or travelling abroad or going to the theatre are occupying a shrinking place in our lives as the squeeze proceeds and what money is left after meeting the household bills must be spread more and more thinly."

By a concomitant policy of incredible inefficiency the Post Office of the land of the Penny Black has managed to produce a remarkable double bill, of second class service at twice the price, so that sending a book through the post now costs as much as would, not many years since, have bought the book. It also costs more to send a book 10 miles in Britain than several thousand miles to the farthest corners of the earth.

To both of these organisations go my sincerest un-thanks.

I hope that readers—Patrons in particular and Postmasters among them in most particular—will excuse these remarks, should they happen not to agree with them. It is a fact, of course, that all who help in bringing out these books do not necessarily agree with all or any opinions expressed in them. But being connected with the printed word in earning my living as well as enlivening my spare time by writing these books I beg leave to say my piece.

Now to the more pleasant subject of thanking those who have helped, not hindered. Some of those Patrons who are listed at the end of the book have assisted me not only with Drama That Smelled but also with Death of a Theatre (1960) and Theatre Un-Royal (1974). Some, in fact, have already trusted me with the money for the intended fourth and last in the series, The Mackenzies Called Compton, of which further details are given later.

For this present book and for the final one I have again been fortunate in securing distinguished Patrons-in-Chief. For this one it is Mr. Harry Greatorex, of Swanwick, Derbyshire, who had taken a proof-reader's interest in Theatre Un-Royal and who readily coughed up the first subscription to this book, on November 27, 1973. His splendid theatre collection and good advice have been of considerable assistance. For the final book Professor Allardyce Nicoll, the doyen of theatre historians no less, has most graciously agreed to be Patron-in-Chief.

Without the Patrons in general I could, of course, do nothing. They provide the capital and in a financial sense it is they who publish the books. When the present project began the target was for 300 Patrons but by the time the aforesaid villains of the piece had done their worst the aim had to be increased to 400; overall costs had gone up by one-third in the interim!

A special vote of thanks must go to Professor William B. Long, of New York City Community College, an early subscriber, who volunteered to help in any way he could, an offer too good to miss. He distributed leaflets in the U.S. and Canada, with a personal recommendation. Richard Chatburn drew the Riding House picture which appears on the dustcover and on Page 152; also the Charles II drawing on Page 95. The text was checked wholly by Mr. Greatorex and Mr. Victor Hatley and in part by Mr. Ian Mayes and Mr. Brian Carter. United Newspapers Ltd. made a donation and Messrs. Ken Nutt and Tony Rowen helped by being custodians of all the funds involved. I wish to thank also the Society for Theatre Research for circulating leaflets and society stalwarts Miss Kathleen Barker, Miss Sybil Rosenfeld and Mr. Jack Reading for general help; and librarians at large but especially those at Northampton including Mr. J. A. J. Munro, formerly Northampton Borough Librarian and now Deputy County Librarian; Mr. J. Kennedy, Northampton District Librarian; Mr. J. B. Stafford, Chief Assistant Librarian; and Miss Marion Arnold, Local History Librarian.

Hoare and Cole Ltd. efficiently and helpfully made the blocks. Some illustrations which appeared in Theatre Un-Royal are repeated in this book because they are relevant and for the sake of the completeness of this volume. Mr. Ray Hedley, of Garden City Press Ltd., who got Theatre Un-Royal out on time despite having to print it during the Miners' Strike of 1974, has again given valued personal attention.

I sadly record the deaths of Patrons of this book and of the last. Insofar as I know of them their names are given following the list of Patrons at the end of the book. Among them is the late the Earl Spencer who took a great interest in the present book and especially the Prologue, which is partly set in the grounds of his home at Althorp, Northants. One of his last acts was to send a cheque covering both this book and the final one. After his having been so helpful I regret that he did not live to read the book—an almost exact parallel with the death of Miss Joan Wake while the proofs of Theatre Un-Royal were being passed.

Finally I must again thank my wife Greta and son Nigel for the silence they have suffered at home while my head has been deep in my notes on noxious drama.

ROYAL CURTAIN RAISER

DEITY IN DRAMA

..." *Sure they are of heavenly race ...*" *With this and similar phrases, written especially by Ben Jonson, the Northamptonshire nobility saluted a Queen Consort on her way to be crowned in 1603. It was an open-air show by a well-bred cast in a parkland setting with a summer breeze for ventilation. Yet still a case may be made out that it was "Drama That Smelled"...*

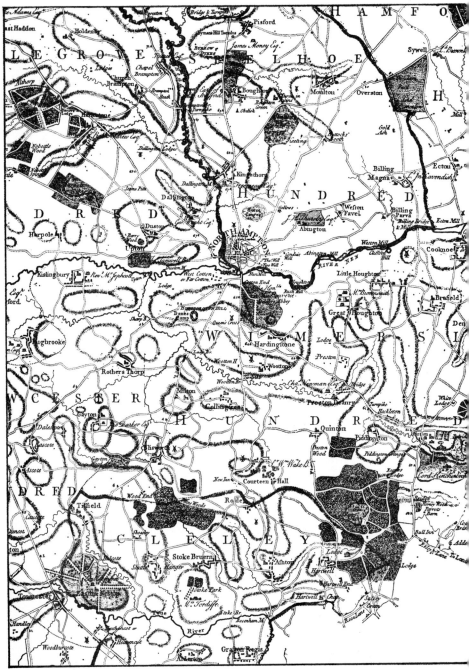

NORTHAMPTIONSHIRE IN 1774—this map by W. Faden covers a number of places mentioned
the text including some of those on the Royal route of 1603—Holdenby, Althorp, Easton Neston a
Grafton Regis. Abington Abbey, home of Lady Elizabeth Bernard, last descendant of Shakespeare, w
well outside the county town of Northampton. It was at the Abbey (or manor house) that Dav
Garrick planted a mulberry tree in February, 1778, which is still growing today. (*Northamptonsh
County Library at Northampton*)

DEITY IN
DRAMA

"Can't you change the title?" was the question most frequently asked during the preparation of this book. One Patron warned: "You're simply asking for people to say that the book smells as well..." And he made a gesture not unknown on the musichall stage, of pulling an invisible chain with one hand while holding his nose with the other.

As to whether the book does indeed smell, the reader must defer judgment until he or she has arrived at the last page. Though, come to think of it, if such is the reaction, he or she may not get that far! Especially as some passages are heavy going for the general reader. I hope, at least, that the pages will be penetrated far enough (or that useful exercise, skipping, sufficiently indulged in) to convince that the title is appropriate and does reflect the theme. Doubly so, in fact.

It may require little persuasion and evidence to justify a smell in respect of stuffy, low-ceilinged, make-shift theatres of old, with the odours of the candles blending with those of the unwashed audience and of the peel of the oranges they had the habit of eating (especially if, as at Northampton, the "theatre" was in fact the town's Riding House). A little more explanation will be needed as to why there should be a nauseous reaction in the nostrils to the first dramatic performance in Northamptonshire of which a detailed account survives.

For this was an open-air auditorium, with a summer breeze for ventilation; the turf of a country parkland substituting for the boards of a stage; and Nature's candles, the moon and stars, according to one account, providing natural lighting. Real trees and shrubs were the stage properties and Althorp, stately home of the Spencer family, formed the backcloth.

The principal members of the audience could scarcely have been more distinguished—a Queen on her way from Edinburgh to London to take her place besides a King on his newly-acquired second throne, with their elder son, a Prince, accompanying her.

The players were no mere strollers: it was, in fact, an amateur perform-ance, with members of the Spencer and other leading county families per-forming in a masque written especially for the occasion, to demonstrate their loyalty to the new monarch and his family.

Truly this was a Royal Curtain Raiser, even though there was no curtain.

Apart from the fact that the performance was in the open the curtain was a theatrical device yet to be invented : the traditional green curtain is believed to have been introduced in Restoration times and was unknown on the Elizabethan stage.

Yet a smell there certainly was, in similitude, despite the open-air surroundings, the high-class cast and the Royal audience. To illustrate the point it is necessary to paint in a little of the background of the events leading to this Midsummer Masque in Northamptonshire.

The Queen was Anne of Denmark who, with Prince Henry, was following James VI of Scotland on his triumphal route to London to be crowned as James I of England in 1603.

It was just over 400 years ago, on December 12, 1574, that Anne was born at Skanderborg Castle, Jutland, to Queen Sophia, wife of Frederick II. Her brother was to become Christian IV, Denmark's most famous King. Legend has it that she was carried about by attendants until she was nine. It does not seem a likely story and if it were true there was certainly no atrophying of the legs for she became well-known for the agility and spiritedness of her dancing.

Two years after she was, if the story be true, not considered old enough to walk, negotiations were in hand for her to become a bride. The projected marriage with James VI of Scotland was not favoured by Elizabeth of England, who had previously executed James's mother, Mary Queen of Scots, at Fotheringhay Castle, Northamptonshire. Although he usually tried to avoid offending Elizabeth, so as not to prejudice his chances of eventually wearing two crowns, James went ahead and the marriage was solemnised in Denmark on August 20, 1589, despite the fact that he was still in Scotland and had yet to meet his fourteen-year-old bride. It was a proxy marriage with the Earl Marshal standing in for the groom.

The bridal party set sail for Scotland but met stormy seas and finished up in Norway. The impatient bridegroom then set out from Leith to fetch his Queen and in Norway a second ceremony took place on November 23. Even after two marriages, all was not plain sailing. High seas prevented their departure for Scotland and the winter was spent in Denmark, where for good measure there was a third wedding, at Kronenberg. They finally arrived in Leith the following April.

James VI and Anne had six children of whom but three survived— Henry, Charles, and Elizabeth. Prince Henry had Elizabeth of England as a godmother, by proxy, and it was at her suggestion that he was called Henry, after her grandfather and father, Henry VII and Henry VIII.

As we know from television series, being a queen was not all honey and for someone as affectionate and quick-tempered as Anne it must have been mortifying to be denied the right to bring up her first-born. She wanted young Henry to be raised at Edinburgh Castle but at the age of one he was taken from her by the King and placed in the charge of the Earl of Mar, who had orders that in the event of the King's death the prince was not to be released to the custody of anyone, the Queen included, until he was eighteen.

It may be considered odd that James should submit his own son to the

* *

childhood isolation from his mother which had been his own lot. James did not see his mother, Mary Queen of Scots, after he was eleven months old and his childhood has been described by his latest biographer, Lady Antonia Fraser, as appalling—a psychologist's dream and a child's nightmare. What is not surprising is that James, described by Henry IV of France as "the wisest fool in Christendom", should emerge as a most complex and contradictory character.

The Scottish historical background to this period is less widely known than the English but this is not the place to go into it at length. Suffice it to mention that James's mother had ascended the throne when a mere week old, her father, James V, having died, of despair it is said, after the defeat of his Army at Solway Moss in 1542; and that James V had succeeded at seventeen months when his father was killed at Flodden Field in 1513.

A King at the age of one, James VI bided his time until March 24, 1603, a day which brought to an end, by death, the long reign of Queen Elizabeth of England and enabled him to ride south to claim peacefully a second throne, obliterating en route a border which had been bloody and turbulent for centuries.

Twelve days after he had been proclaimed in London, James set out from Edinburgh for his new capital. The new Queen, who was pregnant at the time, was to follow. Feeling her new importance she first made a determined effort to gain control of her elder son, taking advantage of the fact, as she no doubt thought, that his guardian, the Earl of Mar, was on the way to London with the King. When she was nevertheless denied her wish Anne flew into such a rage that she had a miscarriage. The King then relented and allowed Henry to be handed over to her. Thus it was accompanied by her nine-year-old son as well as Princess Elizabeth that the twenty-eight-year-old Queen set out on the long trek south.

It had been intended that the two Royal parties should meet at York and had this happened it might well have been King, Queen and Prince who were entertained at Althorp but the Queen's contingent was delayed, possibly owing to this altercation.

Via Berwick, York, Worksop, Nottingham and Leicester the Queen reached Dingley Hall, Northamptonshire, the seat of Sir Thomas Griffin, where Princess Elizabeth left the party for a few days to visit Combe Abbey, which is today the scene of some of those mock medieval banquets which have become a popular and novel form of twentieth century eating out.

From Dingley the Queen moved on to Holdenby (or Holmby) Palace which had been built by Sir Christopher Hatton, Chancellor to Queen Elizabeth, and which in splendour and extent rivalled Burghley House, Stamford. The large number of windows glinted in the sunshine for miles around, giving rise to the Northamptonshire saying of "as bright as Holmby". According to Gifford, in the collected works of Ben Jonson, "the Queen and Prince came from Holdenby to Northampton, where they were received in great state by the municipal magistrates".

All the way south, people used various means to impress the new King and Queen, seeking to show how welcome they were, and, at the same time, endeavouring to ingratiate themselves, with the possibility of a position or a title in recognition. The method chosen by Sir Robert Spencer, of Althorp, was a masque, a dramatic form often used to laud monarchs and monarchy. Sir Robert commissioned one specially, written by Ben Jonson, with a text which included many flattering references to Oriana—the Queen.

Jonson was the author in 1610 of a witty play called *The Alchemist* which was revived at Northampton Repertory Theatre in 1974 in a manner which Jonson could not have envisaged but of which he would surely have approved. A revolving stage was employed and the action went on for some minutes while it was actually going round. A search through the house in the set was carried on by actors treading their way round the circling platform, greatly heightening the effect.

For Jonson's Althorp Masque, entitled *Satyr* or *Masque of Fairies* there were none of the restrictions imposed by a formal stage. It was arranged that the entertainment should be given as the Royal party actually arrived and first entered the park. The piece was a sort of rural or pastoral drama in which fauns, satyrs, shepherds and allegorical characters were mixed together. The original tract in the library at Althorp describes it as "A particular entertainment of the Queene and Prince their Highnesse to Althorpe, at the Right Honourable the Lord Spencer's on Saturday, being the 25th of June, 1603, as they came first into the kingdom."

A preamble explains: "The invention was, to have a Satyre lodged in a little Spinet, by which Her Majestie and the Prince were to come, who (at the report of certain cornets that were divided in several places of the parke, to signify her approach) advanced his head above the toppe of the wood, wondring, and (with his Pipe in his hand) began as followeth:

> *"Here! there! and everywhere!*
> *Some solemnities are neare.*
> *That these changes strike mine eare*
> *My pipe and I a part shall beare.*

"And after a short straine with his Pipe, again:

> *"Look, see (beshrew this tree);*
> *What may all this wonder bee?*
> *Pipe it, who that list for me;*
> *I'll flie out abroad, and see.*

"There he leaped downe and gazing the Queene and Prince in the face, went forward.

> *"That is Cyparissus face!*
> *And the Dame hath Syrinx grace!*
> *Oh that Pan were now in place!*
> *Sure they are of heavenly race.*

"Here he ran into the wood againe, and hid himselfe, whilst to the sound of excellent soft musique that was there concealed in the thicket, there came tripping up the lawne a bevy of Faeries, attending on Mab their Queene, who falling into an artificial ring, that was there cut in the pathe, began to daunce a round whilst their mistresse spake as followeth :

> *"Haile' and welcome, worthiest Queene,*
> *Joy had never perfect beene,*
> *To the Nimphes that haunt this Greene,*
> *Had they not this evening seene.*
> *Now they print it on the Ground*
> *With their feete in figures round,*
> *Markes that will be ever found,*
> *To remember this glad sound."*

And so on. I can almost hear the cries of a twentieth-century audience . . . "Rubbish !" But it has to be remembered that this was a well-dressed spectacle with the main object of flattering the two principal members of the audience. And as we shall see, there was a little more to it than at first appears.

As a climax two deer were led on by young John Spencer and released so that they could be hunted and killed within sight of the Royals.

After the short stay at Althorp there was to have been a parting speech, possibly to be spoken by young Spencer with a group of the youngest sons of gentlemen of the county, but, as the printed version explains, this had to be abandoned "by reason of the multitudinous presse".

Here are the first lines of what the Queen and Prince would have heard, a piece at least as humble and cajoling as those spoken by professional actors and actresses seeking to impress their betters (as will emerge) :

> *"And will you then Mirror of Queenes depart?*
> *Shall nothing stay you? Not my master's heart?*
> *That pants to leese the comfort of your light*
> *And see his day ere it be old grow night?*
> *You are a Goddess, and your will be done;*
> *Yet this our last hope is, that as the Sunne*
> *Cheares objects far remov'd, as well as neare,*
> *So wheresoere you shine, you'le sparkle here."*

Gifford commented : "It is easy, or rather it is not easy, to conceive the surprise and delight with which Queen Anne". . . "must have witnessed the present; she, who in Denmark, had seen perhaps no Royal amusement except drinking bouts, and in Scotland had been regaled with nothing better than 'ane goodly ballad called Philotas. The rich and beautiful scenery of the parkland, music soft or loud as the occasion required, dispersed throughout the woods, the sweetness of the vocal performers, the bevy of fairies composed of the young ladies of the county, foresters headed by the youthful heir, starting forward to chase the deer in sports which ensued, must have afforded a succession of pleasures as rare as unexpected."

As the Queen drove away from Althorp she was saluted at the park gates by a "morrise of clowns" led by Nobody, a grotesque figure with a cap over his face and breeches reaching up to his neck.

Life could be short in the seventeenth century, even for the sons of kings
and lords for, in the field of health, privilege did not cover them. Neither
Prince Henry nor John Spencer were to survive to enjoy their inheritances.
Henry died before he could become king and Spencer died at Blois while still
a minor.

From Althorp Queen and Prince moved on to Easton Neston, home of
Richard Fermor, and there on June 27 they met the King for the first time
since leaving Scotland. He had already visited London after a journey which
had included his reception at Hinchinbrook Priory by Sir Oliver Cromwell,
uncle of the man who was to chop off the head of the King's younger son
some forty-five years later.

In Northamptonshire the King had been greeted on April 23 by the High
Sheriff, William Tate, who met him at the bridge on two shires at Stamford
and accompanied him to Burghley. The Royal progress was strewn with
honours, no fewer than 305 knights being made en route, including a
number of Northamptonshire gentlemen, Sir Thomas Griffin, Sir Valentine
Knightley, Sir Robert Wingfield, Sir Richard Fermor, Sir Nicholas
Haselwood, Sir Edward Watson, Sir Eusebius Andrew and Sir Charles
Montague.

From Easton Neston the Queen went on to Grafton House, also in
Northamptonshire, which belonged to the Earl of Cumberland. Here there
was a touch of farce. Lady Cumberland, a domineering woman who was at
the time estranged from her husband, turned up in the hope that he would
permit her to play hostess to Royalty; instead he sent her off with a flea in
her ear.

More and more people hastened to swell the Royal welcome so that by
the time Windsor was reached Anne had an escort of 250 carriages and
5,000 horsemen. There Prince Henry was invested with the Noble Order of
the Garter and Sir Robert Spencer was elevated. As the Account of
Althorp puts it: "His Majesty, partly in return for the liberality of the
reception of his queen and son at Althorp and still more in consequence of
the long established reputation and great property of the proprietor, created
the then owner, Sir Robert Spencer, a Peer of the Realm—the date of the
creation, according to Dugdale, being July 21." As a testimony of his
gratitude Lord Spencer built a stone hawking stand in the north-west of
Althorp Park, with the Royal Arms on the front and his own, as a peer, on
the west side.

Flattery and self-interest apart, James was welcomed with genuine
warmth. When queens grow old, which, being female, they tend to,
countries often yearn for a male successor. But Anne made a good impression
as she rode through London, "never leaving (off) to bend her body this way
and that, that men and women wept for joy". Her style may be compared
with that of Queen Elizabeth, consort of George VI and later Queen
Mother, in the twentieth century. This was not the case with James, to
whom crowds in Scotland had always been associated with danger and
upheaval. He disliked displaying himself and on one occasion when he was
told that the people wished to see him, commented: "God's wounds, I will

pull down my breeks and show them my arse." Anne was a willing and natural performer; he was not.

Nevertheless, he may not have needed her encouragement in the step he took of adopting the former Chamberlain's Men, as one of the dramatic companies was known, as the King's Men. The Admiral's became Prince Henry's and Worcester's the Queen's. For though James was not a devotee of Shakespeare and was sometimes bored with the lighter fare of the masques, as monarch of England and Scotland he wanted to have a court with entertainments which would be the talk of Europe. It was for this reason, no doubt, that he aided and abetted his wife in the spendthrift spectaculars she was to sponsor, inspired by what she had seen at Althorp.

In case you were one of those who, at least mentally, shouted "Rubbish!" at the extract from the Althorp masque, it should be pointed out that there was more to it than appeared on the surface. The masque was intended not only as simple flattery but as a dramatic recognition of the divine right of kings, a principal point of political controversy. Remember at Althorp :

> *Sure they are of heavenly race ...*
> *You are a goddess and your will be done ...*

Behind the imagery of the masques there was this inner meaning, as Dr. Roy Strong has pointed out. "A deep truth about the monarchy was realised and embodied in the action. When the King was represented as Pan, the Universal God; the Queen as Bel-Anna, queen of the ocean; or Prince Henry as Oberon, Prince of Fairies, they were purposely presented in roles expressing the strongest Renaissance beliefs about the nature of kingship, the obligations and perquisites of Royalty."

The writing of Royal flattery seems to have been a useful source of income for Ben Jonson for apart from the Althorp and other masques there are a number of other hymns to sovereignty among his collected works of 1756. There was the Entertainment at King James the First's Coronation, consisting of congratulatory speeches spoken to His Majesty at Fenchurch, Temple Bar and in the Strand on the way to the crowning, with the author's additional comments; the Entertainment of the King and Queen on May Day in the morning, 1604, at Sir W. Cornwall's House at Highgate; the Entertainment of the Two Kings of Great Britain and Denmark at Theobald's, July 24, 1606; and the Entertainment of King James and Queen Anne at Theobald's, when the house was delivered up into her possession by the Earl of Salisbury, May 22, 1607.

Pleasure was the activity which the somewhat empty-headed Anne took most seriously but in so doing she became a notable, probably unique, patron of the arts. Her £50,000 progress to Bath, for instance, was followed by the licensing of a theatrical company there under the masque author Samuel Daniels and called the Youths of Her Majesty's Chamber.

In effect the Elizabethan age did not end with the death of Elizabeth, any more than the later Edwardian era ceased abruptly with the death of Edward VII. The Elizabethan age spilled over into the reign of James; in 1603 William Shakespeare was not only still alive but had still to write

Hamlet, Othello, Macbeth, Antony and Cleopatra, Coriolanus and *The Tempest* before retiring to Stratford-upon-Avon. But as Elizabeth's time had marked the arrival of a high tide for the drama, Anne's was to be that of the masque.

Probably the first form of English entertainment in which scenery was used, the masque was frequently followed by a masked ball. There is today a tendency to revert to the spelling, mask. Writers of masques included Ben Jonson, James Shirley, Samuel Daniels, William Davenant, Thomas Campion, Frances Beaumont, William Brown and Thomas Middleton. There had been masques since the fifteenth century, involving at first music and dancing, later speech and singing, but nothing to those which were to be staged while James I was on the throne. During this magnificent climax they were one of the most extravagant and spectacular forms of entertainment ever produced. On these State occasions, the talents of poets, musicians, designers, choreographers, etc. were lavished upon shows which were to be given but once. Parts of the dialogue were so full of personal and contemporary allusions as to be almost meaningless today. The performers were mainly amateurs, members of Royalty and aristocracy, and one of the motives was to allow the ruling class to dress up and appear in them. They represented an extraordinary confluence of the professional and the amateur, an exclusive art form only for the elite.

Not long after her arrival in London Anne made arrangements for more masques and on Twelfth Night, 1604, danced in the *Vision of the Twelve Goddesses* in which the goddesses appeared bearing gifts for the king. Some of the materials for the costumes were taken from the wardrobe of the old queen and Anne startled the audience by wearing a dress several inches from the ground, causing one courtier to comment that it revealed to him "that a woman has both feet and legs, which I never knew before". Despite the immoralities of the times it has to be remembered that a glimpse of feminine ankle in public was as daring as a glimpse of thigh was thought to be a few years ago.

Of the Jonson masques some two dozen survive. His *Masque of Blackness* marked the 1605 creation of Charles as Duke of York. In 1610 Charles appeared as a zephyr in a Daniels' Masque, dressed in a short robe of green satin embroidered with gold flowers.

But what began as and was intended to be a splendid, stately, tribute to monarchy could degenerate into a drunken romp at times, especially if the chief sponsor's hard-drinking Danish brother was present. Danes have a reputation for being good drinkers and Christian IV certainly lived up to the image. We have an eye-witness account of what happened when *Solomon and Sheba* was staged for his visit to London in 1606. By the end of the preceding banquet both James and Christian had drunk too much and Sir John Harrington describes how members of the cast were also tipsy. The King of Denmark got a lapful of wine, cream, jelly and cake when the "Queen of Sheba" stumbled while attempting to present him with a gift. After being cleaned up he attempted to dance with her but both fell down and had to be carried out and put to bed. Faith, Hope and Charity fared no better; nor did Victory and Peace. Faith made an unscripted exit "in staggering condition" and by the time Charity had done her unsteady piece her sisters were "sick and spewing in the lower hall". Victory was led away to sleep it off in an outer chamber while back in the hall Peace laid about her with her olive branch. Nearly all the cast "went backwards or fell down, wine did so occupy their upper chambers".

It may be imagined what harm was done to the image of the Divinely Right King when the story of the squiffy Solomon and Sheba in all their expensive glory got around the city and the country houses, and what Members of Parliament thought, they only recently having been prevailed upon to grant the King £400,000 "to relieve his necessities". As James Willson put it in his Life of James : "The spreading tales of court scandals and debauches . . . marked the beginning of that rift between court and country which was to be James's worst legacy to his descendants and was to make the pattern of politics for the next century."

Jonson's *Masque of Queens* was dedicated not, as the title might suggest, to Anne but to her son Prince Henry. A good dancer, he had appeared in Jonson masques as early as 1606, though his real interest was in outdoor pursuits. He was created Prince of Wales in 1610 and when Jonson's *Oberon, The Fairy Prince* was staged the following year in the new banqueting hall in Whitehall the Prince danced the title role, watched by his parents and sister. The Venetian Ambassador noted that the masque was "most remarkable for the grace of the Prince's every movement".

For the performance, a large curtain—this may well have been one of the earliest recorded uses of some sort of curtain—had concealed the first scene until the King and Queen had taken their seats. Among the Knights Masquers who danced with the Prince were two earls (one of them the Earl of Southampton, Shakespeare's Patron), three baronets and five knights. The first scene was an "ugly hell" and all the characters witches, witchcraft being a subject which James found of absorbing interest. Halfway through, the scene changed suddenly to a "magnificent building figuring the house of fame". To achieve this Jonson and his collaborator, Inigo Jones, used scenery shutters, another innovation. The budget allowed meant that the producers could innovate and experiment with expense virtually no consideration whatever, a situation in which very few authors and artistic directors have found themselves in Britain.

The following year Prince Henry died of typhoid fever, though his distraught mother was sure he had been poisoned. He was only eighteen and it must remain conjecture whether his survival might have changed the course of English history—whether, had there been a Henry IX, there might have been no period of Commonwealth.

Charles, who now became heir apparent, also had a dramatic company named after him. With the death of his brother, their title changed from the Duke of York's Men to Prince Charles' Men.

Anne of Denmark never cared as much for Charles as she did for Henry. When, as a boy, Charles refused some medicine his nurse expressed the fear that he might die. "No," said Anne, "he will live to plague three kingdoms by his wilfulness." She did not live, of course, to see her prophecy come true, dying on March 2, 1619, at the age of forty-four. She died as for many years she had lived, in debt, and even her funeral was held up for many weeks by lack of funds, until May 13. James had not attended the funeral of his son and nor did he turn up at that of his wife, having a great fear of death. In any case, they had not lived together for thirteen years, the King preferring his homosexual companions. She lived at Denmark House, now known as Somerset House, while he was often on the move between the extravagant number of houses always kept ready for his occupation.

After Anne's death the masque tended to give way at court to the bawdy song. But the masque had not ceased to figure in the Stuart story. When Charles went to Spain to seek the hand of the Infanta Maria Anna, daughter of Philip III and Margaret of Austria, there was a seeming conspiracy against his being allowed even to talk to her and he was able only to gaze at her in adoration . . . during court theatricals. Then came the successful wooing of the French Henrietta Maria, sister of Louis XIII, and Charles' first sight of her was at a court masque.

On March 27, 1625, at the age of fifty-nine, James died and following Charles' accession there was at first little court drama but then it came back in full flower and extravagance. Again the Queen was the sponsor. As Ian Bevan states in his book Royal Performances : "Certainly there has never been anything else in the life of the British Court to compare with the spending by James I and Charles and the instigators of it all were their wives. James' Danish-born consort Queen Anne and Charles' French-born Henrietta Maria both amused themselves by commanding more and more costly entertainments until their masques were a source of amazement throughout Europe."

If they were a source of amazement throughout Europe what must have been the reaction of the drama-hating Puritans at home? The masques must have been positively putrid in their nostrils. Especially as Charles was ill advised enough to use a masque as propaganda against the Puritans. This was *Salmacida Spolia,* the last masque before the Civil War, with both King and Queen appearing. As Davenant put it : "The title allusion is to the King who out of his clemency sought by all means to reduce tempestuous and turbulent natures unto a sweet calm of concord." If that was the intention it was not only a failure but produced the opposite effect. Some say it was a factor in leading on to the outbreak of war.

Whether the Civil War was started by this masque which had its origins in Northamptonshire in 1603 must remain a point for argument but what is a fact is that as well as having its climax in the county, in the Battle of Naseby, the war's first action was also here—in the Puritan village of Kilsby where Royalist troops rode in and shot a number of villagers on August 9, 1642. During the war Grafton House, which had been visited on the 1603 Royal Progress, was laid siege to by Parliamentary forces and burnt down on a Christmas Day.

Then came the arrest and execution of Charles in which Northampton-shire again provided some of the settings. He was held in the Royal Palace at Holdenby and from there allowed to play bowls at Althorp, both of which had been on the 1603 route of his mother and brother.

In 1650 the Palace was sold to Adam Baynes, M.P. for Leeds (the only

ANNE OF DENMARK, Consort of James VI of Scotland and James I of England, who was welcomed at Althorp, Northants, in 1603 with a masque specially written by Ben Jonson. In the background is the Palace of Oatlands, with Inigo Jones's new classical doorway. Paul van Somer's painting is reproduced by permission of Sir Gyles Isham, Bart., of Lamport Hall, Northants, where the picture hangs.

26

ALTHORP, Northamptonshire home of the Spencers, was the scene of the 1603 masque which greeted Anne of Denmark on her way to London for the Coronation of her husband, James VI of Scotland, as James I of England. The picture was drawn by a member of the retinue of Prince Cosmo of Tuscany when he visited Northamptonshire during his Grand Tour of 1669. (*Northamptonshire County Library at Northampton*)

ABINGTON ABBEY as it was in the eighteenth century. Lady Elizabeth Bernard, last descendant of Shakespeare, lived there and was buried in the adjacent church. A century later, when it was owned by John Harvey Thursby, the Abbey (or manor house) was visited by David Garrick who planted a mulberry tree which is still growing. (*Northamptonshire County Library at Northampton*)

IN 1932 spectators of and characters in the 1603 masque at Althorp were brought to life there in an historical pageant. Countess Spencer (left) appeared as Anne of Denmark and Lady Delia Peel (nee Spencer) as a court lady. (*Northampton Chronicle and Echo*)

"THE BEGGAR'S OPERA", written by John Gay and originally produced in 1728, was admirably presented by Northampton Theatre Guild in 1974 (above). This was the comic opera which helped to bring on the repression of the Drama. In this condemned cell scene two of his amours argue over the condemned highwayman Macheath (John Lott). They are played by Avril Plunkett (who had to appear pregnant as Lucy Lockit and in fact was!) and Jenny Curtis (as Polly Peachum).

Member Leeds ever had until after the Reform Act of 1832) who had the place pulled down. The lands were restored to the Crown after the Restoration.

During the period when Cromwell held sway attempts were made to abolish the drama, as will be mentioned later. All this can be traced back to the June day at Althorp in 1603.

Today the masque is virtually dead but in 1932 a pageant based on the one seen at Althorp in 1603 was staged there, with members of the Spencer family taking part. More recently the masque itself was recreated at York Festival by students of St. John's College of Education. Among the audience was Sir Gyles Isham, Bart., an actor in the first company to appear at the present Royal Shakespeare Theatre, Stratford-upon-Avon, and later one of its governors : it is at his home, Lamport Hall, Northants, that the picture of Anne of Denmark, reproduced with his permission, now hangs.

How it came to be there is an interesting speculation. One theory is that it came from Pytchley Hall (demolished 1824) where Anne stayed in 1605 as a guest of Sir Euseby Isham. On that occasion the King was accommodated at Apethorpe, neither house being able to cope with both courts. After Sir Euseby's death and, six months later, that of his son John, Sir Euseby's grandchildren sold the Hall and that branch of the family ended up in Virginia where the male line failed in 1678 but the women married Virginians and were the forebears of many distinguished Americans including Thomas Jefferson. Another theory is that the portrait came from Holdenby Palace which had been bought by James I. The artist, Paul van Somer, may have painted this version especially for Holdenby. There is a smaller picture in the Royal Collection but the Lamport one is considered the better and was selected by Dr. Roy Strong for inclusion in the Elizabethan Exhibition at the Tate Gallery some years ago. Wherever it came from, the portrait was at Lamport by 1676 as it appears on a list drawn up by Sir Thomas Isham that year.

Anne of Denmark is placed on the north wall of Lamport's lofty music hall; facing her directly on the south wall is a Van Dyck of her younger son, Charles I. At Lamport, too, is a Bible which belonged to Charles I. He gave it to Brian Duppa, Bishop of Salisbury, who presented it to Sir Justinian Isham, second Baronet.

Unlike her ill-fated son, the Princess from Denmark is comparatively forgotten today. But her life was so full of colour and incident—in a word, of drama—that if the devisers of TV serials are looking for a good Royal subject . . .

A series on Anne could scarcely miss the spectacular opportunity to recreate what went on at Althorp on June 25, 1603.

ACT
THE
FIRST

THE EARLY YEARS

...in which the Northampton stage is taken successively by Mr. Jones and Company, who then repaired to Preston Guild; the Warwick Company during whose brief tenure the gallery fell down; the Durravans Company of Comedians, who appeared without a drum; and the impecunious Mr. Carleton; together with some interesting facts about Mr. Garrick, who could prescribe the guest list of a Northamptonshire Countess, and Lady Bernard, the last descendant of our Great Bard.

NORTHAMPTON'S old Town Hall at the corner of Abington
Street and Wood Hill where Mr. Coysh and company appeared in
1705. For some years the lower part served as a gaol. The hall was
supplanted in 1864 and demolished.

Scene One

DRAMA IN THE NEWS

From 1603 to 1721 there is virtually a complete gap in the available theatrical history of Northampton and hereabouts. Only one sentence have I been able to find. This does not mean, of course, that there were no theatrical events, merely that there appears to be no record of them.

A period when there was perhaps indeed nothing to record is that of the Commonwealth, when drama was banned because it was odious to the Puritans. With the restoration of Charles II in 1660 was also restored the theatre, but whatever activity may have gone on in the home county of John Dryden, then the leading dramatist, at the time when he was writing his plays and having them performed in London, little or no evidence of it remains.

This lack of information is one which Northamptonshire shares with the rest of the country, as opposed to the capital. It was precisely because the period was so ill-served in the field of theatrical history that Sybil Rosenfeld wrote her Strolling Players and Drama in the Provinces, 1660–1765, concentrating on Bath, the Kent Circuit, Norwich and York, where some material is available.

As Miss Rosenfeld states : "The players figure infrequently in town records and it is because we have to rely on Mayor's Books and Chamberlains' Accounts for the years 1600–1700 that so little has come to light. We can form no idea at all of the number or quality of strollers in Restoration times since only the Norwich records have anything to tell us of them. The Puritan opposition may have been strong enough to curtail their activities in most places or it may not."

In the seventeenth century we look in vain to provincial newspapers for evidence of local theatricals, for the simple reason that there were no country newspapers.* These did not start until the turn of the century but

* There are two possible exceptions. The Stamford Mercury has been produced continuously since 1712 but the traditional starting date is 1695. Berrow's Worcester Journal dates, under various titles, from 1709 but its traditional origins go back to 1690. Other early newspapers are the Nottingham Weekly Express (1710), Newcastle Courant (1711), Bristol Postman (1713), Hereford Journal (1713), Norwich Mercury (1714), Kentish Gazette (1717), Leeds Mercury (1718), Derby Postman (1719) and Ipswich Journal (1720), which was also the commencement year of the Northampton Mercury.

by 1760 there were 160 of them. They sprang up especially in centres of growing industrial activity such as Derby and Nottingham and also in other county capitals and centres such as Stamford, Northampton and Worcester. In fact the two newspapers with which we shall have particular concern have a special place in newspaper history. The Stamford Mercury (now the Lincoln, Rutland and Stamford Mercury) claims to be the oldest surviving paper while the Northampton Mercury (now the Mercury and Herald) appears to be the oldest of which every copy survives.

Miss Rosenfeld continues : "It is thus almost impossible to dig out anything about a company such as Herbert's in Lincolnshire whose circuit does not include a town which had a local paper." In point of fact some rays of light on the Herbert Company are thrown by the Stamford Mercury which mentions its appearances at the times of the races at Spalding and covers the period when Herbert combined with Jemmy Whitley for seasons at Stamford and elsewhere. But with Miss Rosenfeld's comment in mind it will be interesting to see just how much Squadron Leader John Richards, formerly of Oakham, Rutland, and now at Cardiff University College, manages to "dig out" about the Herbert Company for the thesis on the Lincoln Circuit on which he is currently engaged.

Complicating the newspapers' role as a source of theatrical history are two failure factors—some newspapers themselves failed; and copies of some of those which succeeded failed to survive. In eighteenth-century Lincolnshire, in addition to the Stamford Mercury, there were the Boston Weekly Journal (1731-9), the Doncaster, Nottingham and Lincoln Gazette and Yorkshire, Nottinghamshire and Lincolnshire Advertiser (1786) and the Lincoln Gazette or Weekly Intelligencer (1727).

Generally speaking the journalist who reported the news and the printers who made up the advertisements were among the principal "historians" of the period, in the sense that where they did not exist nor does the available history.

Even in the eighteenth century there were not provincial newspapers in all the provincial centres. The Warwickshire Advertiser did not begin until 1806; the Bedford Mercury did not appear until 1837; while at Banbury the Guardian did not have its first issue until 1838 and even then was at first only a monthly Poor Law journal.

In Northampton there is just one tantalising glimpse of dramatic happenings between 1603 and 1720. This is in 1705 when the Borough Records list a payment :

£3 4s. 6d. paid to Chamberlain by Mr. Coysh for use of the Town Hall to act their playes.

This Town Hall was the one at the corner of Abington Street and Wood Hill which was pulled down in 1864 after serving the town for several centuries. Towards the end of the eighteenth century it was again used for entertainment purposes and in 1822 became the first concert hall of the Northamptonshire Philharmonic Society who after a few meetings found it too small and moved to the Theatre, Marefair, opened in 1806. We shall also come across this Town Hall when its basement was used as a gaol.

If Mr. Coysh used this hall in 1705 it would seem likely that he did so on other occasions; and so may other companies have done. However, a scrutiny of the Borough Records fails to disclose any further evidence.

Miss Rosenfeld has discovered the company of John Coysh at Cambridge in 1667 and at Norwich in 1672, 1683, 1684, 1686 and 1696 while from 1674–81 he was engaged at Drury Lane. In 1682 there is a mention of his planning to appear at York.

Apart from this single entry in the accounts of the town I have found nothing else about stage or other entertainment until the launching of the Northampton Mercury in 1720 by Robert Raikes and William Dicey.

It was in manner similar to that used by theatre managers that these pioneers of print solicited the patronage of the town—at least of those citizens who could read and afford the price of the newspaper : "It is sur-prizing to think that this famous, this beautiful, this polite Corporation has not long ago been the object of those many printers who have established printing offices in towns of less note. And certainly it argues their want of thought : for the soul of conversation must be absolutely necessary to a body of people that excel therein. With this view 'twas that the Proprietors hereof sought that gracious leave, which the worshipful Mr. Mayor, the Court of Aldermen and Common Council have unanimously granted to them; and which they will study to improve as to make this excellent, this admirable mystery, as useful an ornament to Northampton, as That is an Honour to the Art."

After this bit of puffing, the proprietors assured their new readers "that they shall be furnish'd with this news early every week, according to the distance of their respective habitations; and that advertisements are taken in by the printers hereof as also at the Printing-Office in St. Ives in Hunting-donshire; by Mr. Gibson, bookseller in Wisbech; and by the men that carry the news."

The promise made by Raikes and Dicey 255 years ago has been well and truly kept. Though it is now fused with the opposition Herald, which began in 1831, the newspaper has come out with the news every week since May, 1720.

There was not a line about drama or entertainment of any kind in that first issue of 12 pages, measuring $7\frac{1}{2}$ inches by 6 inches, unless one counts public executions as entertainment. The paper reported eight men and women being sentenced to death in one day at the Old Bailey, including John Kean for murdering his wife and George Davis for robbing the Sword Blade Company; the same session saw "about 33" ordered for transportation.

Northampton's first three Press advertisements were in the realm of Property, Transport and Stolen. The property being a house to be let at Sumersham in Huntingdonshire, with a good granary, barns, stables, out-houses, dovehouse and an acre-and-a-half of pasture; the transport being the Northampton Flying Wagon stagecoach which set out at five in the morning from the Fleece Inn, reaching the Rose and Crown, St. John's Street, London, on Wednesday, fare 6s.; while the third was from a man who had had his horse stolen while he was in the Red Lion Inn and who offered a reward.

If you go to Northampton Public Library, where every copy of the newspaper is on the file, you will have to thumb through sixteen months' issues before finding the first reference to dramatic entertainments. It appears in October, 1721, significantly following a list of "Horses entered to run for the £10 Plate on Pye-Lees near Northampton on Thursday October 19" : "For the entertainment of the quality there will be a play each night at the Talbot Inn by Mr. Toller's Company which now being completed and made one of the best companies that ever was in the country will continue for some time to perform the most celebrated tragedies and comedies now acted at the theatres in Drury Lane and Lincoln's Inn Fields."

It is appropriate indeed that the first recorded play performed in Northampton should have been by the county's own John Dryden. This was *The Spanish Fryar* or *The Double Discovery*, staged at the Hind Inn in January, 1723, "by desire of several ladies and gentlemen". The announcement added : "N.B. The part of Torrismond by a gentleman for his diversion." This is another local first—the earliest mention of an amateur inviting himself into the cast and probably paying for the privilege. The company is not named.

The Spanish Fryar (or Friar) was the play which Charles II saw many times despite its being plagiaristic, his comment being, "You steal me another like it and I'll go to see it as often." He appears to have been more tolerant than his successor James II, who suppressed it because of an untoward reference to Royalty. By June, 1689, after the "Glorious Revolution", it was back in favour, being the first play seen by the new Queen (Mary) at her command.

First produced at Dorset Garden in March, 1680, it was a tragi-comedy and Dryden was proud of having combined the two elements, declaring that audiences had grown weary of continued melancholy scenes—"I dare to prophesy that few tragedies except those in verse shall succeed in this age if they are not lightened with a course of mirth."

Of the Northampton performance of 1723 there are no further details but the play forms the subject of a theatrical budget in an account book kept at about this period in Malmesbury, Wiltshire, by a group of players who had quarrelled with their manager in Cardigan and set off on their own. The balance sheet for one night's performance was : "Musick 6d., Candles 10½d., Ale 1½d., Paper 4½d., Rent 2s., Nails and Packthread 2½d., Entertainment at Newland 4d. Total charges 4s. 5d." The takings amounted to 16s., leaving 11s. 7d. to be divided between the company.

On February 10, the company at Northampton performed *Hamlet Prince of Denmark* with "N.B. The part of Hamlet by Mr. Berriman, Gravedigger by Mr. Phipps."

One can only speculate whether there was any connection between the theatrical advertisement and the one immediately below it, referring to a truant servant with a talent to entertain : "John Steele, an Irishman about 5′ 6″ plays a little on the violin and trumpet, dances indifferently on the rope, a covenanted servant of Dr. Richard Smith of Berkhamsted, did on Saturday last in the evening desert his master's service. This is to give notice that whoever secures the said John Steele and brings him to his said master at the Hind Inn, Northampton, shall have a guinea reward and reasonable charges." The missing man appears to have been little more than a slave for the notice added this warning : "N.B. All persons are desired not to entertain the above said John Steele at their peril."

Next in the Northampton play parade comes a company somewhat more identifiable. Early in July, 1727, the Mercury stated : "We learn that the Comedians from Bath (of Mr. Power's Family) acting a Medley who have gained so much reputation and received so high a compliment from the nobility and gentry for their excellence in going through so many different characters and playing without a prompter are expected here in a few days."

Mr. Power himself was almost certainly deceased by this time but (assuming it is that same Mr. John Power who is referred to) his company was the one which had been "The Duke of Grafton's Men" in times when a link with a titular head was a safeguard against persecution.

John Power himself had been a member of the King's Company in London. At Bristol, then a twin star in the theatrical firmament with Bath, he had erected a theatrical booth in Tucker Street and taken his company there early in the century. Shortly afterwards the Common Council of the city requested the Mayor and Aldermen that "by regards to the ill consequences by the introduction of lewdness and debauchery, by the acting of stage plays, players should not be allowed to act within the city". Power returned in 1705 and 1706 and on the latter occasion was "presented" to the Grand Jury at the Assizes and ordered to be suppressed. Subsequently the theatre in Tucker Street was sold to the Presbyterians who converted it into a meeting house.

In November, 1707, the company performed in Norwich. Meantime in 1705 Bath's first theatre had been erected by the subscriptions of "persons of the highest rank" whose names were engraved on the inside of the house in acknowledgment; this was for the use of John Power's Company so that Bath appears to have been more tolerant than Bristol.

By 1727 the company was owned by Power's widow and seemingly managed by a man named Hornsby. No names appear in two scant references to the Northampton season of 1727 but the personnel of the company had been given at Exeter in March that year where an advertisement of "The Bath Company of Comedians, servants to his Grace the Duke of Grafton" listed the performers in *The Busie Body* as Messrs Copen, Howell, Eldred, Agnew, Haynes and Rous and Mrs. Howell, Mrs. Copen, Mrs. Rous and Miss Power. This would be Miss Jacobella Power, daughter of the late manager.

Expected in mid-July, the Northampton appearance of the Bath Company did not materialise until September. There seems to have been some elasticity of timetable. They probably stayed at one place as long as the takings merited it (and as long as they could avoid being thrown out!), also picking up engagements at country houses. The Mercury reported on September 4, 1727 : "The Comedians from Bath, who were expected here some time since are now arrived from the Rt. Hon. the Lord Leigh's (where they were detained some time) and intend to give our gentry an evening's diversion or two at the Hind before they go to Banbury Races. There was a vast concourse of people to see their performance at Warwick, to whom we hear they gave general satisfaction." Nothing further appears. But in 1728 they were reported in Bristol.

A few weeks after the Powers' season in Northampton came a fire-eater named Edward Price who was billed as having appeared before George II and Queen Caroline at the Court at Richmond "to their great satisfaction as he has also done before most of the nobility of the kingdom in such a wonderful manner as seems beyond the capability of human nature".

Wonders indeed! Not only eating "all sorts of combustible flaming fire" and lifting a red-hot heater of 2 lb. weight but also "He takes a man on each arm of 16 stone each and carries and dances with them; he breaketh a flint stone of four or five pounds weight only with his hand upon a table into as many pieces as any person can do with a sledge hammer. He commands (with dexterity of hand) a pinch of snuff off the table upon the hand of any lady or gentleman. He causeth a penknife to dance in a pint of beer and jump out of it into another empty pint. He takes three pieces of burning coals in his mouth and sufferes them to be blown with a pair of bellows till he hath broiled upon a gridiron over the said coals a piece of raw flesh until it be full dressed and fit for eating. He charges his mouth with gunpowder as much as will charge a fowling piece and sufferes it to be fired upon his tongue. He performs many more curious novelties perfectly new and unknown to others and never before done by any in Europe but himself."

In addition to his shows at the Sign of the Swan and Helmet, Gold Street, at 11 a.m., 2 p.m. and 7 p.m., fire-eater Price was "ready at an hour's warning to wait on any ladies or gentlemen in private".

In July, 1728, "We hear that a Company of Comedians from the Theatre-Royal are coming to this town in order to divert the gentry with the most celebrated tragedies and comedies now in vogue and shortly after their arrival will be performed *The Beggar's Opera*." They duly arrived and began with this celebrated piece on July 23, repeating it the following Tuesday and Wednesday. This was an early provincial performance, for the London premiere had been on January 28 that year. On Thursday came another popular attraction *The Provok'd Husband*.

When the company, "who gave so much satisfaction with their performances last summer", returned the following June this play was the only one mentioned in the Press. No venue is given for either season. It was said that they would "continue to entertain the gentry etc., with the best tragedies and comedies".

Again in 1730 there was a company from London, "from both the theatres", this time at the close of the year. On Monday, December 28, they gave *Cato*, followed on Tuesday by *The Beggar's Opera* and on Wednesday by *The Provok'd Husband*. These performances were at the Talbot Inn.

Inns have played a leading part in the development of the drama in Britain. In his Short History of English Drama, Sir Ifor Evans states that the Elizabethans "had not theatres but played in inn yards or bear gardens". Whether they played in the yards of the inns or in outbuildings and assembly rooms has recently been a topic of controversy. Some towns had suitable town halls or assembly rooms where a visiting company might be accommodated : in others these did not exist or were not available and then the inn often came into use.

Sometimes it is not possible immediately to identify the particular inn. Where the playbill states, "Theatre, Old Swan Inn, Wellingborough", there is no room for doubt but when it merely says "Theatre, Buckingham" this does not mean that it was not at an inn. Such is the bill heading in the 1820s when the Jackman Company performed at the Swan and Castle, Buckingham, where the room, the last surviving of that company's tour of "theatres", can still be seen today.

Some people might object to attending a performance in an inn; although many of those who objected to "the drink" would equally object to the drama so that their non-attendance would not be affected.

More lowly premises also served as "fit-up" theatres, including barns, cowsheds, stables and riding houses, not to mention booths. It never does to accept at its face value the word "theatre". During my early researches I innocently did this in the case of a "theatre" at Peterborough in 1866, until I came across an advertisement stating that "a new waterproof cloth has recently been placed upon the theatre".

At Northampton, as we have seen, at least some of the early performances of plays were in inns, the Talbot and the Hind being mentioned. It is highly likely that the first establishment to be described as a "Playhouse" was also an inn, as we shall see. But the three great coaching inns of the town, the Peacock, the George and the Red Lion, do not appear to have come in for much dramatic use.

Placed almost in the very centre of England, Northampton was an important town on the stagecoach map. The three inns mentioned coped with the provision of fresh horses, which were changed every few miles; meals and refreshment for the travellers; and overnight accommodation.

The Peacock, which stood on the Market Square on the site of what is now shops and offices (where I am typing this piece in fact), dated back to at least 1456 when a hospice called Le Pecok was sold by George Longueville, Lord of the Manor of Little Billing, to Roger Salisbury, the Squire of Horton whose granddaughter married Sir William Parr, also of Horton, uncle of the sixth and last wife of Henry VIII. The Assembly Room of the Peacock was frequently used for balls and concerts and once or twice for theatrical events. The inn was demolished as recently as 1960.

The George had been erected at the top of Bridge Street by John Dryden (not the playwright) immediately after the Dreadful Fire of 1675. His will of January, 1707, left it to be settled as his executors, with the advice of the Mayor and Corporation, "should think most convenient to charitable purpose within the town". In 1806 it was sold to fifty-four subscribers on a tontine basis, so that when only four remained alive the property was to be divided between them. This did not happen until 1887. On their late nineteenth-century visits to the town theatrical people staying at the George included Robert Courtneidge (father of Cecily), Bransby Williams, Ellen Terry and Frank Benson.

Not a great deal is known about the Red Lion, which stood at the lower

end of Sheep Street, where the covered market is today. But inns served
all manner of purposes in those pre-railway days and in March, 1736, the
Red Lion was the overnight resting place of the corpse of Sir Gilbert
Pickering, on its way following his death at his London home in Cavendish
Square, to the family estates at Titchmarsh, Northants.

In the eighteenth century many of the managers and actors stayed at
the large number of lesser inns and when they had benefit nights these
served as points of sale for tickets. Even when the inns did not have Thespian lodgers they seem sometimes to have sold tickets, whether for a percent-
age or free tickets for the landlord is not clear. There was no problem of
multiplicity of sales points as normally there was no reservation of seats.
To effect this you could, however, send your servant along to book it with
his body, so that he would surrender it to you when you arrived. He would
then often retire to the gallery where he might make a nuisance of himself.

The first mention of a "Playhouse" in Northampton comes in May, 1735 :
"We hear that a Company of Comedians from the Theatres in Drury Lane
etc. are coming to this place to divert the gentry with their performances
this summer and that they have taken the New Playhouse in Abington
Street for that purpose." This early announcement is the only one of that

> *By a Company of* COMEDIANS,
> AT the Play-houfe in Abington-ftreet,
> Northampton, on Monday the 26th of this Inftant December,
> will be acted a Comedy, call'd,
> *The* PROVOK'D HUSBAND:
> OR,
> *A* JOURNEY *to* LONDON.
> With Entertainments of DANCING between the Acts, by
> Mr. Williams and Mr. Whitaker,
> And an EPILOGUE of Addrefs to the Town.
> To which will be added, A Farce, call'd,
> *The* MOCK DOCTOR:
> OR,
> *The* DUMB LADY Cur'd.
> Pit 2 s. Middle Gallery 1 s. Upper Gallery 6 d.
> To begin exactly at Six o'Clock.
> N. B. Great Care will be taken to make the Houfe warm and
> commodious for the Reception of the Gentlemen and Ladies that intend
> to honour us with their Company. Vivat Rex.

THE FIRST "display" theatrical advertisement in the
Northampton Mercury, in December, 1743. Judging by the
number of repeated performances "The Provok'd Husband"
was Northampton's most popular play of the eighteenth century.

Mr. Jones's Company of Comedians, from the Threatres in London, have taken for a Play-houfe the Riding-houfe in this Town, and will open there this Evening with the laft new COMEDY, call'd,

P A M E L A; *or,* V I R T U E R E W A R D E D.

The Place is fitted up to the beft Advantage in a Theatrical Manner, The Company will ftay here but fix Weeks, being obliged to be at Prefton Guild (or Grand Jubilee) in Lancafhire, which begins the 30th of Auguft next,

THE FIRST mention of the Riding House being in use as a playhouse comes in June, 1742. (*Northampton Mercury*)

season. There are no further advertisements or reports to give any extra information or clues as to this first named "Playhouse" but it was probably an inn under another name.

The year before this first mention of a playhouse in Northampton had seen an attempt to put on to the Statute Book a law placing all playhouses outside the legal pale, except a couple in London and a few others holding the Royal "Patent" (or sanction). The drama was looked upon as permissive, revolutionary and a menace to corrupt Government. The Bill did not become law but a subsequent one was passed in 1737, virtually outlawing all "legitimate" drama if that is not too contradictory. On the oath of a credible witness an actor was liable to be fined and/or thrown into prison. Such penal legislation might have been expected to put an end to provincial acting but this was by no means the case. The situation is examined in more detail in the Interlude.

It was six years after the passing of the Act before the Abington Street Playhouse was mentioned again, in December, 1743, with the first theatrical "display" advertisement in the town. On Boxing Day, a Monday, they presented *The Provok'd Husband* with entertainments of dancing between the acts by Mr. Williams and Mr. Whitaker and an epilogue of address to the town plus a farce *The Mock Doctor* or *The Dumb Lady Cured*. Admission was 2s. pit, 1s. middle gallery, and 6d. upper gallery. The performance was to begin "exactly at six o'clock".

But the previous year, 1742, the first "significant" playhouse in Northampton had come into use when it had been announced that Mr. Jones' Company of Comedians from the theatres in London had taken for a playhouse the Riding House of the town.

There do not appear to be many examples of the use of a riding house as a playhouse. One other instance was at Salford, Lancashire, in 1760. In the present century there was, however, a further example of Northamptonshire drama in equestrian surroundings. At her then home, Harpole Hall, Mrs. Jessie Knight, one of the county's leading patrons of the drama, had

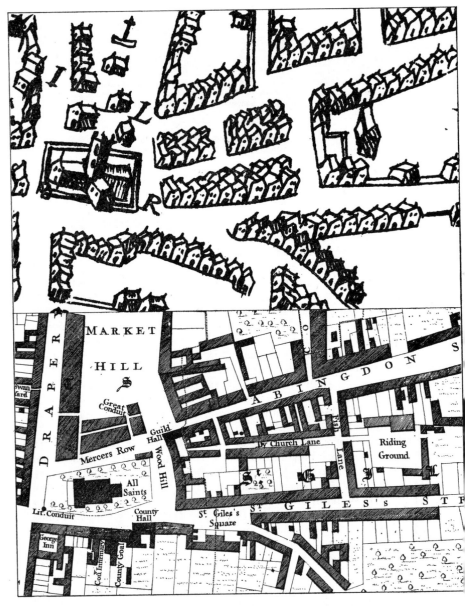

BEFORE AND AFTER the Dreadful Fire of Northampton of just over 300 years ago. The same part of the town is shown, embracing the area which after the 1675 fire was used as the Riding Ground. In the top picture (from the John Speed map of 1610) the Gobion farmhouse appears to have stood there. The lower map is by T. Jefferys and of 1747. (*Northamptonshire County Library at Northampton*)

the old stables converted for use as an Arts Theatre Club, complete with its own bijou theatre. It continued as such from 1958–68. After Mrs. Knight lost her husband she moved to The Priory, Weston Favell, Northampton, and rehoused the club in a former Rechabite Hall and public house, the Pytchley Arms, in Pytchley Street.

The Riding House or School appears to have been on an estate called Gobions, after a family of which there were two branches, one in Northampton, the other at Yardley Gobion, a village some nine miles away. The Gobions of Yardley were descendants of Henry Gobion, younger son of Richard Gobion, of Northampton and Yardley, grandson of Hugh Gobion, who was Sheriff of Northamptonshire from 1161–4.

A manor house or homestead called Gobions was destroyed in the Dreadful Fire of Northampton in 1675 and remained unrestored until 1689 when Richard Lee agreed to rebuild it on being granted a lease for sixty-one years from Lady Day, 1678, at £1 6s. 8d. rent. Whether this became the Riding School or when the School was founded is not clear.

The Riding School and other properties on the Gobions estate appear to have been a Corporation leasehold and it is likely that this arose as a result of the fire, when a special Act of Parliament was hurried through for the rebuilding of the town, modelled on the one following the Great Fire of London in 1666.

I find surprising a statement by the Northampton newspaper editor Samuel Smith Campion in a "Homelands" guide to Northampton in June, 1907, that the Riding School had a pit, gallery and upper gallery and would hold nearly 2,000 persons. The pit might have been standing room needing no seating but even so from where would a town with a population of about 5,000 be able to produce an audience of 2,000? Where Sammy Campion obtained this figure is not clear and the reference makes one wish that he was one of the academics who sprinkle their sources at the bottom of each page.

From some later references to entertainments it would appear that equestrian feats, for example, were performed in some sort of amphitheatre, presumably in the Riding School yard which is indicated on the map of 1747.

The theatrical performances must surely have been in part of the Riding House itself. As to the layout or architecture of the buildings there are few clues, nor as to its interior or fittings. Perhaps the latter were something like those described by an actor member of Jackson's Company at Fareham, near Portsmouth, in the 1770s. This was in a room at the Black Bull where the manager had "suspended a collection of green tatters along its middle for a curtain, erected a pair of paper screens right hand and left for wings; arranged four candles in front of the said wings to divide the stage from the orchestra (the fiddlers' chairs being legitimate divisions of the orchestra from the pit) and with all the spare benches of the inn to form boxes and a hoop suspended from the ceiling, perforated with a dozen nails to receive as many candles to suggest the idea of a chandelier". Scenery and props were most elementary, with two drop scenes and a few chairs and a table. Manager Jackson would play many parts himself, some from behind the scenes.

On the whole I fancy that, lowly though it may have been, the North-ampton Riding House was a cut above the antics of Manager Jackson. Nevertheless in theatrical matters one must always read between the lines. The manager puffeth ever. Even into the beginning of the present century quite a few theatres had bench seats in the pit, including the Northampton Theatre Royal and Opera House, Guildhall Road, and in make-shift theatres of the eighteenth century the seating was probably very rudimentary—planks perched on boxes perhaps.

Even in some of the lesser London theatres of the eighteenth century conditions were very cramped. George Colman the younger suggested that patrons of the Little Theatre in the Haymarket should have bells round their necks like wagon horses, to give notice of their approach—"The avenues to the side boxes were so incurably narrow that when two corpulent gentlemen endeavoured to squeeze past each other there was great danger of sticking in the way."

As regards what conditions were like backstage (or "behind the scenes" to quote the contemporary expression) we have Hogarth's pictures. Writing of a performance at Brentford in 1766 that talented but unpredictable actor George Frederick Cooke noted : "We dress male and female in one room." If such goings on were known to the audiences it can scarcely have raised the Drama in their estimation. Though in some amateur groups today, such as those performing in village halls, it occurs.

If this early Northampton theatre in The Riding ever had a device upon its escutcheon it might well have been that of the nosegay—the floral or herbal garland carried by the Law. Judges of old felt it necessary to have this unofficial badge of office as they walked through the streets from the church, where the Assize service had been held, to the courts. In church they had joined in prayers for the spiritual elevation of mankind in general ; on the bench they decreed the physical elevation on the gibbets of mankind in particular. Such a nosegay would have been useful when passing up the Riding School passage, into the yard and thence to the "theatre". I suppose that if a table of ratings of strong smells was drawn up those of equestrian source would come high up. In Vanbrugh's *A Journey to London* Colonel Courtly says of a rural visitor to London : "The man's a walking stable."

The first record of a performance in the Riding House (as it was then referred to) comes in the Mercury on May 31, 1742 : "We hear that Mr. Jones' Company of Comedians from the theatres in London have taken for a play-house the Riding House in this town and will open there on Monday, June 14, with the last new comedy called *Pamela* or *Virtue Rewarded*. The place will be fitted up in a theatrical manner. The company will stay but six weeks being obliged to be at Preston Guild (or Grand Jubilee) in Lancashire which begins on August 30."

In fact the season was even shorter, for it began a week late, as a further announcement on Monday, June 21, shows : "... will open this evening". After that there is no mention of the performances so the only names we have are "Mr. Jones" and "Pamela".

Who was "Mr. Jones"? Apart from Smith and Brown it could scarcely have been a less easily identifiable surname. But there was a Mr. Charles

Jones in the 1742-3 company at the Lincolns Inn Fields theatre and at the Theatre Royal, Drury Lane, in the season beginning September, 1743.

And who was "Pamela", whose virtue was thus rewarded? This was presumably the Pamela of Richardson's novel of 1740. In the Stamford Mercury I found the same piece offered in literary form in June, 1741. Under the identical title a two-volume account was published of "the letters of a beautiful young damsel to her parents, published in order to cultivate the principles of virtue and religion in the minds of the youth of both sexes". It was, claimed the blurb, "divested of all those images which in too many pieces calculated for amusement only tend to inflame the minds they would instruct".

Perhaps, however, the reader wanted to have his mind inflamed? If so he could read further and decide to purchase instead Anti-Pamela or Feigned Innocence, a series of Sirana's Adventures showing the mischief that arises from a too sudden admiration, published the same day as "a necessary caution to all young gentlemen".

It may appear surprising that the Jones' Company should travel 170 miles from Northampton to an engagement in Lancashire but the Preston Guild was, and still is, something rather special. From the second half of the twelfth century Preston had a Guild Merchant whose members formerly had exclusive command of markets and trading in the town and enjoyed exemption from certain taxes in the country at large. Many Royal Charters confirmed the rights of the burgesses and celebrations of the Guild have been held since 1328. At first the intervals between them were irregular but since 1542 they have been held every twenty years, up till 1922, the event being missed in the war-time year of 1942, and resumed in 1952 and 1972. The Guild Merchant is held to enable freemen to renew their privileges and enrol their sons and the feasting and jollifications last for a week or so beginning on the Monday after the feast of the Decollation of John the Baptist.

In 1742 this Monday fell on August 30 and the town would have attracted players, musicians and itinerants of all kinds. Disappointingly, however, there is no record of the entertainments provided. This is especially frustrating because the Preston Journal had started up two years earlier and copies do survive of September 10-17 but they do not mention the event.

There is no subsequent mention of the Jones' Company in Northampton. After the 1743 performances at the Abington Street "Playhouse" there are no references to entertainment until July, 1750, when "the playhouse in St. Giles Street" was taken by Widow Rayner's Company from London "with several new feats of activities on the stiff rope, tumbling etc." In fact Widow Rayner was a Shakespearian actress and because of legal restrictions the wording was probably guarded. The description of the playhouse as being in St. Giles Street is intriguing, as will be seen.

When the King or a member of the Royal Family died it was the custom for the playhouses, certainly those in London, to close and this closure sometimes lasted quite a long while, especially if the funeral was not held immediately. In March, 1751, the Prince of Wales died of pleurisy and the Lord Chamberlain instructed the playhouses to close until further notice.

Marks of outward respect are not always in accord with popular feelings and on this occasion a ballad reflected an astonishing measure of open disloyalty :

> *Here lies Fred*
> *Who was alive and is dead*
> *Had it been his father*
> *I had much rather*
> *Had it been his brother*
> *Still better than another*
> *Had it been his sister*
> *No one would have missed her*
> *Had it been the whole generation*
> *Still better for the nation*
> *But since tis only Fred*
> *Who was alive and is dead*
> *There's no more to be said.*

Even our most strongly left-wing elements of today would scarcely come out with such an insult to Majesty.

The deceased Prince had apparently been a patron of a Mr. Powell, another fire-eater, who came to the Saracen's Head, Abington Street, early in 1752 having previously appeared before the Lord Mayor at the London Guildhall ("where never man besides himself was ever admitted"); Windsor Lodge, where he entertained the Duke of Cumberland; and Kew, where the Prince of Wales and Prince Richard were among his audience. From Northampton he was to proceed to Warwick, Coventry, Birmingham, Derby, Nottingham, York and Scarborough. Four years later, in October, 1756, he was back in Northamptonshire, at Kettering, Wellingborough and Oundle. In 1752 Powell described himself as "original for 30 years" and eighteen years later he was back in town consuming his combustibles, after entertaining the Duke and Duchess of Grafton at Wakefield Lawn, Potterspury, Northants. A fire-eater named Powell is also mentioned in an announcement at Stamford in June, 1778, which said that he would proceed from the Swan and Talbot there to Rippingdale, Gosberton, Tattershall, Spilsby, Horncastle, Louth, Caistor, Brigg, Barton and Winteringham.

The Shrove Tuesday of 1752 found the Mayor of Northampton forbidding the ancient amusement of "throwing at cocks in the streets and lanes of the town". He also initiated public house raids on Sundays—"The publick inns and alehouses were visited in time of Divine Service and people found tippling were obliged the next day to pay penalties according to the Statutes of Edward VI, Elizabeth and James I."

The playbill which is reproduced at the start of the book and on the dustcover is a reminder of how much of Northampton's eighteenth-century theatre history may have left no clues for the historian. It is the earliest Northampton playbill which I have traced, indeed the only one relating to that century, although there are one or two for places in the county. Despite its being the last night of the season, when a flowery farewell might be expected, the bill does not even name the company and does not give the venue. Even the year is left out but from the date, "Monday, September 18, N.S.", it seems to have been of 1752. "N.S." refers to New Style, the calendar change when twelve days were skipped. The playbill appears to have been issued within days of the change for the "New Style" Act of Parliament decreed that the day after September 2, 1752, should become September 14. Previously the English legal year began on March 25. Thus England came into line with the Continent, just as it is doing in our day in such matters as metres and feet and decimalisation of weight and coinage.

As to the company, it seems possible that it was that of Mr. Quelch who, with his wife is among the cast of *Theodosius* or *The Force of Love,* a tragedy which had been first produced in 1680. Quelch is mentioned in theatrical memoirs of this period, including those of Henry Lee who recounts his experiences at Huntingdon.

Quelch had played at Oundle, Northants, at the end of 1752 or the beginning of 1753 and then "opened in a barn at the lower end of Crown Inn yard, Huntingdon" at the time of an election. The first night was paid for by the honourable candidate, Captain Montague of Hinchingbroke Castle, who sent 20 guineas with orders not to take other money nor to admit anyone without a ticket signed by one of his agents. "This night's entertainment was designed as a compliment to the voters that were in the captain's interest with their wives and country cousins." A case of drama that smelled—an electoral bribe.

"But poor Quelch, without any other design than to promote the interest of his company, had, before this order came despatched a person to Cambridge to distribute bills among the several colleges." A party of young bucks arrived and caused a rare old disturbance, first on being refused admission, and then, on being admitted, when their money was refused.

As regards the Northampton playbill, the point is that there is *no mention whatsoever* of the Quelch season in the Mercury, which leads one to wonder how many other seasons failed to leave an imprint on the pages of the newspaper.

As the season ended on Monday, September 18, it was most likely connected with the autumn races. On Wednesday, August 26, there had been a gentlemen's ordinary at the Peacock, a ladies' ordinary at the George, and a ball at the Red Lion; on the Thursday the same three events were switched round, the gentlemen's function being at the Red Lion, the ladies' at the Peacock and the ball at the George.

With this 1752 season at Northampton in mind the fact that nothing appears in the Press between 1752 and 1756 is no certain evidence that nothing dramatic was happening : it may have been happening but left no traces.

On October 11, 1756, the Mercury reported : "We hear that the Warwick Company of Comedians (who have some time been expected here) will open their theatre in this town on Monday next with the new tragedy of *The Earl of Essex* and the last new farce of *The Apprentices.*"

Thus the company which had been "expected some time" were due to give their first performance on Monday, October 18, but in fact they didn't.

We hear that the Warwick Company of Comedians (who have fome Time been expected here) will open their Theatre in this Town, on Monday next, with the new Tragedy of *The Earl of Essex*, and the last new Farce, call'd, *The Apprentice:*

Advertisement to the Town.

New Theatre in St. Giles's-Street, Northampton.

NOtwithstanding that we might, according to last Week's Paper, have been in a very tolerable Degree of Readiness to have perform'd this Evening; yet, as we are defirous to entertain the Town in the best Manner we possibly can, and as the Place is not so completly finish'd as we were in Hopes it would, we think it a Duty incumbent upon us rather to fuftain the Lofs of a Night's Performance, and poftpone our first Play till Tuefday the 19th, than to prefume to begin till we have gain'd that Point of Perfection to which our weak Endeavours can arrive: And, as there is no other View in this Delay than the better Entertainment of the Town, we humbly hope the Difappointment will not be imputed as a Fault, fince we rather chufe to fuffer in Profit than in Reputation.

N. B. On Tuefday Evening will be prefented an excellent Comedy (written by Mr. Baker) call'd, *Tunbridge Walks, or, The Yeoman of Kent*; with a Farce, call'd, *A Wonder! An honeft Yorkfhireman*. To begin at Six o'Clock.

We hear that an Accident happen'd at the Theatre in this Town on Wednefday laft, fome of the Gallery Seats falling down, but providentially no Damage was fuftain'd ; however, they are now fo effectually repair'd, and fuch due and proper Care has been taken to make them fafe and firm, that no fuch Misfortune need again be fear'd.——This Evening will be acted the celebrated Hiftorical Tragedy, call'd, ROMEO *and* JULIET, with the Mafquerade-Dance, folemn Dirge and Funeral Proceffion of *Juliet*; together with a Farce, call'd, *The Miller of Mansfield*.

☞ *At the Theatre in this Town, this Evening, will be acted a Tragedy, call'd,* HAMLET, *Prince of* Denmark; *to which will be added a Farce, call'd,* LETHE, *or* ÆSOP *in the Shades. To begin at Six o'Clock.*——N. B. *There will be Fires in the Pit.*——*The Company's Stay in Town will be fhort.*

FOUR REFERENCES in the Northampton Mercury to the 1756 season at Northampton by the Warwick Company, respectively dated October 11 and 18, and November 8 and 15.

Just why was explained in one of those verbose but friendly and unsophisticated announcements which punctuate eighteenth-century provincial theatre history : "Notwithstanding that we might according to last week's paper have been in a very tolerable degree of readiness to have performed this evening, yet as we are desirous to entertain the town in the best manner we possibly can and as the place is not so compleatly finished as we were in hopes it would we think it a duty incumbent upon us rather to sustain the loss of a night's performance and postpone our first play till Tuesday the 19th, than to presume to begin till we have gained that point of perfection to which our weak endeavours can arrive. And as there is no other view in this delay than the better entertainment of the town we humbly hope the disappointment will not be imputed as a fault since we rather chuse to suffer in profit than in reputation."

On the Tuesday they staged *Tunbridge Walls* or *The Yeoman of Kent* with a farce called *A Wonder! An Honest Yorkshireman*. On Friday, October 22, it was *Oronooko* and other plays of the season included *The Recruiting Officer*, *The Lying Valet*, *The Constant Couple*, *George Barnwell*, *Miss In Her Teens*, *Romeo and Juliet* and *The Miller of Mansfield*.

The late start was not the only mishap of the Warwick Company's Season. On Wednesday, November 3, some of the gallery seats fell down but "providentially no damage was sustained" and "they are now so effectually repaired and such due and proper care has been taken to make them safe and firm that no such misfortune need again be feared".

In the Northampton accident no one seems to have been hurt but that there could be a real danger in "theatres" which were improvised in barns, etc. (apart from the fire perils of thatch) is illustrated by a happening at Melton Mowbray, Leicestershire, which was reported in the Mercury on February 16, 1778 : "Last Monday night a most melancholy accident happened. A company of comedians having fitted up a barn for the purposes of a theatre (and the play being that night bespoke by a gentleman of the neighbourhood) the place was so uncommonly crowded that great numbers were refused admittance for want of room."

They were the lucky ones. "About the middle of the entertainment a large beam which had been put into the wall for the support of the upper gallery, but not properly secured, gave way and one end drawing out of the wall fell down upon the company below. A young lady, daughter to a gentleman of that town, was unfortunately struck with the end of the beam and had her leg and thigh broke and now lies in the utmost danger of her life. Numbers were also much bruised and hurt. The town became instantly alarmed and supposing the place on fire burst open the door and forcing themselves forwards prevented the audience from getting out. In this situation they continued a considerable time but at last were relieved, some much wounded and others with their cloaths stripped off their backs."

Between the apparently single season of the Warwick Company in 1756 and the arrival of Messrs. Durravans Company of Comedians in 1759 for the first of five seasons there is again scant reference to entertainment, apart from a dromedary and camel being on show at the Chequer Inn, Northampton, in October, 1758. These animals, which were looked upon as great curiosities, afterwards moved on to Market Harborough in what was no doubt a nation-wide tour.

Meantime the cost both of buying a newspaper and of advertising in it had gone up. In July, 1757, the raising of the newspaper duty led to an increase in the price of the Mercury from 2d. to 2½d. And any theatre manager who wanted to take space had to pay 1s. a time tax, along with all the other advertisers.

Governments in those times did not like the Press any more than they favoured the Drama and prices of newspapers were to go a lot higher before the importance of the dissemination of knowledge was accepted and duty and prices tumbled to a level at which the Press could begin to become the Popular Press.

Thus the Governments of those times may well have been to blame for the gaps in theatrical history, quite apart from the fact that they had tried to make provincial theatre illegal. The manager would think twice about advertising if, on top of the cost, he had to pay the admission price of one seat in tax as well.

In effect it was an early example of Entertainment Tax, which was not to be introduced officially until 1916.

"The stage should either be wholly depressed or laudably encouraged . . . example is of more force than precept, so virtue personiz'd and heightened by action must make a deep impression on the soul."
—Mr. Durravan

PHILOSOPHY as well as information in the Northampton Mercury in a Durravan advertisement on August 2, 1762.

By Meff DURRAVANS' *Company of* COMEDIANS,
AT the Theatre in the Riding in Northampton, on Monday Evening, Aug. 2, will be prefented a TRAGEDY (never acted here) call'd,

MACBETH, by SHAKESPEAR.

With all the Original *Mufick*, both *Vocal* and *Inftrumental, Scenes, Machines, Sinkings, Flyings,* and other Decorations proper to the Play.----To which will be added, the two *Favourite Scenes* out of the Farce of the UPHOLSTERER, after the Manner of the Originals.

☞ On Monday laft was acted, by Defire of Major DICKENSON, a Comedy, call'd *Love for Love,* with *High Life below Stairs* for the 4th time. This Effort fhews the Goodnefs of the worthy Gentleman who favour'd this Performance with his Company and Intereft ----On Wednefday Evening, *Hamlet,* with *The Intriguing Footman.*---And on Friday Evening, by Defire of the Hon. SPENCER COMPTON, Efq; *The Mourning Bride,* with *Harlequin Triumphant* for the 4th Time, to a Houfe fill'd with Ladies and Gentlemen.----Mr. DURRAVAN, on his Part in particular, and in refpect of his People in general, fenfible of the Honour done him, and the Regard paid to his Company, by repeated Inftances of Generofity and Protection, pays, for himfelf and all concern'd, the profoundeft Acknowledgment of Thanks and Refpect. The Stage has ever been the Attention of the Learned, the Delight of the Public: Royalty has fecur'd it, and the Legiflative Power tolerated and encourag'd it; and Arguments, however fpeculative and conclufive, tending to depreciate it, muft lofe their Effect and Force, from fuch united Support. The Stage fhould either be wholly deprefs'd, or laudably encourag'd; but as its chief End and Motive is the Promotion of Virtue, and Difcouragement of Vice, and as all Dramatic Pieces are refus'd Reprefentation, which do not tend to that Purport, it has ever defervedly been the Object of the higheft Concern, and the Publick are themfelves interefted in its Behalf. Theatrical Exhibitions have ftill continu'd the firft in the long Lift of Entertainments, as the moft rational Amufement of the Mind. Example is of more Force than Precept, fo Virtue perfoniz'd, and heighten'd by Action, muft make a deep Impreffion on the Soul.

Scene Two

THE DRUMLESS DURRAVANS

With the arrival in Northampton in 1759* of Messrs. Durravans Company of Comedians we enter a period in which much more detailed evidence is available of theatrical activities in the town.

Through their Press advertisements the Durravans not only provided more information to the public about the plays they were to stage, the players who were to appear in them, the circumstances in which performances would take place, the costumes and scenery which would be used to heighten the illusions, the plots of the plays, their authors, where tickets might be obtained, where the actors were lodging, etc., but also advanced philosophical arguments in favour (or defence?) of the Drama.

The Durravans were to appear in five seasons at Northampton : 1759, October to December; 1762, May to September; 1764, May to July; 1768, May to September; and 1771, April to July.

Of their debut in the autumn of 1759 there is no advance notice in the Mercury nor a reference to the first night but on October 22 the paper recorded : "On Monday last the play of *The Suspicious Husband*, by command of the Rt. Hon. the Earl of Northampton, was performed by Messrs. Durravans Company at the theatre in this town before a numerous and polite audience." On Bonfire Night, November 5, the paper mentioned that the Rt. Hon. John Spencer, of Althorp, had commanded *The Busy Body* and *The Upholsterer*. Other productions in a season lasting into December were *The Drummer, Romeo and Juliet, The Adventures of Half an Hour, The Miser, Lethe or Aesop in The Shades, The Inconstant, Wit at a Pinch, The Country Lasses*, and *High Life Below Stairs*.

The "command" performances were patronage occasions when some leading local figure, a nobleman or member of the gentry, lent support by promising to take all or part of the house and they constituted a vital element not only in the financial sphere but also as upper class condonement of what was of doubtful legality.

At Bath, a city where theatre was relatively strongly entrenched, there was this doggerel poem entitled The Pleasures of Bath :

* 1759 was their first season in Northampton, not 1762 as stated in Theatre Un-Royal.

4—TDTS * *

Pray Madam bespeak
Or the Playhouse must break
We've had a bad season
And hope for that reason
You won't see three
For a whole company.

We'll strut you Cato
Or speeches of Plato
Farce, comedy, pastoral
We can master all.

Days of playing at Northampton appear to have been elastic to a degree for while in 1762 they were stated to be Monday, Wednesday and Friday it was made clear that if a member of the upper set wanted a command performance on another day this could be arranged.

Equally prominent was the "benefit" and similarly this could be a vital feature in the finances of the individual actor or actress. On these nights one or more of them received the whole or part of the takings, subject usually to certain (or in the case of unscrupulous managers, uncertain!) deductions.

Among the Durravan benefits it is interesting to note that *The Inconstant* or *The Way to Win Him* staged on December 3, 1759, was for the benefit of Mr. Didier and Mrs. Quelch—whether the same Mrs. Quelch who appeared with her husband in 1752 one can only speculate, lacking initials, Christian names or other evidence. In their first season, probably in an effort to get into the town's good books, the company staged a different sort of benefit, with the aim of helping Mr. Thomas Greenhough who had been in gaol for four years, not for crime but debt. As a result, as related in the Interlude, he was released.

Thus there were two main types of benefit—for members of the company, as a means of supplementing their income; and for good causes, sometimes local, sometimes national; sometimes charitable, sometimes patriotic. There is not space here to go into the whole question of the benefit system which has in any case been dealt with admirably in The Benefit System in the British Theatre, written by the late Sir St. Vincent Troubridge and published by the Society for Theatre Research.

But as they were a form of extra remuneration it was in the beneficiary's interest to see that as many tickets as possible were sold and this he or she would do by going the rounds selling them and making them available at his or her lodgings and at as many other points of sale as possible. When it was a joint benefit for Mr. Ward and Mr. Benson in August, 1768, tickets were to be had "as usual and at the George, Peacock, Red Lyon, Angel, Saracen's Head, Black Lyon, Spread Eagle, Blue Boar, Mr. Froggatt's, barber; Mr. Hickman, confectioner and of Mr. Ward and Mr. Benson at their lodgings in the Riding School Yard". A remarkable feat or organisation on the part of this pair, to recruit so many assistants to sell their tickets for them. Did they invest a certain amount of capital in patronising all these public houses and inns beforehand? If so, it must have been a boozy circuit of the town. The selling points varied from benefit to benefit. When Mrs. Durravan had hers that same month the list was : George, Red Lyon, Peacock, Angel, Mr. Lacy and Mrs. Pasham, booksellers; Mr. Froggat, barber; Mr. Hickman, confectioner; Mr. J. Durravan at Mr. Dyer's in the Market Place; and Mr. M. Durravan at Mrs. Palmer's in Fish Lane. Mr. Durravan himself (the lack of an initial indicated seniority) stayed at "Mr. Dyer's china shop in the Market Place".

In Northampton the benefit system survived vestigially into the twentieth century though sometimes in an entirely artificial form. Edward Compton was not only the proprietor of the Compton Comedy Company but also joint proprietor of the Northampton Theatre Royal and Opera House where they played, so whatever benefit there was to be had from the performances would surely come his way in any case. But, very much a traditionalist, he carried on announcing his own benefit night (and nobody else's).

After their 1759 season at Northampton the Durravans announced that they would open at the New Theatre, Leicester, on Monday, December 24, and continue to perform there on Monday, Wednesday and Friday. On January 14, 1760, the Mercury reported hearing from Leicester that on the 4th they had performed *The Recruiting Officer* and *High Life Below Stairs* by command of Her Grace the "Dutchess" of Hamilton and Brandon; and on the 9th *The Stratagem* and *The Devil to Pay* by command of the Rt. Hon. Lady Hamilton; and that that evening, the 14th, they would give *The Suspicious Husband* and *High Life Below Stairs* again, this time by command of the Rt. Hon. Lady Rous.

From another source one learns that the "New Theatre" at Leicester was in fact the Assembly Rooms and that the company were still in the city in April. Mr. and Mrs. Blanchard, who were in the cast of *The Busy Body*, were probably the parents of the then infant, Lomas, who later achieved some eminence in the profession at Bath and Covent Garden. Mrs. Quelch was still with the company then but later moved on to Bath.

An interesting comment on the performance of *The Busy Body* is made by Harry Greatorex, Patron-in-Chief of this book : "In total 13 names appear on the bills, three more than the author actually wrote parts for and three more than performed in the comedy when it was produced at the Drury Lane and Covent Garden theatres. Obviously wanting to make a favourable impact with his opening production, Durravan introduced the three new characters so that he could show off the size of his company."

There was no theatre company in Northampton to take part in the celebrations marking the Proclamation of George III in November, 1760. The report which appeared in the Mercury about the local festivities indicated, however, that the town had some form of musical establishment —the "Town's Musick" took part in ceremonials on the Market Square (or Place as it was also referred to) and in the evening the gentlemen of the Corporation met at the Red Lion Inn, to drink the health of His Majesty.

To mark the Coronation the following year a large fat ox was roasted whole on the Market Hill (yet another name for the central open place), several hogsheads of strong beer were provided for the populace, and a pole with a crown on top was a feature of the decorations. Mayor and Corporation announced however that they would "punish with the utmost rigour any throwers of crackers, squibs, or other mischievous fireworks".

The following spring, 1762, the Durravans were back and this time their Northampton season was preceded by one at the Leicester theatre on the Coal-Hill, which had begun on Wednesday, January 20, with the tragedy *Tamerlane* and *The Oracle* and continued until April.

Although, as will emerge, they refrained from banging the drum, in their more expansive Press advertisements the Durravans were keen, like showbiz folk throughout the ages, to trumpet their talents, praise their equipment and vaunt their capabilities. Such as, in May, 1762 : "Messrs. Durravans take this opportunity of informing the ladies and gentlemen of Northampton that they have with great diligence and expense provided and improv'd their stock of cloaths, scenery, machinery, etc., in order to entertain the publick in the best manner with the best plays. As a farther inducement to the taste of a polite audience, all the new plays, farces, interludes that have lately taken a run in London and never performed here shall with great care and propriety be exhibited. As a proof of the goodness of the performers no trouble has been spar'd in collecting the best from several companies and particularly from London and Dublin. The house is commodiously fitted up and the company humbly hope for encouragement."

Despite being "commodiously fitted up" the house was exceedingly modest in theatrical facilities, for a report said that "The pit was crowded with almost all the ladies and gentlemen in and about the town nor could any person pretend to say that Northampton ever produced so numerous and so bright an audience at the theatre before. The utmost regularity was observ'd and candour, not ill-nature, play'd the critic." If the "ladies and gentlemen" were in the pit, this means that there were no boxes in which they could segregate themselves from the common folk and this is borne out by the price list : Pit 2s., Gallery 1s., Back Seats 6d. Whether a fit-up or the genuine article, a theatre which had boxes was one up the scale from one which had not.

In times when superstition still retained a powerful hold and the occasional witch could still find herself being dipped in the river or village pond (one was dipped at Mears Ashby, Northants, as late as August, 1785), if not burned in fire, or, the more usual British remedy, hanged by the neck, plays with a supernatural theme and a ghost or two among the dramatis personae were popular. This point was touched on in a prologue delivered at the Northampton theatre by Almeria, title character in Congreve's *The Mourning Bride*. It appears in a book of oddments called Hope's Curious and Comic Miscellaneous Works, Started in His Walks, which appeared in April, 1780, and includes the following :

A Gothic taste hath reigned in latter Age,
To raise the dead—to spout upon the Stage;
Here Murder'd Kings, stabb'd wives and poison'd Maids,
Start up to Life—and hail you from the Shades
Thus we tame Players, when our Authors bid
Tho' slain, must rise (pointing to the floor) our coffin has no lid.

She went on to say that although a mourning bride she would be a happy one if only the audience would applaud.

The plot was one of murder by mistake. Furious at his daughter's marriage to Osmyn, the King of Granada took Osmyn's place in a cell so that when she came to rescue him she would be thwarted. Through some small administrative slip the King himself was executed but when his daughter found the decapitated body in Osmyn's clothes she imagined it was indeed her beloved and took poison. Congreve's only tragedy, the play is mercifully forgotten today but some lines in it are remembered

> *Heaven has no rage like love to hatred turned*
> *Nor Hell a fury like a woman scorned.*

The actual date of the prologue being given at Northampton is not stated but the only reference to the play being performed in the town is by the Durravans, in July, 1762, commanded by the Hon. Spencer Compton.

Other patrons of performances in 1762 included Major Dickinson, the officers of the Royal Cheshire Militia, Mrs. Isteds and Mrs. Clavering.

The Intriguing Footman which the Durravans presented on July 26, 1762, in support of *Hamlet* was the only play written by the theatrical manager James Augustus (Jemmy) Whitley who was a real card and will turn up later in these pages.

When the Durravans staged *Jane Shore*, one of the most popular and long-lasting plays, it was described as "containing the tyranny and usurpation of the Duke of Gloucester, then Protector of the Realm. The difficulties and lamentable end of the unfortunate fair one Jane Shore, concubine to Edward IV, who perished in a ditch for want of food, it being proclaimed by order of the cruel Duke that whoever gave her comfort, food or harbour should suffer death. With many other historical beautiful passages."

Characters in some of the pieces presented bore names signifying their nature. *When Love Makes a Man* or *The Fop's Fortune* was staged on Monday, August 23, 1762, for the benefit of Mr. and Mrs. Stanton there were names like Clodio alias Don Dismallo Thickscullo de Halfwitto (Mr. Clarendon) and Don Lewis alias Don Choleric Snapshorto (Mr. Parsons.)

For this joint benefit Mrs. Stanton excused herself from touting personally with tickets—"indisposition renders a personal application on her part impossible". On a number of occasions one finds an actor or actress avoiding the chore, distasteful to many, of making themselves pleasant to possible patrons, using either legitimate reason or trumped up excuse. One of the Durravans did it during the last month the company appeared in Northampton, July, 1771, when there was a benefit for "Mr. J. Durravan and the Company". A footnote stated "As Mr. Durravan's indisposition is such that it may render him incapable of making a general application he humbly hopes for the indulgence of the public on this occasion which will be gratefully acknowledged among the many favours that have already been conferred upon him."

A warning that there was to be no backstage admission was given in May, 1762 : "As it must greatly injure the performance we hope that no person will take it amiss they are refused admittance behind the scenes." In August that year the announcement of *The Tempest*, with all its machinery, was accompanied by a more categorical warning off : "No person whatever can be admitted behind the scenes, it being impossible to perform unless the stage be entirely clear."

To the playgoer of today who is used to being strictly segregated from the stage, entering the foyer and taking his numbered seat, to sit his side of the proscenium arch while the player remains his side of the footlights (in conventional theatres, that is to say) it may seem hard to believe that the audience was ever allowed to invade the sanctum of the backstage, probe its mysteries, penetrate its magic aura. Yet such was not only the case, but gallants, aristocrats, Royal mistress-seekers, and others whose interests were not confined to touching reverently the hem of the muse could enter the dressing rooms of actresses while they were dressing and were even allowed to seat themselves on the stage itself.

Genest's history of the English stage says that critics and wits often occupied stage seats, attended by pages with pipes and tobacco, which was smoked there and in other parts of the house at private performances. During the time of Charles I the custom disappeared but with his son on the restored throne it was revived. Tate Wilkinson, the ramblingly loquacious and best known provincial actor-manager of the eighteenth century, recalled Mrs. Cibber playing Juliet in the tomb scene with 200 of the audience in the tomb with her !

Only exceptionally, on a first night for example, would a ban be operated. When Cibber's *She Would and She Would Not* was produced at Drury

---

By *Meſſ* DURRAVANS' *Company of* COMEDIANS,
A T the Theatre in the Riding in Northampton, on Monday
 Evening, Sept. 6, will be preſented,
   The BEGGARS OPERA.
With all the Original Songs, &c. and a Country Dance by the
      Characters.
The Whole to conclude with the laſt new Muſical Entertainment of
  A BRITON, the Son of a BRITON,
a Poetical and Muſical Rhapſody, occaſion'd by the Birth of a
PRINCE of WALES, between Mr. Bridges, Mrs. Godwin. Mr.
Blanchard, Mrs. Blanchard, Mr. Nepecker, and the reſt of the
Company.
  ☞ On Monday laſt was perform'd *The Tempeſt, or the Enchanted
Iſland*; on Wedneſday Evening, for the ſecond Time, *The
Tempeſt*; and on Friday Evening, *The Tempeſt*, with *A Briton,
the Son of a Briton.*
  N. B. The Company will entertain the Public with ſelect Plays
and Farces, Interludes, &c. during the Races.

A POETICAL and Musical Rhapsody occasion'd by the
Birth of a Prince of Wales in 1762. (*Northampton Mercury*)

Lane in 1702 it was "humbly desired that no gentleman may interrupt the action by standing on the stage the first day".

A playbill for Lincolns Inn Fields in 1720 mentions that "because of rioting and disturbing the audience occasioned by gentlemen going behind the scenes none for the future shall be admitted but who shall take tickets".

Thus it was not entirely the principle that was involved, but the question of payment. The price of a stage seat could be the highest in the house. For a play called *Whig and Tory* by Griffin in 1720 admission tickets for back-stage were to be had at the stage door at half-a-guinea each. But many were willing to pay : it was easier to pick up an actress close at hand on the same level than from a seat yards away and at lower or higher level.

When Dalton's *Comus*, staged at Northampton during the later Kemble regime, in October, 1774, had been given at Drury Lane in 1738 the play-bill carried the footnote : "N.B. To prevent any interruption in the musick, dancing, machinery, or other parts of the performance 'tis hoped no gentle-man will take it ill, that he cannot be admitted behind the scenes, or into the orchestra." The musicians too, apparently, were accustomed to invasion. Many a fiddler's elbow must have been jostled by a tipsy spectator, for those who wished to be nearer the stage were often well primed.

This business of stage seating provided a few lines of dialogue for Alder-man Sharp to say to Captain Smart in *Sir Giddy Whim* in 1703 : "You get your first load of claret by seven—then to the playhouse where you reel about the stage, and expose yourself to all the world at once."

The most recent instance of a Northampton audience sharing the stage with the players comes as late as mid-Victorian times when the Jackman and Morgan Company took their leave and a family link with the Marefair theatre lasting twenty-one years came to a close. Times had been bad for them but when it came to parting the houses were full and they wished to make the most of it. For the farewell benefit for Frederick Morgan and his wife Harriet (nee Jackman) in February, 1861, "every available space where a sight of the stage could be obtained was crammed and the stage itself accommodated a considerable number of people who were packed into the wings, somewhat to the inconvenience of the performers".

During the 1762 season a ballad on Northampton beer, written by Mr. Cunningham, was given by Mr. Blanchard. The inference is that this had been written specially to honour the Northampton beverage but one suspects that the song was one which could be adapted for use in any town where the company happened to be playing. Certainly such a song could not be sung today for in the 1970s the beer breweries have been replaced by one making Danish Carlsberg lager and for the first time in centuries there is no Northampton beer, apart from that which Northamptonians make in kitchen, bathroom or garden shed with "do it yourself" kits.

During the season a Prince was born, the first of fifteen children whom George III was to sire by his Queen, Charlotte. It was the future George IV who was to have to wait a further half-century before ascending the throne (though he did gain the powers of a Regent, through his father's madness) and was to spend some of the impatient years in dalliance with actresses. George III was notable theatrically for making exceptions to the rule that Royalty did not patronise individual benefits.

The Royal birth was reflected in three ways on the Northampton stage. First on August 16, when Mr. Stanton recited a special prologue on the birth of a Prince, written by Mr. Clarendon. The same advertisement announced the postponement of Mr. Durravan's benefit night from Friday to Monday "on account of the universal rejoicings made on the birth of the Prince". These included the firing of three vollies on the Market Hill by the Bedfordshire Militia, then quartered in Northampton. They were drawn up under their Colonel the Marquess of Tavistock, who commanded a performance of *The Beaux Stratagem* on June 21. Later than season, on Monday, September 6, in support of *The Beggar's Opera* there was a "poetic and musical rhapsody occasioned by the birth of a Prince of Wales" in which took part Mr. Bridges, Mrs. Godwin, Mr. Blanchard, Mrs. Blanchard, Mr. Nepecker, and the rest of the company.

The following week the Durravans returned thanks to the town and county and announced that they were off to Litchfield (Lichfield). Subsequently they appeared at Derby from November, 1763, to February, 1764.

Many companies, particularly in former times, had announced their presence in a town by parading about beating a drum and shouting out the name and merits of their "forthcoming attractions". The Durravans, however, announced in May, 1764: "The company use no drum but bills will be properly distributed the day preceding the play." Discarding the drum was evidently regarded as an elevation in status. When Herbert's Lincoln-shire Company omitted the drum at Grantham they are said to have played to empty houses, so that they reinstated it, nominally at the request of the Marquis of Granby. I must say that I find this story hard to swallow: surely people wanting to see a play would not all stay away simply because the company did not bang a drum?

In addition to all the day-to-day particulars given in the Mercury one finds this absorbing Durravan defence of the drama in general: "Mr. Durravan on his part in particular and in respect of his people in general, sensible of the honour done him and the regard paid to his company by repeated instances of generosity and protection, pays for himself and all concerned the profoundest acknowledgement of thanks and respect. The stage has ever been the attention of the learned, the delight of the public: Royalty has secur'd it and the legislative power tolerated and encouraged it; and arguments however speculative and conclusive tending to depreciate it, must lose their effect and force from such united support. The stage should either be wholly depressed or laudably encouraged but as its chief end and motive is the promotion of virtue and discouragement of vice and as all dramatic pieces are refused representation which do not tend to that purport it has ever deservedly been the object of the highest concern and the public are themselves interested in its behalf. Theatrical exhibitions have still continued the first in the long list of entertainments as the most rational amusement of the mind. Example is of more force than precept so virtue personiz'd, and heightened by action must make a deep impression on the soul."

It sounds almost as though Mr. Durravan was pleading his case before a magistrate trying him for illegal play acting. But how eloquently he pleads : how well-worded is his exposition of the cause of the Drama. No ignorant, illiterate showman here. No mere drum-banger at a booth.

In May and June, 1764, a Mr. Robertson turns up in the Durravan Company, playing Fryar Lawrence in *Romeo and Juliet*, Sancho in *Love Makes a Man*, Sir Jasper Wilding in *The Citizen* and Sir Jealous Traffick in *The Busy Body*. There had also been a Mr. Robertson with the company in *The Busy Body* at Leicester in 1760. Was he one of *the* Robertsons? The infuriating custom of the day of not giving initials or Christian names is a hindrance to our knowing. Robertson is one of the most significant names in the history of local companies such as we are discussing. The family was to provide the manager of the Lincoln Company which was to open the new theatre in Northampton in 1806; a Robertson was to be the last manager of that company before its disintegration in 1846; the family was to provide a dramatist who would write a play which was a turning point in the drama, T. W. Robertson, and his *Caste*; and an actress who was to become a Dame for her services to the stage, Dame Madge Kendal, nee Robertson. But the granddaddy of the Robertsons was James Shaftoe Robertson who ran away from Ludlow Grammar School to go on the stage. This was about 1740 and by 1764 he would have been approaching or just turned forty.

The Riding School was the cradle not only of drama but of religion too. It was the first place in Northampton where Methodism was preached. In the spring of 1766 a Regiment of Horse Guards was stationed in the town under Captain Scott who was anxious to spread the cause of evangelistic religion. He wrote to John Wesley asking him to send a preacher and Richard Blackwell came and held services in the Riding School. On October 28 the following year Wesley himself paid the first of some two dozen visits to the town and, as his journal tells us : "We rode into Northampton where in the evening, our own room being far too small, I preached in the Riding School to a large and deeply serious congregation." On another occasion Wesley heard that a man was to be hanged on the Racecourse the following morning, visited the prisoner in his cell and travelled with him on the cart next morning, both of them sitting on the coffin.

In its primary function, however, there are indications that the Riding School was not prospering. In April, 1766, there was an auction sale at the Sign of the Fish (i.e. the Fish Inn) of "a close, several gardens, stables, a coachhouse, a new-built sash'd house in The Riding a good dwelling house, and a tenement adjoining in Abington Street, and several other tenements, with the Riding School, a good wine vault, the Riding Yard and other appurtenances". The following month there came an announcement that John Scofield and Samuel Thompson had taken over the Riding School business from Mr. Deacon and that they would "break horses for the saddle and the coach in the quickest and most reasonable manner." To overcome a slow start the new firm advertised a "don't pay if not satisfied" offer. This was on September 9, 1766, when they said that "not having the business they reasonably expected they attribute it to some prejudice the gentlemen may perhaps retain of their inability to perform it as before done. They therefore (flattering themselves with ability) in this public manner declare not to demand or to receive any thing for their trouble if due satisfaction be not given."

The special offer does not appear to have had the desired effect for in 1778 we find John Scofield cast in a new role—as Town Gaoler, doubling it for a special performance with that of seller of theatre tickets, as will emerge in the Interlude.

When the Durravans turned up for their 1768 season it seems that either new premises were brought into theatrical use or that the old ones had been considerably tarted up. Stating that they would present *The Stratagem* in the New Theatre, St. Gyles Street, they claimed that "the house will be fitted up in a more elegant and commodious manner than any Thing of the Kind that has ever been seen in this town." Bearing in mind the flatulence of managerial language this could mean anything, but the significant thing is that there were now boxes. These were priced at 3s., with the pit at 2s. and the gallery at 1s. The lighting was "in the manner of the London theatres".

To ask whether the theatre in The Riding was the same one as that in St. Gyles (or Giles) Street may seem self-answering to the reader not familiar with Northampton but in fact the two present-day streets are parallel and back on to each other. At the time in question the Riding was the Riding (place) and not yet a thoroughfare.

I had hoped to solve the question of whether there were two different playhouses by reference to the rate books of St. Giles Parish, some of which are at Northampton Public Library and others at Northamptonshire Record Office, at Delapre Abbey, but as often happens in such cases the evidence is not precise or clear-cut. A consecutive annual series is not available. The

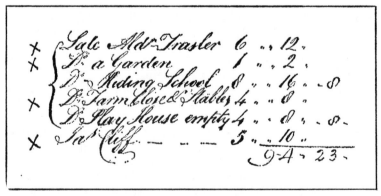

THE PLAY HOUSE, listed separately from the Riding School, is described as "empty" in the St. Giles Parish Rate Book of 1803. (*Northamptonshire County Library at Northampton*)

> *By Defire of* ROBERT CLAVERING, *Efq*;
> AT the NEW THEATRE in St. Gyles's-Street, Northampton, by Meff. DURRAVANS' Company of Comedians, on Monday, June 13, will be prefented a Comedy, call'd,
>
> ## ALL IN THE WRONG.
>
> End of Act II. a SONG by Mifs Hopton.
> End of Act III. a SONG by Mrs. Jacobs.
> End of Act IV. a SONG by Mifs Hopton.
> End of the Play a SONG by Mrs. Jacobs.
> To which will be added (by Defire) a Farce, call'd,
>
> ## The Spirit of Contradiction.
>
> To begin exactly at Half after Six.
> The Houfe is lighted in the Manner of the London Theatres.
> ☞ The Days of Playing are Mondays, Wednefdays, and Fridays.

"LIGHTED in the manner of the London Theatres" . . . June 1768. (*Northampton Mercury*)

first actual mention of a playhouse comes in 1773 but the books of 1767 and 1768 do not cite it by name.

The 1771 and 1772 listings of the Riding School Yard and other properties were in the name of Mr. Hillyard, Mr. Scofield having by then become Town Gaoler, and then, in 1773, comes the interesting entry : "Mr. Trasler, House (5s.), Close (1s.), Riding School (5s.) and Playhouse (2s.)". After that separate Playhouse entries continued until at least 1803 when it was noted that it was "Empty".

We are indebted to a political source for a street guide which clearly places the theatre in St. Giles Street in 1768. This was the year of a Parliamentary election which was the most notable, or notorious, in the history of a town which has had more than its share of political incident (e.g. Charles Bradlaugh, the Radical Member who was thrown bodily out of the House of Commons; and Adolphus Drucker the Dutch-born Tory M.P. who fled abroad in debt and died in a New York ward for alcoholics at the age of thirty-five).

In 1768 the Earls of Northampton and Halifax and the Earl Spencer are said to have spent a quarter of a million pounds on election expenses. Earl Spencer threw in the liquid contents of his cellar. The finances of all three families were severely strained. But as far as we are concerned the significance of all this electoral hurley-burley is that someone in charge of getting the voters out made a detailed street guide to the town and "The Playhouse" is clearly marked on it, in St. Giles Street.

George De Wilde, editor of the Mercury from 1830–71, wrote a series of articles called Rambles Roundabout, which were afterwards published in book form. In 1866, for one of the series, instead of going on a real ramble

A VOTE-PURSUING election map of 1768 clearly locates a make-shift theatre as being in St. Giles Street. It was elsewhere stated that the premises had formerly been used as a malting. (*Northamptonshire County Library at Northampton*)

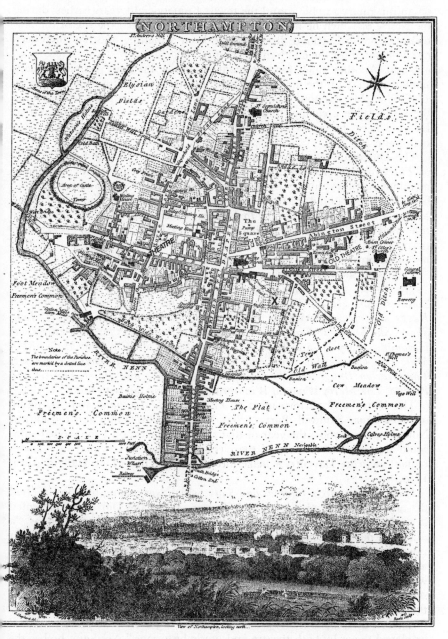

LOCATION of the St. Giles Street make-shift theatre (marked Old Theatre) and of the
purpose-built theatre (marked Theatre) opened in Marefair in 1806. The map was made by
J. Roper and G. Cole in 1807. (*Northamptonshire County Library at Northampton*)

in the county, he fished out this electoral guide of 1768 and took his readers
on an imaginary ramble round the town of ninety-eight years earlier, during
the course of which he noted : "The Playhouse occupied the site of the new
houses opposite Castilian Street. It had been a malting and had then been
newly-adapted for the children of Thespis."

Hmm. Another smell for our nasal palate. A malting. A smell perhaps
similar to that at the first permanent theatre at Stratford-upon-Avon in
1836 when Mr. Leyton, landlord of the adjacent Shakespeare Hotel, hired
the under-stage area for storage of empty casks, etc. at £2 a year. Or at
Derby where James Whitley built his theatre on the site of a former
malthouse.

The Durravans gave three performances, one in 1762, and two in 1768
of *The Provok'd Husband*, which is revealed by a count of the newspaper
mentions of plays during the eighteenth century in Northampton to have
been the most popular. Its author was Colley Cibber, who based it on
Vanbrugh's unfinished *Journey to London*, which was in fact the alternative
title used by Cibber. First produced at Drury Lane in January 1727–8 its
purpose was "chiefly to expose and reform the licentious irregularities that
too often break in upon the peace and happiness of the married state".

The count shows performances at Northampton in 1728, 1743, 1762, 1768,
1771, 1778, 1781, 1784, 1787 and 1793. Other plays with good
"ratings" are *Midas, The Beggar's Opera* and *The Wonder! A Woman
Keeps a Secret*, all with six mentions; *Thomas and Sally, Hamlet, Jane
Shore, She Stoops to Conquer* (first performed here in 1772), *The Suspicious
Husband, Henry IV* and *High Life Below Stairs*, all with five; *Maid of the
Mill, The Clandestine Marriage, The Padlock, The Merchant of Venice,
The Grecian Daughter, The Earl of Essex, Romeo and Juliet, Florizel and
Perdita, The Merry Wives of Windsor* and *Macbeth*, all with four.

The Durravans' performances of *The Provok'd Husband* were by desire
of Sir Thomas Samwell, Bart. (1762), Mrs. Thursby (1768) and the Earl of
Northampton (1768—the year of that sensational election I mentioned—this
could well have been part of the election expenses). The play was also a
request item at Daventry's makeshift theatre in the Moot Hall in April,
1770.

Isaac Bickerstaffe's *Thomas and Sally*, which was among the "fivers", had
the alternative title of *The Sailor's Return*. When the Durravans presented
it at Northampton on Monday, June 24, 1771, it was described as "a
dramatic pastoral concluding with a country dance by the characters". It
is worth a mention because it was typical in two respects. First it was musical
and music played a part in eighteenth century playhouse entertainments
which has not always been sufficiently emphasised, a fact which Roger Fiske
stresses in his book, Theatre Music in the 18th Century. As he puts it : "In
the last forty years of the century the sheer quantity of operatic music performed in the playhouses is astonishing yet it has been continuously ignored
or played down by both theatre and music historians." No doubt he has the
London playhouses mainly in mind but the trend was amply reflected in the
provinces, though there the "pit orchestras" must have been painfully lacking
in numbers and competence at times.

Thomas and Sally was all-singing. The opening called for the sound of horns and clarinets from the wings. How the musical resources of the Durravan Company coped with this it is difficult to imagine. Secondly it was simple and rural. No doubt this suited rural tastes. But the links with "the land" of a town such as Northampton were much closer than they are today. Also, as Mr. Fiske points out, it suited the palates of the London playgoers, along with a great deal of similar rusticity, because it contrasted pleasantly with their own degree of sophistication and, to a degree, degeneracy. The plot is of the simplest kind : wicked Squire pursues Sally but she is saved at the last minute by the return of her sailor lover, Thomas. The first performance at Covent Garden in 1760 had been delayed by the death of George II on October 25, and did not take place until November 28. In the Garrick era at Drury Lane it received more performances than any other afterpiece, musical or otherwise, and continued popular until the end of the century.

Nicholas Rowe's *Tamerlane*, which the Durravans staged at Northampton in July, 1768, was a form of tribute to another English monarch, William III, whose character was represented in the title part. Its first night had been at the Lincolns Inn Fields Theatre, London, on November 4, 1702, the date being the birthday of William III. The dedication by Rowe (who later became Poet Laureate) spoke of Tamerlane's (i.e. the King's) "courage, piety moderation, justice, and fatherly love of his people, but above all his hatred of tyranny and oppression and his zealous care for the common good of mankind".

Two more pieces with a rural flavour were *Love in a Village* and *The Maid of the Mill*, both examples of a new brand of pastiche opera. *Love in a Village* had been first produced in London on December 8, 1762, and had forty consecutive performances at a time when a dozen were remarkable.

When the King and Queen attended a performance on December 30 a "down to earth" touch was provided by a dancer named Miss Poitier— "Her low-cut dress allowed her breasts to flab like a couple of empty bladders in an oil shop", reported the Theatrical Review. Worse was to follow. "One of her shoes came off and those in the front row were able to observe that she was not wearing any drawers. The pit was astonished."

Appropriately the first Northamptonshire performance of *Love in a Village* appears to have been in a village. In the village of Brixworth, half-a-dozen miles north-west of Northampton, I have found but one reference to the drama and that includes the performance there on Monday, January 23, 1769, by Mr. Jackson's Company of this piece. There is little more to be learned about where the theatre was (almost certainly in a barn), about the company, or where they came from and where they went to. There is just the one advertisement in the Mercury, of one week's performances on Monday, Wednesday and Friday. *Love in a Village*, which was presented on the Monday, included *A Statute for the Hiring of Servants*, and was followed by *Miss in Her Teens*. On Wednesday the 25th came *Richard III* and *Damon and Phillida* while on the Friday there were *The Way to Keep Him* with *Hob in The Well* or *The Country Wake* which introduced "the usual diversions of a country wake as ballad singing, cudgel playing, country dancing etc."

The only other early mention of entertainments at Brixworth appears to be in the diary of Thomas Isham of Lamport (1658–81). On the instructions of his father this young man kept a diary in Latin from 1671–3 and on May 12, 1673, he wrote: "Brixworth Fair. My brothers Justinian and John went and there met Sir William Haselwood and Mr. Saunders and Mr. Ashfield with whom they went to see a Punch and Judy Show." This, incidentally, appears to be one of the earliest references to the Punch and Judy Show in contemporary literature. As far as local theatrical perform- ances are concerned the diary is negative—it contains nothing in this category.

The Durravans introduced *Love in a Village* to Northampton in April, 1771, when it was described as an English comic opera. The piece had also been played at Oundle, Northants, in January that year by a company headed by Mr. Moore who had previously performed at Kettering and Wellingborough. At the latter the last night had been Monday, January 14, when there was an "extra band of music" to support *The Busy Body* and *The Citizen*. The opening at Oundle was on Thursday, January 17, when they played *Hamlet* and *The Lying Valet*. *Love in a Village* followed on the Saturday, teamed with *Miss in Her Teens*, with further perform- ances to follow on Tuesdays, Thursdays and Saturdays. Another company which I have discovered at Oundle at a later period is that of Messrs. Humphreys and Seabrook. Advertising their last night at Newport Pagnell, Bucks, on Monday, December 9, 1811, the managers presented their

AT the THEATRE at Brixworth, in Northamptonfhire, by Mr. J A C K S O N's Company of Comedians, on Monday, January 23, will be prefented

LOVE in a VILLAGE.

In which will be introduced a S T A T U T E for the HIRING of SERVANTS.
To conclude with a D A N C E by the Characters.
To which will be added,

MISS in her TEENS.

On Wednefday, January 25, will be prefented,

King RICHARD the Third.

To which will be added,

DAMON and PHILLIDA.

And on Friday, January 27, will be prefented,

The WAY to KEEP HIM.

To which will be added,

HOB in the WELL: Or, The COUNTRY-WAKE.

THE FIRST Northamptonshire production of "Love in a Village" was in the village of Brixworth in 1769. (*Northampton Mercury*)

For the Benefit of Me/Irs..DURRAVAN,
AT the NEW THEATRE in St. Gyles's-Street, Northampton,
by Meff. DURRAVANS' . Company of Comedians, on
Monday, Auguft 29, will be prefented a COMEDY, call'd,
The CLANDESTINE MARRIAGE.
With Entertainments of SINGING, &c.
To which will be added a COMEDY of Two Acts (Never
Acted Here) call'd,
The INTRIGUING CHAMBER-MAID.
☞ TICKETS to be had at the George, Red Lion, Peacock,
and Angel Inns; of. Mr. Lacy, and Mrs. Pafham, Book-
fellers; Mr. Froggat, Barber; Mr. Hickman, Confectioner;
Mr. J. Durravan, at Mr. Dyer's, in the Market-Place; and
of Mr. M. Durravan, at Mrs. Palmer's, in Fifh-Lane.

TEN POINTS of sale for tickets in August, 1768. (*Northampton
Mercury*)

respectful compliments to their friends at Oundle, Stilton, Stony Stratford
and Leighton Buzzard.

Brixworth also figures in the dramatic record because one of its principal
residents commanded a performance at Northampton. It was "by desire of
Mrs. Raynsford of Brixworth" that the Durravans staged the comedy *The
Inconstant* or *The Way to Win Him* on Monday, May 16, 1771. A local
gentleman had written a special prologue which was spoken by Mrs.
Glocester "in the character of Bisarre".

The following Wednesday was another "request night", the command
this time emanating from Mr. Woolley's and Mrs. Pasham's Boarding
Schools whose young ladies and young gentlemen were in the audience.
The surprising choice was the semi-bawdy *The Provok'd Husband*. The
previous December the Young Gentlemen of Mr. Woolley's Grammar
School had performed the tragedy, *The Countess of Salisbury*, to an
audience which included the Hon. and Mrs. Bouverie, Mr. and Mrs.
Thursby and "most of the gentry of the town", at a venue unstated.

Other "commands" of 1771 included *The Merchant of Venice*, at the
desire of Col. Hesilrige, and *The Busy Body* (Sir William Wake).

Whole volumes and indeed complete libraries have been filled with
examinations in the closest detail of the works of William Shakespeare. What
is said here is addressed to the reader who is as unfamiliar with "the Bard
in depth" as I am.

To him it may appear that the text of the works of our master playwright are sacrosanct and sacred, whatever mod costumes some of them
may now be presented in. It was not always so. Not merely sentences were
re-shaped and lines deleted; sections amounting to whole scenes, indeed
complete acts, were thrown out and in the re-writing, adaptation and

alterations characters disappeared and new ones were introduced. Bits of "business" were brought in to liven up the proceedings such as the grave-digger in *Hamlet* wearing a couple of dozen waistcoats which he peeled off one after the other. Masques were interposed, songs injected, and mechanical scenery brought in for spectacle.

Sometimes the name was the same, such as *The Tempest* which was "altered" by Northamptonshire's John Dryden and Davenant. Described as "Never acted here" when staged by the Durravans in August, 1762, it introduced two quite alien characters—Hippolito, who "never saw a woman," and Dorinda, an extra daughter for Prospero, "who never saw a man except her father".

Great stress was laid upon the scenic effects. "Two entire new sets of scenery proper to the play with all the original music, vocal and instrumental; scenes, machines, sinkings, flyings, and all other necessary decorations; the ship, sea, an artificial shower of hail and fire and all incidentals to a beautiful Tempest scene. The play to conclude with a beautiful view of a calm sea on which appear Neptune and Amphitrite in a chariot drawn by seahorses, Ariel, and her attendants descend in three aerial chariots." Doors for *The Tempest* opened at five, the play beginning at half-an-hour before six o'clock by reason of its length. In view of the great expense in "getting up" the play nothing under full price could be taken.

Shakespeare had inserted a masque into *The Tempest* and Purcell composed one for *Timon of Athens*; it was also heard in other plays. Dido and Aneas was performed in *Measure for Measure* and Peleus and Thetis in *The Jew of Venice*, one of the adaptations.

It was hard for the ordinary spectator to know just where Shakespeare ended and the adaptors began. Pepys described *Macbeth* in 1664 as "one of the best plays for a stage and a variety of dancing and music that I ever saw". Needless to say, what he had seen was one of the versions, by Davenant, with some minor characters deleted and the parts of Macduff and Lady Macduff built up.

Sometimes the title was altered, as well as the contents. During the Durravan period we find *Catherine and Petruchio* which was a re-hash of *The Taming of the Shrew*; and a dramatic pastoral called *Florizel and Perdita* or *The Princely Shepherd*, which the Bard himself might not have recognised as *The Winter's Tale*. This was performed at Northampton on May 6, 1771.

When the Durravans presented *King Lear and His Three Daughters* the propaganda leads one to conjecture whether Shakespeare was presented for the beauty of his language or the goriness of some of his plots—"Shewing the distresses and real madness of King Lear who is driven to extreme want by the cruel ingratitude of his two daughters Goneril and Regan, after resigning his kingdom to them. The loves of Edgar and Cordelia who to secure himself from the rage of his father and the treachery of his brother puts on a feign of madness and wanders as a lunatic in which disguise he rescues Cordelia from the hands of the Russians. The cruelty of Edmund who is the instrument of his father, the Earl of Gloster's eyes being torn out. The deaths of Goneril and Regan, the fall of Edmund. Concluding with the restoration of the king, the marriage of Edgar and Cordelia with many other historical passages". Other variations of King Lear were *King Leer* and *King Lear and His Daughters Queer.*

There were a number of reasons why Shakespeare was butchered. For one thing he had written for a stage on which women did not appear and their introduction during the reign of Charles II led to some re-writing involving giving more lines to the actresses.

Later alterations could be a means of getting round the law making drama generally illegal. A few songs and dances interpolated could make legitimate what would otherwise not be. And there were some who altered to improve from the point of view of attracting audiences and securing their approval. It is idle to pretend that the man-in-the-street idolises universally our Great Bard. How often dare our Repertory companies of today include his works in their repertoire? In Fielding's *Pasquin* in 1736 a dancer says: "Hang his play and all his plays: the dancers are the only people that support the house; if it were not for us they might act their Shakespeare to empty benches." In the epilogue to *The Jew of Venice* the drawing power of Shakespeare sans music was questioned by its author-adaptor Granville:

> *How was the scene forlorn and how despis'd*
> *When Timon without Musick moraliz'd.*

Perhaps one of the greatest liberties taken was with the corpse of Juliet. Her supposedly dead body was carried in state across the stage. The Durravans' 1768 performance included: "In Act 1 Masquerade dance; end of Act 4 Funeral procession of Juliet." Arne provided a processional dirge for the work with trumpets, drums and a tolling bell, ending with a three part chorus "Ah Hapless Maid" accompanied by flute and strings. The spectacle survived for many decades. Writing in 1878 Fanny Kemble said she was glad this "dreadful piece of stage pageantry" had been suppressed. She recalled: "It had gone on in my time. About 1830, it was still performed. An exact reproduction of a funeral procession such as one meets every day in Rome, with torch-bearing priests and bier covered with its black velvet pall, embroidered with skull and crossbones, with a corpse-like figure upon it marched round the stage chanting some portion of the Roman Catholic Requiem music."

Probably the most spectacular Shakespearean occasion during the Durravan seasons came on Monday, May 27, in the final season of 1771 when they staged "A Musical Piece call'd *Shakespeare's Garland* or *The Warwickshire Ballad* containing the ballads, catches, glees etc. as performed at the Grand Booth in Stratford-upon-Avon and now at the Theatre Royal, Drury Lane, in which will be introduced a pageant or procession of the principal characters in Shakespeare's plays preceding the comic and tragic muses with a portrait of Shakespeare crown'd with laurel and performing with general applause at the Theatre Royal, Drury Lane." This was such an ambitious production that the company numbers could not run to filling all the roles so that characters were played by "the comedians and others of the town". Young Northamptonians also made up the numbers—"Fairies by the children of the company and others".

The words of the "Garland" were by David Garrick and the music by Dibdin. The piece had been constructed for the Jubilee celebrations at Stratford in 1769, nominally in honour of Shakespeare but which, cynics said, did more to enhance the lustre of Davy Garrick than Willy Shakespeare. Rain played the leading role.

Garrick, incidentally, was a pioneer in clearing audiences off the stage. This was a battle he won at Drury Lane and an example which was copied at Covent Garden. The other principal reform he attempted was to do away with second price admission : in this he failed.

Though he does not appear to have performed on the stage of the lowly Northampton theatre he gave readings in stately surroundings only five miles away and had other links with the county, which are dealt with in the following Scene. As far as Shakespeare was concerned Garrick was something of a Jekyll and Hyde. Some plays he restored to their original state but others he mangled himself. From Hamlet he cut the graveyard scene and fencing match altogether.

As Romeo he gave himself sixty-five extra lines to say and it was he who woke up Juliet in the tomb :

> *Twixt death and life I'm torn, I am distracted*
> *But death is strongest.*

From the Durravans season of 1771 there is an interesting survival—a record of a speech of thanks made by Mrs. Glocester on June 2 during the benefit night for her and her husband. It is a fair reflection of the deferential attitude of those on stage to their betters in the seats, more especially in the boxes :

> *When I look round this crowded house and see*
> *Each generous heart that appears for me*
> *Who by their presence striving to abate*
> *The unpleasing rigours of a Wanderer's Fate*
> *Heavens how I feel! My grateful soul would pay*
> *In more than words the Favors of this day*
> *To you (the gallery) and you (the pit) and chiefly YOU*
> *   (Mrs. Thursby's box) my friends*
> *I humbly bow—you've gained your generous ends*
> *You always strive in every different part*
> *By well tim'd praise to assure my doubting heart.*
> *You strove at last nor here you strive in vain*
> *To fill an empty purse quite full again*
> *We'll fear no more th'imperious landlord's frown*
> *But pass with cheerful heart from town to town*
> *And yet believe me ladies from this place*
> *I cannot go but with a lingering pace*
> *With you my grateful heart would still reside*
> *Regardless of its interest or pride*
> *But duty calls, my Husband's strict command*
> *Bids me away to Shakespeare's native land*

And we poor souls in spite of all our wit
Must to our husbands, yes we must submit
To Rank alone this privilege is given
To break the vow that's registered in Heaven
This world's a stage; to different scenes I go
Unconscious if they lead to joy or woe
Ah should I meet my critic's surly rage
How should I sigh for this good natur'd stage
Where o'er my faults a friendly curtain's thrown
And I am praised for merits not my own
Yet let me boast that free, quite free from Art
I've one perfection—'tis a grateful heart.

And so we say farewell to Madame Glocester and with her the Durravans. What became of them all? The Durravans are by no means the best researched of the provincial companies of this era. The name is unusual, however, and we can feel confident that it is the same family which turns up seventeen years later in the Bath and Bristol Company. From December, 1788, we find a Durravan senior playing broad comedy and a son James looking after the light variety. This James Durravan married a Miss Sutton, daughter of a Salisbury clothier, on October 25, 1792, and his death is recorded in Felix Farley's Bristol Journal in 1793: "Same day (October 28) died at his lodgings in Prince's Street (Bristol) Mr. James Durravan, late of our theatre. The seeds of native genius and the richest buds of comedy would have blossomed into professional excellence had not death prematurely deprived the stage of this promising young actor." Durravan senior's death is also recorded, on April 25, 1796, when it was stated that: "Since the death of his son he had owed his support to a voluntary weekly subscription which the performers of the theatre laudably agreed to allow him."

It will be recalled that the Northampton advertisements refer to a benefit for a Mr. J. Durravan and there is also mention of a Mr. T. Durravan and Mr. M. Durravan. It would appear from the wording of the Bristol announcements that the Mr. J. Durravan acting at Northampton in 1768 could not have been the same one showing promise at Bristol in the 1790s. The recruitment of a Mr. J. Durravan is also referred to by Henry Lee in his memoirs. With his partner James Shatford "we engaged Mr. J. Durravan, a very clever actor at Bath". The name of Durravan crops up too in play-bills at Worcester, including the opening night of a new theatre in Angel Street on March 29, 1781 : the cast included a Mr. Durravan and a Mrs. Pero—another name we shall come across.

The information given by the company at Northampton conveniently mentions their seasons elsewhere. In January, 1762, the Mercury reported : "We hear from Derby that Messrs. Durravans Company of Comedians intend opening the theatre on the Coal-Hill in Leicester on Wednesday next, the 20th instant . . . and that they purpose continuing until the beginning of April." By May they were at Northampton and there they remained until September when they announced that they would "go hence to the city of Litchfield". Which appears to complete their pattern of movement for that year—Derby, Leicester, Northampton, and Lichfield. From the other towns and other sources, however, little information about the company is available.

No great names leap to the eye from the Durravan cast lists (with the possible exception of Robertson) and the company's name is not one which has gone down to posterity. Which is certainly not the case with the next company to play a number of seasons at Northampton—the Kembles. Before moving on to their scene there is one other manager to be considered, one with a doubtful distinction, and it is also an appropriate moment to take in some other contemporary entertainments.

At the Peacock in November, 1765, there had been the "Celebrated Lecture on Heads", possibly by its originator Mr. Stevens who had found it so profitable that he had given up the managership of the Lincoln Company to tour with it. The "Lecture" was in three parts, the subjects being given in staccato style in the advertisement. Part Three, for example, consisted of : "Physical Wig. Dissertation on Sneezing and Snuff Taking. Life of a Blood. Woman of the Town. Tea Table Critic. Learned Faces. Gamblers' Funeral and Monument. Life and Death of a Wit. Head of a Well-Known Methodist and a Tabernacle Harangue."

That same year, and again in 1769, there were brief visits by the Sadlers Wells Company who performed on tight ropes, slack rope and wire and did tumbling and acrobatics, with plays as an extra.

Very confident of the merits of his display of tricks with cards and other deceptions was Mr. John Rea who appeared at the Saracen's Head in March, 1769. He charged 1s. 6d. for front seats and 1s. for back seats but promised in his advertisement : "As many bunglers and common pretenders to dexterity of hand are imposing on the public Mr. Rea takes this opportunity of acquainting the company that no money is taken at the door. If he don't give general satisfaction, will desire nothing for his pains." Than which he could scarcely say fairer?

Next comes the manager who was responsible for taking the largest and most detailed advertisement to date. Indeed I cannot call to mind a larger one until the boastful Mr. William Thomas opened his musichall in Gold Street in the 1860s.

The first Press mention of Mr. Carleton on September 21, 1772, provides his immediate place of origin : "We hear that Mr. Carleton's Company of Comedians who have given such general satisfaction in Derby and its environs intend opening the theatre here at the Races and will perform a regular play and farce three nights a week till the end of November. Among the many pieces which the company will perform for the entertainment of the town the following have already been got up and in rehearsal : *The Grecian Daughter, Cyrus, Zenobia, Zobeide, The Fashionable Lover, Lionel and Clarissa, The Recruiting Sergeant, Cupid's Revenge*, etc. N.B. Their cloaths and scenes are entirely new."

The subsequent announcements of October 12, 19 and 26 were brief but two nights before the season ended Mr. Carleton had a burst of extravagance and took the long (and therefore expensive) advertisement which is

"THE MAID OF THE MILL" was given "by
special desire" during the Durravans' last
season at Northampton in 1771. (*Northampton
Mercury*)

LONGEST of the eighteenth-century
theatrical advertisements in the
Northampton Mercury is that of the
garrulous Mr. Carleton in 1772. He is
the actor who at Nottingham made a
benefit appeal from behind bars.

reproduced on Page 75. Its air of wheedling yet bombastic flatulence cannot be conveyed by a transcript.

Together with this eulogy in the advertisement columns there was a matching piece of unusual length in the editorial section of the paper, which, judging by its phraseology, was a quid pro quo to the manager's dictation : "The very great success Mr. Carleton has met with during his company's Stay in Town, calls for his warmest acknowledgments to the public in general; but as no words can express the grateful sense he entertains of the many favours conferred upon him, he can only present his best respects to the ladies and gentlemen, with all possible Thanks and humbly take his Leave, with a most sincere and grateful heart; at the same time hopes to have the honour of awaiting on them the next year; and begs leave to assure them that at all times it shall be his constant study to merit a continuance of that countenance and Patronage he has now so happily experienced, being determined to take every step in his power to give satisfaction, and add to the entertainments and better amusement of the public, as far as shall any way come under his direction."

A single, equally wordy, prior announcement is the only confirmation that Carleton did achieve his hope of "having the honour of awaiting on them next year". On July 3, 1773, the Mercury carried this : "Mr. Carleton begs leave to acquaint the ladies and gentlemen of Northampton and its environs whose patronage and generosity he so amply experienced last year that in consequence of their approbation for the honour of appearing before them at the ensuing races he has engaged some of the most capital performers from the Theatres Royal in Dublin, Edinburgh and Bath and has made such additions to his apparatus in general that his company's performance of that grand and universally admir'd entertainment of *The Jubilee* is now admitted the most elegant and pleasing representation ever exhibited at a country theatre, the dresses, scenery and decorations being entirely new and copied from the Theatre Royal, Drury Lane.

"As Mr. Carleton will use every endeavour to give entire satisfaction in all respects he humbly hopes for the countenance of the ladies and gentlemen having in particular prepared for their entertainment all the new plays that have succeeded in London, *She Stoops to Conquer*, *Alonzo*, *Alzuma* etc., etc., and being determined to merit the esteem and patronage of the public begs leave to subscribe himself with the utmost gratitude for past favours—Their much oblig'd, Very Humble and Devoted Servant, J. Carleton." This is the only place where Carleton's initial is given.

This is the last local mention, there being no further advertisements and no editorial reference to this second season. Whether J. Carleton's high but humble hopes were not achieved and it collapsed in disaster we can only speculate, bearing in mind what happened to him at Nottingham in 1779 as a member of the Nottingham and Derby Company.

An advertisement for the last night of the season at Nottingham called attention to J.C.'s predicament : "As Mr. Carleton's melancholy situation prevents him from waiting personally upon them to solicit their support he begs leave to embrace this method" (a newspaper advertisement) "of conveying his most respectful compliments to every individual whose patronage (in whatsoever degree whatsoever) he humbly entreats and ever remember them with the greatest gratitude." J.C. was in gaol and tickets could be got from him there, or of Mrs. Carleton, more fortunately situated at Mr. Bramley's on the High Pavement, Nottingham.

Although he presumably could not attend in person J.C. did contribute to the performance for he had composed a song of address to the ladies of Nottingham called The Loves and Graces, which was sung by his wife. The main piece for the benefit was *Edward the Black Prince* or *The Conquest of France at the Memorable Battle of Poitiers* presented with "all the necessary decorations and attendance of banners, trophies, drums and trumpets and the characters of the English and French armies dressed in the proper habits of the time and country".

In 1801 we find a Carleton in the Nottingham and Derby Company at Stamford in March, July and August; and in September, 1802, a Mrs. Carleton, of the Theatres Brighton and Margate, was appearing with His Majesty's Servants from the Theatre Royal, Cheltenham, at Warwick under the management of Mr. Watson.

And so we leave J.C., a theatrical character of whom we are afforded just a few glimpses but sufficient perhaps to convince us that he would not have been out of place in the pages of a Dickens novel, a man who was so skint that he could not get out of gaol but who could marshal the English and French armies on the Nottingham stage, all properly accoutred.

"You relish satire (to the pit): you ragouts of wit (boxes)
Your taste is humour and high season'd joke (1st gallery)
You call for hornpipes and for Hearts of Oak (2nd gallery)"

—Garrick's Epilogue to Murphy's
"All in the Wrong", 1761

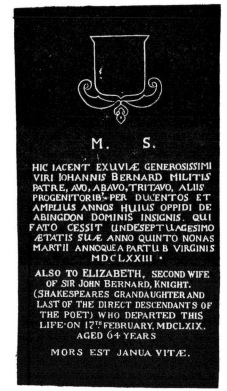

MEMORIAL in Abington Church to
Sir John Bernard. The reference to his
second wife, Lady Elizabeth Bernard,
Shakespeare's last descendant, was
added in late Victorian times.
(*Northampton and County Independent*)

M.   S.

HIC IACENT EXUVIÆ GENEROSISSIMI
VIRI IOHANNIS BERNARD MILITIS
PATRE, AVO, ABAVO, TRITAVO, ALIIS
PROGENITORIB; PER DUCENTOS ET
AMPLIUS ANNOS HUIUS OPPIDI DE
ABINGDON DOMINIS INSIGNIS. QUI
FATO CESSIT UNDESEPTUAGESIMO
ÆTATIS SUÆ ANNO QUINTO NONAS
MARTII ANNOQUE A PARTU B VIRGINIS
MDCLXXIII ·

ALSO TO ELIZABETH, SECOND WIFE
OF SIR JOHN BERNARD, KNIGHT.
(SHAKESPEARES GRANDAUGHTER AND
LAST OF THE DIRECT DESCENDANTS OF
THE POET) WHO DEPARTED THIS
LIFE·ON 17ᵀᴴ FEBRUARY, MDCLXIX.
AGED 64 YEARS

MORS EST JANUA VITÆ.

Scene Three

GARRICK—THE GREATEST?

The name of David Garrick is about the most prominent in English theatrical history. As far as I know he did not appear on the stage of Northampton's lowly theatre in a riding house or the one in a malting but he does have two important local links which merit a separate scene.

As far as I know he did not appear in Northampton productions . . . but it is intriguing to speculate that he *might* have done, being a close friend of Earl and Countess Spencer, of Althorp, and of Ann Thursby, lady of one of the local Manors, who were all prominent patrons of the local drama. If the leading actor of the English stage did ever mix it with the provincial Thespians of the Durravan, Carleton or Kemble troupes, there appears to be no record of it.

Born at Hereford, on February 19, 1717, the son of an officer in the Dragoons, he was brought up in the cathedral and garrison city of Lichfield studying under Samuel Johnson in his schoolmastering days. As a boy he delighted officers of the garrison with his mimicry and sometimes they took him to the theatre in London. When various companies visited Lichfield, young Garrick would be among the keenest spectators. He made few provincial appearances, stepping straight up into London theatre, having gone to the capital to become a wine merchant.

Because of and yet despite his calling as an actor he came to be on equal terms with members of the nobility, among them two with Northamptonshire connections. He was particularly friendly with Lady Spencer, of Althorp, who had been born at St. James's Palace, London, in May of 1737, the year of the passing of Walpoles's repressive Act against the drama, and christened Georgiana after her godfather, George II. This was the year when the twenty-year-old Garrick arrived in London. They appear to have met for the first time in 1759, two years before her husband was created a Peer. Garrick and Georgiana exchanged scores of letters which were published privately in 1960 by the late Earl Spencer, for presentation to members of the Roxburghe Club, of which he was president.

The second friendship with nobility was even more surprising in view of Garrick's calling for it was with the second Duke of Grafton, who was Lord Chamberlain (and therefore cast in the legal role of oppressor of the players) at the time of the 1737 Act.

Garrick cannot have been favourably impressed by his first encounter with the Duke. Tired of not being paid his salary by Fleetwood, then manager of Drury Lane, Garrick refused to perform and devised a scheme for the company quietly to secede and meantime approach the Duke to get a licence for a new theatre, which he felt confident would be forthcoming. The Duke agreed to receive the deputation but when he learned that Garrick received (or rather should have received) £500 a year he commented "And do you think it is too little ... when I have a son who has to venture his life for half that sum?" He turned down the application.

The Duke took his name from Grafton Regis, Northamptonshire, and in the 1740s built Wakefield Lawn at Potterspury in the county and founded the Grafton Hunt, which still survives. At one time the family owned vast areas of Northamptonshire and the county connection diminished only in the 1930s after three Dukes had died within little more than a decade and death duties decreed their departure. Today Wakefield Lawn (or Lodge) is the home of Mr. and Mrs. R. N. Richmond-Watson.

When Garrick took over the management of Drury Lane Theatre it was in partnership with James Lacy who was well in with the Duke through a mutual interest in hunting. In 1755 the Duke was a guest at the Garricks' home at Hampton-on-Thames, along with Horace Walpole.

The Garricks and the Spencers were already well acquainted by the time they met on holiday in Italy in 1763. From Naples Garrick wrote: "We dine and sup with Lord Spenser (sic), Lord Exeter, the Minister, the Consul, almost every day and we have balls twice a week and parties innumerable." They were together also in Rome where Joseph Nollekens did a bust of Garrick which was the first he modelled and both Lady Spencer and Garrick sat for portraits by Batoni. The Nollekens bust and the Lady Spencer portrait, with Vesuvius in the background, are both now at Althorp, along with Benjamin Van Der Gucht's painting of Garrick in his special uniform and bearing his special wand at the Shakespeare Jubilee at Stratford in 1769. One of Garrick's memoranda for that event was "Lodgings for Lord Spencer and Family".

It was on a July day of 1768 that the Garricks' carriage drew up at Althorp for the first of many visits. The actor used to give readings there, largely from his favourite author, and was very upset when the Earl of March, later Duke of Queensberry, fell asleep during one of them. So much so that he wrote to fair Georgiana requesting that the Earl be left off the guest list when he, Garrick, appeared on it.

Lady Spencer would often send her coach to meet the Garricks at Newport Pagnell. In October, 1776, for example, she wrote: "If you set out from thence about one o'clock you will be here full time enough to dress for dinner. I shall likewise send directions to have Holywell House" (at St. Alban's, where she lived after the death of her husband, it being pulled down soon after her death in 1814) "ready in case you should like to lie there on Friday night. The beds and rooms are well aired and more comfortable than at an inn and that will make the journey to Newport Pagnell easy for your own horses. We have no servants there so that you must have your dinner or supper sent from the inn which you will have no difficulty in as they are used to it."

Both David and his wife, Anne-Marie, a former Viennese dancer, were members of the exclusive Althorp Hunt, which later became the Pytchley Hunt (which is still operating today) and are listed in the Chace Books kept by Lady Spencer. Such as on Wednesday, October 16, 1766: "Met at Holdenby Green with the old hounds, found several foxes in Cank as soon as the hounds were thrown in but one went away after taking a turn by Holdenby Spinneys to the cover again and back to the Spinneys; he was killed in one of them. The chace lasted an hour. Lady Spencer and Mr. Garrick were out in the cabriolet and viewed the fox several times over Holdenby Grounds." Along with Lord Althorp, Lord Jersey, Sir William Hamilton, Lord Thomas Clinton, Lord Richard Cavendish, Sir Thomas Clarges, Mr. Raynsford and Mr. Bouverie, those listed as being in the field that day included Mr. and Mrs. Thursby.

Ann Thursby and her husband lived at Abington Abbey (or manor) in the vicinity of Northampton, which is now a museum in a public park. She was the daughter of William Hanbury who, as related later, had his own private theatre at Kelmarsh, Northants.

Abington is today an integral part of Northampton but it was not so in Ann Thursby's time. In the 1780s the Northampton Association for the Prosecution of Felons was concerning itself with the problems of dealing with people who were "Breaking down the stiles and gates between Northampton and Abington and Weston Favell".

It was at Mrs. Thursby's request that Garrick planted a mulberry tree at Abington early in 1778. The inscription on the plaque read "This tree was planted by David Garrick Esq. at the request of Ann Thursby as a growing testimony of their friendship". It served as an almost immediate memorial to her for she died within a few weeks of its being planted. Garrick wrote to Lady Spencer: "We have not been able to overcome by any philosophy the late melancholy accident."

In the same letter he asked Countess Spencer to attend a benefit performance at Drury Lane for old actors. Sheridan had allowed the performance of *The School for Scandal* for which Garrick had written the prologue. This, and the one he wrote for Isaac Jackman's farce *All the World's A Stage* were his two best-known prologues.

The Northampton tree, which is still growing today, could not, as has been stated, have been a direct cutting from the famous mulberry which Shakespeare planted in his garden at Stratford in about 1609. Along with his fellow actor Charles Macklin, Garrick had sat under that tree in 1742, conversing with the then owner of the house, Sir Hugh Clopton, who regarded himself as Curator of the House and Guardian of the Tree. After Sir Hugh's death, however, house and garden were disposed of to the Rev. Francis Gastrell who was less impressed with the dramatic associations, especially when he found that the tree overhung his windows and darkened his house, and when worshippers of the Bard came from near and far to view the arboreal shrine and to steal cuttings from it. So, in 1756, he had the tree cut down, an act which made him most unpopular. Three years later, in an early example of a Rates Protest (he objected to paying rates all year round when only using the house as a summer residence), he had the house pulled down as well. Stratford vowed never again to allow anyone with the name of Gastrell to live in the town.

Abington Abbey has an even more interesting dramatic connection for which we must step back a further century to when Shakespeare's last descendant lived and died there and was entombed in the adjacent church.

Shakespeare's favourite daughter Susannah married a Dr. Hall and their daughter, Elizabeth, married Thomas Nash, of Welcombe, Warwickshire, in 1626. After his death she married Sir John Bernard (or Barnard), in 1649, and this brought her to Abington Abbey which had for two centuries been the home of his family. She died in 1669 and he in March, 1674, after selling the property to William Thursby.

All sorts of speculations have arisen and mysteries made about possible Shakespearean connections with the manor, including some by the leading Shakespearean scholar, James Orchard Halliwell. It should be remembered that part of the time Lady Elizabeth Bernard lived there was that of the Commonwealth when the drama smelled to high heaven and being Shakespeare's grand-daughter was not necessarily something about which a lady would boast. Halliwell asked whether this lady would not have put her grandfather's papers out of sight of the Rector, Mr. Howes, who was a Presbyterian.

The matter was summed up by Ernest Reynolds, author of Early Victorian Drama and other books, in an article he wrote for the monthly magazine, the Northampton and County Independent, of which I was editor, and which he has kindly consented to my reproducing here.

It was entitled : "The Curious Case of the Missing Coffins" :

"Three hundred years ago Lady Elizabeth Barnard, Shakespeare's grand-daughter and his last descendant, died at Abington Manor, now the Abington Park Museum, Northampton. She was 64. The mystery of Shakespeare's missing manuscripts, which she presumably inherited along with the rest of the poet's estate, has never been solved and probably it never will. For many years there was a lively legend that the precious papers were concealed somewhere in the present Museum, with the panelling of the famous Oak Room as a probable hiding hole.

"The fable is now generally discredited though in fact the panelling has never been completely dismantled to investigate. But the Manor was finally sold by Lady Elizabeth's husband to the Thursby family and they largely rebuilt it around 1740 when any valuable relics would surely have come to light. The Thursbys were besides, interested in Shakespeare, and Garrick, the most famous Shakespearean actor of the eighteenth century, actually stayed at the house as their guest. Also a general search of the house was made some years back to see if anything could be discovered, but nothing whatever was found.

"But the whole business begins to take on a touch of Sherlock Holmes with the curious affair of Lady Elizabeth's grave. She definitely died at Abington Manor and the entry of her burial can still be seen in the Abington Parish Register for February, 1669. It is presumed that she must have been buried in the same grave as her husband (in the south aisle of the church), but there was no inscription recording this until fairly recently when a brief statement about her was cut on the flagstone tomb. And both the coffins of Sir John and Lady Elizabeth seem to have vanished.

"Did someone anticipate a rich reward from the opening of the tomb? Could the coffin of Lady Elizabeth have been known to contain valuable mementoes of her famous grandfather? Has the coffin been removed to some nearby place, either in the churchyard or somewhere in the park or its vicinity? Are the precious papers somewhere at Abington still? Did the theft from the tomb take place when the church's plate was stolen in 1807?

"We can probably rule out the possibility of any manuscripts of the actual plays of Shakespeare having ever been at Abington at all. They would far more likely have been retained in London after the poet's death, either at the Globe Theatre (they would have been the theatre's property) or at the office of the printers of the First Folio, which appeared in 1623. And if so they may well have perished in one of the many fires of the seventeenth century, perhaps the Great Fire of London in 1666. But Shakespeare wrote much poetry other than the plays, and Elizabeth would surely have inherited some specimens of this. And if so she would have brought them with her when she married Sir John Barnard.

"Did she perhaps hide them for safety's sake during her own lifetime and die without revealing their hiding place? She lived at Abington during a time when the theatre was in disgrace. The Cromwellian and Puritan regime was at its height; the theatres were closed, and anyone with theatrical connections was certainly not anxious to advertise the fact.

"Whatever the truth may be, the mystery still awaits its detective. Where is Lady Barnard's coffin? Where are the famous papers? It is a problem for one of the great heroes of detective fiction."

In 1669 Sir John sold the Manor to William Thursby, of the Middle Temple and Chief Justice of Ely, along with the manors and estates of Little Billing and Weston Favell. The price was £13,750.

Thursby, who served as Northampton's Member of Parliament, devised his property to two nephews and it was because they did not survive that it passed instead to Ann Hanbury, who had married John Harvey, a wealthy landowner from Essex. A condition of the will was the assumption of the family name and he therefore became John Harvey Thursby. John and Ann's son became M.P. for Stamford and their grandson, the Rev William Thursby, was Vicar of All Saints, Northampton, until he inherited the family estates in 1824 and moved to their other ancestral seat, Ormerod House, Leicester.

The Abington property was then purchased by Lord Overstone, a millionaire who was so careful with his money that in the 1880s it was noted in the Northampton Mercury that when he took a cab from Northampton railway station he always stopped it a few yards short of the gate of his Overstone residence so as to save the few coppers which the few more yards would involve, being another fare stage. His daughter, Lady Wantage, gave Abington Manor and part of its parkland to the citizens of the town and with equal perspicacity, sold them the rest.

The Thursby line continued until 1941 when it failed with the death of Sir George Thursby Bart., at his seat in Scotland. His only son had died in infancy. Sir George was one of the few amateurs to have ridden in the Derby, in which his mount John O'Gaunt came second in 1904. In 1941 there died also Lt. Basil Shuckburgh, son of Sir George's sister-in-law, Honor, Lady Shuckburgh who was the only daughter of Mr. Neville Thursby, of Harlestone. He was killed in Palestine.

It is now necessary to adjust the controls of our time machine to take us back to 1789 and to another death, that of Garrick himself, and to his funeral which was described as the most splendid the country had ever seen, Royal ones not excepted.

There seems little doubt that Garrick ought to have stayed at home at Hampton and not made the usual Christmas journey to Northamptonshire. Despite being in poor health he succumbed to the pressing invitation of Lady Spencer, though not arriving at Althorp until December 30. Dr. William Kerr, the Earl's physician, was called in from Northampton and diagnosed shingles. The Garricks set out on the return journey on January 15, in sunshine and snow. En route, at Dunstable, he wrote: "I am alive my good lady but such a journey as Northampton to Dunstable I never went before and hope never to go again." The Spencers made the trip to London and Lady Spencer paid him a final visit at his home, where he died on January 20.

Garrick and a number of other actors of the top rank make an exception to the rule about the smell of the drama, though a rumour in 1771 that he was to be knighted had proved to be a false one. The string of carriages at his funeral at Westminster Abbey stretched back to the Strand. Lord Spencer was a pall bearer along with the Duke of Devonshire, and Lords Camden, Ossory and Palmerston. He was interred at the foot of Shakespeare's statue, where his widow was laid to rest alongside him forty-three years later, at the age of ninety-eight.

Lady Spencer, who had attended Garrick's farewell performance at Drury Lane on June 10, 1776, remained a keen supporter of the drama and gave 90 guineas for her box at a Drury Lane benefit for Mrs. Siddons in 1783. Over the years the Spencers were also patrons of the local drama, both at the early make-shift theatres and at Northampton's first permanent theatre, erected in Marefair in 1806.

Was David Garrick the "greatest"? Was the 5 ft. 4 in. actor the towering giant of theatrical history? Lacking film and sound records, which will be such an invaluable aid to future historians and students in evaluating the leading personalities of the present century, we have to rely on contemporary witnesses. What is superb to one generation or century can prove laughably inadequate or exaggerated to the ones that follow.

But in terms of money he was indeed the most successful for he left over £100,000, most of this from his 1747–76 management at Drury Lane.

From the proud David Garrick, who could prescribe the guest list of a countess, we turn to the Interlude, a self-contained examination of the manner in which the Drama Has Smelled, a theme in the greatest possible contrast to the noble friendships of "Davy".

THE INTERLUDE dealing with "The *Pariah Profession*" is self-contained. To continue with the history of the North-ampton theatre turn to Page 141.

INTERLUDE

The Pariah Profession

SMELLS Literal and Metaphorical
THE CHURCH found it Nauseous
THE INFLUENCE of The Drink
POLITICIANS found it Revolting
THE DODGES around The Law
HOW ACTORS got into Gaol and helped others get out
VILLAINS in real life too
SLANDERS on The Stage
THE ACID TEST
  The Officer and the Actress

WILLIAM CHARLES MACREADY
(1793–1873), the somewhat haughty
and imperious actor who coined the
expression "my pariah profession". He
appeared in Northampton in 1829.

SMELLS
Literal and Metaphorical

The title of this book is copied from a chapter heading of my previous volume, Theatre Un-Royal, so that an eight-page chapter has become a 232-page book. In that book, Drama That Smelled was a reference to the fact that one of Northampton's early fit-up theatres was in the town's Riding School.

The reason for the choice of chapter title is obvious. And quite apart from the equestrian smells which must have been present in such surroundings, it should also be remembered that there was the smell of the illuminations, of the oranges the spectators customarily consumed, and of the audience themselves.

The amount of thought and propaganda which today goes into persuading people that they must smell like anything but people is almost a joke. Previous ages were in general much less sweet-smelling and odour-conscious than the present era of men as well as women tipping body talc ad lib into the top of their underwear (with who knows what long-term effects on the intimate areas of the body), spraying perspiration killers (likewise of dubious effect) under their arms, washing with soap which is guaranteed to dispel body odour, using facial lotions (after-shave) after every application of the razor, not to mention the fact that weekly, let alone daily, bathing is a comparatively recently discovered necessity to the survival of the species. One of the things which Anne of Denmark, principal artiste in our Royal Curtain Raiser, did not like about her husband, James VI of Scotland and James I of England, was that he seldom washed, let alone bathed. So that while some of those in the boxes may have masked their body odours with pomade or lavender water, the greater proportion of the eighteenth-century audiences, especially the galleryites, must have taken their own atmosphere along with them.

Added to the smell of the people, of the horse flesh, harness, saddle and excreta, there was the smoke of the candles which provided the illumination throughout the performance (the auditorium was not in darkness in those days).

In his memoirs the actor-manager Henry Lee tells the story of a false alarm at the Aylesbury Theatre in about 1790. The "theatre" stood "very near the yard of one of the principal inns". The innkeeper wanted to get hold of his ostler, whose name was William Squire. Suspecting him to be in the audience the landlord went up the gallery steps shouting "William, William". Getting no response he heeded a suggestion that there might be a dozen Williams in the packed house. Instead he shouted "Squire, Squire" and caused a panic. The audience thought it was "Fire, Fire".

There was screaming, scrambling from the gallery down into the boxes, from the boxes to the pit; every passage was soon clogged up and, the outward doors being hung on the inner side ("A great error in public places" commented the observant Lee), could not be opened, so that no one could get out.

He describes the atmosphere (and remember that there was NOT in fact a fire) : "The heat, the reeking heat of the gallery, was almost unbearable. A cat, even a cat (notwithstanding its nine lives) could not have lived long in such an exhausted atmosphere. I say exhausted because there was no vital air, no oxygen, left unconsumed within it . . . the poor devils puffing and panting were gasping for breath as fish do when they are first drawn out of the water. In short, the top of the gallery was as offensive as it would be to blow out a large candle, and immediately hold your nostrils over the smoking wick of it."

Low ceilings must have compounded the problem. At the Bath theatre in the 1780s the curtain had to be drawn up between the play and the farce on account of the intolerable heat. The Northampton theatre was so hot in May, 1784, that people complained and for her benefit night Mrs. Hudson announced that several ventilators had been fixed "in order to remedy the inconvenience".

What Lee described in such a colourful, slightly exaggerated manner was corroborated in scientific terms by Sir Frederick French in the *Mechanic and Chemist* in June, 1839. He said that one wax candle consumed as much oxygen as two men while 240 candles would deteriorate the atmosphere as much as 700 men. The chemist Lavoisier worked it out that oxygen in a theatre diminished by a quarter from start to finish of a performance.

Not that there would be anything like 240 candles in Northampton's Riding House theatre. In this respect it probably paralleled the Chichester theatre visited in 1809 by Lord William Pitt Lennox who wrote of "a man in a carpenter's dress lighting six tallow candles that were stuck into wet clay and partly screened by dirty tin shades". The level of lighting must have been quite dire by modern standards but this was a shortcoming shared with most other facets of life. Imagine, for instance, how dark the streets must have been in the days before gas (Northampton was first lit by gas in 1824) and how eyestraining it must have been to read or sew by oil lamp or candlelight.

And even candles were not to be lit without forethought. Their cost was an important item on the theatrical budget and an actor's remuneration might well include the remains of the candles at the end of the evening or season. Tate Wilkinson relates how when David Garrick advised him to get some provincial experience he played at Maidstone in 1757 and on his benefit night the fruits of his endeavour amounted to 1s. 6d. and two pieces of candle. Along with 3d., two pieces of candle represented his evening's wages for an actor named King early in his eighteenth-century career. To earn this he had "performed King Richard, given two comic songs, played in an interlude, danced a hornpipe, spoken a prologue and played Harlequin". Mrs. Shatford, wife of the Wessex manager James Shatford, was described by Henry Lee as being "so very careful of the pieces of candle left burning in the sockets that she would burn or spoil a silk handkerchief or shawl by collecting them or by putting them into the tail of her gown or the crown of her best bonnet".

The actual smell of the illuminations is referred to by Matthew Macintosh in his 1866 Reminiscences of an Old Stager. Recalling days at Greenock before gas was installed he described the arrival of Edmund Kean : "At seven o'clock Kean arrived in the theatre, dressed and ready to go on, with his fur travelling cloak over his stage costume. When he heard the tumult in front and surveyed the miserable looking stage, dingily lighted with the smoking, smelling fat-pans, I thought he looked very unhappy." To be accurate, it was not the smell of the fat-pans which put Kean in his despondent mood. Not long before this he had lost £1,000 in a court case when sued by a London alderman for seducing his wife.

When gas lighting first arrived in Northampton in June, 1824, the initial demonstration was in the Theatre, Marefair. Even when gas did eventually replace tallow and wax it sometimes created a new "smell" problem, such as at Covent Garden itself. Gas first lit the auditorium there in 1817 but eleven years later it was taken out again as locally manufactured gas proved so offensive. The theatre switched to oil and wax.

Lighting apart, it has to be borne in mind, without going into unnecessarily grim detail, that the drains and water supply were not then what they are now. Just as houses did not have baths, nor did they have flush toilets, nor even running water. Water was toted around by men and women carrying two buckets on the ends of a yoke, for which they charged a penny —it was called a "gate" of water. The "bog" was very much a term of true derivation and the attendant odours of the privy must have been very penetrating.

Adding all the factors together, the drama must indeed have smelled in the Riding House theatre.

Even in a booth (a tent) the atmosphere could be oppressive. Dramatic performances of this lower order used to take place at the annual fairs at Boughton Green, a couple of miles to the north of Northampton, and an amateur poet composed a poem about it, a long piece in three cantos. The writer, in 1776, was Dr. Lucas, Vicar of Pattishall, who described :

> *The gay confusion—and the sweet distress*
> *That heats the fervent booth still more and more*
> *Till Fahrenheit would rise to ninety-four*

So much for the literal smell and oppressiveness.

It was only after Theatre Un-Royal, covering mainly 1806–84, had appeared and I had decided to write about earlier drama, that it occurred to me that this chapter title, Drama That Smelled, would be a suitable banner under which to marshal material reflecting the degree to which the drama has smelled in a metaphorical sense—in the nostrils of the Church, the Law, and of the community in general.

THE CHURCH
found it Nauseous

Actor and Parson, and Actor and Gaoler, have been closely linked at various stages of our history. Some of the origins of the drama were in fact in the church, in the shape of Miracle and Mystery plays, which were later brought out into the open air and performed on wheeled platforms trundled about the streets, for instance at Coventry.

At some periods Church and Stage have been regarded as two sides of a coin so that a male member of a quite respectable family might hover between the two. Indeed as I write in 1974 I hear that a top acting award has gone to Patrick Drewry, a student at the Royal Academy of Dramatic Art, London, who was previously training to be a priest. The Agnostic might claim that a good deal of religious practice consists of dressing up and playing a part. Both trainee priest and student actor may be said to be entering pulpits where they will mouth other people's ideas and sermonise upon their life and times; in the case of the actor, as far as the authorities of the day will permit. In 1758 the Rev. John Stockwood drew a direct comparison between the drawing power of pulpit and stage. Preaching at St. Paul's Cross, London, he asked " Will not a filthy play, with the blast of a trumpet, sooner call hither a thousand than an hour's tolling of a bell to bring to the sermon a hundred?"

The most sensitive nostrils to the drama have been those of the Church, though politicians have sometimes provided strong competition.

As the seventeenth century was about to expire, there came a direct clerical attack by Jeremy Collier on the theatre as it had emerged after the Commonwealth. In his Short View of the Profaneness and Immorality of the English Stage Collier declaimed that the business of the stage was to "recommend virtue and discountenance vice". His words had some effect, there being a reaction against the indecencies of the Restoration comedies, with their plain-spoken sexual banter and bawdy bits of business.

Another clerical arch-enemy of the stage was the Rev. Arthur Bedford, Vicar of Temple Church, Bristol, Chaplain to the Duke of Bedford and later to the Prince of Wales. In 1706 he wrote a book citing 2,000 examples from plays "showing their natural tendency to destroy religion and introduce a general corruption of manners." He described actors as emissaries of the devil travelling from place to place throughout the land as if they designed to sow their tares in every town. Later he brought out a new edition enlarging to 5,000 the number of citings of dramatic debauchery. An example? The imitating of the Almighty in his wonderful acts of Lightnings, Thunder Storm and Tempest. Dropping peas on a drum to simulate rain amounted to sacrilege in Mr. Bedford's ears. In 1705 he particularly attacked *The Provok'd Wife* which had been given by Mr. Power's Company, describing Power's own role as Sir John Brute, husband of the provok'd wife, as "the most scandalous, profane, and atheistical part of the whole play". Perhaps what really narked Rev. Bedford was the inclusion of one of those ridiculous stage parsons.

Later in the eighteenth century Tate Wilkinson could not stomach a parson's declaration that "No player or any of his children ought to be entitled to Christian burial or even to lie in a churchyard" and that "Anyone who enters into a playhouse is, with the players, equally certain of damnation". In his book, The Wandering Patentee, Wilkinson wrote : "There is a gentleman of the church I should have had reason to make complaint about but that his foaming at the mouth and being over earnest has created me friends and himself the contrary; which will ever be the case with over-burning zeal." This "gentleman" was a Mr. Garwood of the Low Church at Hull and his words so stuck in the manager's gorge that he thought of appealing to the Archbishop of York for redress. In fact he merely expressed the hope that his book might find its way into the Palace at York.

A century after this suggestion that Christian burial should be withheld from actors and actresses the song "God Bless the Little Church Around the Corner" was sung by Mr. J. Arnold when Matthews Bros. Christy Minstrels performed at Northampton Town Hall. Its words tell how a parson in New York refused to bury the body of an actor, saying that they should take him to "the little church around the corner". This was in April, 1872.

There was at least one eighteenth-century Northamptonshire clergyman who patronised the stage. In the memoirs of Charles Mathews (senior) Mrs. Mathews mentions a Northamptonshire preacher who always went to London when Mrs. Siddons and John Kemble performed. "He admitted to me, however, that this was unknown to his connexion, but he saw no impropriety in such a gratification; still he had no right, he said, to shock the prejudices of his sect by thus proclaiming his opinion of their narrowness of mind." And in December, 1793, during Mr. Beynon's management of the Northampton theatre, an address to the ladies and gentlemen of Northampton and its environs read by Mr. Bristow was stated to have been written "by a clergyman of the town".

But even when an actress showed her faith in the Lord by going along to Sunday service she was not safe from insult. In February, 1819, the Litchfield Mercury reported that the Stafford Theatre had closed after a most unprofitable season. The "only novelty" was Miss Booth and "We regret to hear that on the occasion of this accomplished actress going to church, the Curate commenced a very unjust and indecorous attack on the theatre, from the pulpit; and turning the eyes of the whole congregation on this interesting female, she burst into tears."

If this could happen when a Princess of the Stage went to church it may be imagined how unlikely it was that a Prince of the Church should turn up on the stage, in a theatre. It was in fact half-a-century after the Stafford incident before we find the Bishop of Manchester, James Fraser, daring to go into a theatre to address a congregation of actors and actresses. If his claim was correct, in speaking at the Theatre Royal and the Princes Theatre, Manchester, in February, 1877, he was the first bishop of the Church of

England to address a congregation in a theatre, if not the first bishop of a
Christian Church.

After quoting how St. Paul was advised not to adventure himself into
a theatre, the Bishop said Christians ought to penetrate into theatres and
he personally would be satisfied if purity and modesty in word, deed and
gesture, and conduct were the ruling principles of the theatre. He did not
think that anyone would say that it was overrighteous if he wished that no
woman was ever called upon to pose herself in any way that would compro-
mise her maidenly and womanly modesty and purity; they were as often
old men as young men who sat in the pit with opera glasses and gloated
upon the poor girls. It was not the women who were the offenders, but the
men who degraded the theatre. On the practical side he said he wished the
skirts of the ballet dancers were a little longer.

Seemingly it's all in the mind, or to fit my theme, in the nostrils.

In contrast to Manchester, London was totally anti-stage, a fact which
became crystal clear in 1878 when a curate in Bethnal Green said in a
lecture that the average entertainment offered by theatres and musichall was
innocent enough. This drew a rebuke from the Bishop of London (James
Jackson): "I pray that you may not have to meet before the Judgment
Seat those whom your encouragement first led to places where they lost
the blush of shame and took the first downward step to vice and
misery."

When a meeting was held in St. James Hall, London, in October, 1889,
to back a campaign to "purify the musichalls", a couple of bishops were
there to lead the troops. London was in the chair and Bedford moved the
principal resolution backing the efforts of the licensing committee of the
London County Council.

Many Nonconformists remained as anti-theatre as Mr. Garwood had been
in the 1700s. In Victorian London one Baptist minister, the Rev. C. L.
Spurgeon, "ex-communicated" playgoers from his congregation at the
Metropolitan Tabernacle.

A Northampton Church of England parson was also severe. He was
Canon Robert Bevan Hull, third son of the Rev. John Hull, of Poulton-le-
Fylde, Lancashire, and vicar of All Saints, Northampton, from 1877–99.
Speaking in a series of Sunday afternoon sermons on amusements at the
round Church of the Holy Sepulchre, in December, 1889, he prefaced his
remarks on the theatre with some on football and cricket. At first sight, he
said, nothing could seem more harmless and cheering. But he had heard
of the constant practice of playing cards for money on the way to and from
cricket matches and as regards football, he was told there was constant
swearing and bad language on the field. The most harmless recreations
might thus become a source of spiritual degradation. This applied even more
to the theatre.

Here I must interpose to mention that atop the portico of All Saints
Church stands a statue of Charles II, who gave 1,000 tuns of timber towards
the church's rebuilding after the Dreadful Fire of Northampton in 1675
had largely destroyed it. Considering how much Charles was a patron of
the theatre and of the bedrooms of its actresses, Canon Hull, had he pon-

THE STATUE of Charles II atop the portico of All Saints Church, Northampton, for the rebuilding of which he gave 1,000 "tuns" of timber. One of the church's Victorian vicars, Canon Robert Bevan Hull, was very much a dramaphobe. "Considering how much Charles was a patron of the theatre and of the bedrooms of its actresses Canon Hull, had he pondered on the matter, might as soon have had the devil himself as a trademark over the church entrance." (*Drawing by Richard Chatburn*)

dered on the matter might as soon have had the devil himself as a trademark over the church entrance.

Canon Hull said that he would not be doing his duty if he did not refer to the danger encountered by the presence of a large number of the worst characters and bad women of the town inside or outside the theatre. In considering whether it was lawful for them to enter the theatre they must take into account the peculiar fascination it had for most people. Some were quite carried away and were obliged to return again and again. He was glad to say that he very seldom went to the theatre but he had many years ago gone to a ballet. Instead of watching the women dancing he had looked at the faces of the audience and what he had seen was enough to convince him of the harm it did, in the low, coarse, vulgar, sensual expressions of those who were witnessing it. He was sure that in a great many instances the insufficient dress and the form of the dance led people to indulge their sensual natures. Their duty was to keep their sensual nature down. How should this be achieved, while still amusing oneself? Canon Hull recommended the alternatives of botany, geology or astronomy from which they could never obtain that which was false or base.

Hull was criticised in the Northamptonshire Guardian for his "Pharasaic virtuous indignation" and his consistency challenged when he accepted the proceeds of some theatrical performances towards a fund to erect a mission church in honour of St. Gregory on The Green. The newspaper writer, "Man About Town", also quoted the case of a Scottish minister, the Rev. Jno. MacTavish, who implored the Inverness authorities not to grant a theatrical licence to a Mr. Walter Bentley because a refusal would be "contributing to the glory of God".

Another amusement with which Canon Hull found fault was one which had close links with the drama, theatrical seasons being often timed to coincide with it—racing. Northampton had had races since at least 1736 but in the late 1880s there arose a Society for the Suppression of the Races. You may be able to guess who was presiding when it held a meeting in Northampton Town Hall in October, 1889. Canon Hull had got an excellent house of over 1,000 for this particular race meeting (if you will excuse the mixture of metaphors). Unfortunately the majority had him cast as the villain rather than the reforming hero. The strong contingent of book-makers, backers, publicans and other agents of the devil enlivened the preliminaries with shouts of "Race card or pencil gents?", "Now then, three to one, bar one," and "All in, run or not". It must have been rather puzzling for the parson.

After information had been given about how the Racecourse had been enclosed by an Act of Parliament of 1779 and left in the charge of the Freemen of the Borough, and how it had in 1882 passed to the control of the Town Council subject to a proviso that nothing should be done to "take away, diminish or restrain the holding of races", Canon Hull got up to have his say. There is not room to mount all his pearls of wisdom on a subject not the direct concern of this book; in any case, most of what he said could not be heard. As soon as he stood up, as the Mercury recorded, "the temperature rose from tepid to boiling : he could scarcely make himself heard above the hisses, cat-calls, groans and yells." When the Mayor (Mr. J. Barry) took the vote there were about 100 in favour of suppression and 1,000 against.

To be fair, what Canon Hull objected to was not so much the races themselves as the attendant betting. In fact the Races were "suppressed" at Northampton in 1904 when the last meeting was held. The grounds were, however, that the course was dangerous.

Northampton Theatre Royal and Opera House was visited on a number of occasions by Frank Benson's Shakespearean Company, which for many years held unchallenged sway at the Shakespeare Memorial Theatre, Stratford-upon-Avon. Benson was a nephew of the Archbishop of Canterbury and when the Mercury wished Benson well for his opening of *A Midsummer Night's Dream* at the Globe Theatre, London, on Thursday, December 19, 1889, the columnist added: "Someone even whispered that a bishop will occupy the dark corner of a box. Fie! Fie!" Many an officer of the Church would at that time no more think of entering a theatre than a brothel.

This was at a time when changes in the licensing of theatres brought the position of God and the Stage into discussion in Northampton Town Council. Councillor Samuel S. Campion, Liberal and local newspaper owner, did not like a regulation banning anything on stage "which in any manner tends to bring into contempt the Christian religion". The Christian religion, said Campion, should be left to look after itself and could not in any case benefit from attempts by a Town Council to prop it up. Dr. Buszard, a leading Tory Councillor, claimed that Campion was inconsistent. If they did not adopt the religious rule why should they adopt the rest, referring to impropriety of language, offensive personalities, public decency, etc. According to Mr. Campion the public were to be the censors of what was right and wrong and there was to be no other authority. "If we are to have any rules for the protection of public morals and manners we must have them all or strike them all out." In the event Campion got no seconder but in times when we have virtually, since 1968, "struck them all out" and almost anything goes on the stage apart from physical fornication it is illuminating to look back to Victorian attitudes as expressed in a provincial council chamber.

Madamoiselle Beatrice (Binda), whose company played many successful seasons at Northampton, both at the Marefair theatre and at the Opera House, both before and after her death at the age of thirty-nine, was said to kneel in prayer at the side of the stage before every performance. Whether this took the form of "For what I am about to perform may the Lord make me truly repentant" only the late Madamoiselle and her Maker can know.

Ought the Church itself to provide amusement? The Baptists of the Young People's Society of College Street Church, Northampton, held three weekly meetings to discuss the matter. In the chair was Mr. Henry Cooper, one of the town's pioneer photographers and a prime mover in an abortive attempt to build a new theatre in the early 1880s. The Rev. T. Gasquoine wanted to see the number of amusements lessening rather than increasing.

Mr. H. Berrill thought the Church suffered spiritually even by providing
penny readings. On the other hand, Mr. George S. Whiting, a local music
shop proprietor, felt the Church had a bounden duty to provide amusements
while Mr. J. Williamson agreed that if they were to have a man's soul they
must first have his body. But the Rev. F. W. Pollard said that if they were
going to lay hold of people by amusements they would be outrun by
Franklins Gardens (one of the leading amusements centres in the town) and
by the theatre.

As late as 1908 we find the Rev. R. Moffat Gautrey, of Nottingham,
addressing a rally of Northampton Wesley Guilds at Queen's Road Chapel,
Northampton, appealing to young people to guard their innocence—"I have
often been asked whether it is wrong to go to the musichall, the theatre or
card party. My reply is that one cannot explore the seamy side of life
without being affected, cannot play with the flame without being
scorched."

The Church of England and the Roman Catholic Church, on the other
hand, were involved in the frenzy of amateur theatrical activity which
occurred in the latter part of the Victorian period. St. Matthew's, the
Northampton church erected in memory of the leading local brewer,
Pickering Phipps, formed an amateur dramatic society even before its con-
secration by the Bishop of Peterborough in September, 1893. St. Michael's
Church had a flourishing group of amateurs and other churches indulged
in or gave parish room to theatrical activities, often with the aim of raising
money for the church and other "good causes".

When the church went in for drama in the Northamptonshire town of
Kettering it at first imposed a restriction harking back to Elizabethan times :
no ladies allowed. In 1882 Kettering Church Institute formed a dramatic
club and in 1887 put on *Richard III* with an all-male cast. Two years later,
for *The Taming of the Shrew*, presented in the Victoria Hall, the rule was
dropped and the Mercury breathed a tempered sigh of relief. "We shall not
forget the amusement caused by seeing the female parts sustained by male
actors attired in skirts. The Institute has fortunately discarded that dreadful
rule of prohibiting ladies. On February 15, when *The Taming of the Shrew*
was produced we were not, at any rate, subjected to the infliction of seeing
young men whose chins were developing hirsute appendages trying to make
themselves look and talk effeminately." Even so, the Mercury was not
enthusiastic. "Some would say it is arrant folly for amateurs to try to
represent Shakespeare's works."

In 1890 Northampton Roman Catholics formed an amateur dramatic
society and six years later a troupe of Catholic Amateur Minstrels. Both
appeared at the Catholic Schools in Clare Street.

In 1914 the Roman Catholic Bishop of Northampton (Dr. Keating)
referred to the "curious relationship" between the Church and the stage
when he addressed the Roman Catholic Congress at Cardiff. The Church
claimed to have inspired the stage and to be the mother of the drama just
as she was the mother of literature, the fine arts, of music, poetry and
sculpture. Of course there were wayward children of the Church and he
was afraid she had spanked the dramatic profession more fiercely than any

other. What caused standards to fall was when writers and performers began to play to the gallery. "Once the sense of austerity is lost anything in the way of great drama or great literature is at an end."

An anecdote linking Church and stage is told by Jimmy Glover, who was musical director at the Theatre Royal, Drury Lane, in the 1890s and early 1900s. A chemist's assistant in his native Dublin he was organist at two churches. "On many occasions I played the early service at the Pro-Cathedral in the morning, sold senna and salts till 6 p.m., played another service in the evening at my mother's church, St. Michael's in Kingstown, or at Mount Argus, which I then left for the greatest honour of all—in my view—to carry the red fire which, as a chemist, I had made in the daytime, to the property man of the local Theatre Royal." Because he was over-anxious to keep his theatrical appointment he got a thrashing from Canon, later Cardinal, MacCabe. "It was owing to my anxiety to 'scamp' the Benediction service at Kingstown for fear that I should miss the train and disappoint the clown with his two pounds of red fire that I was subjected to castigation at the hands of the Cardinal."

Jimmy Glover also tells the story of how Cardinal Cullen, with whom he served Mass on many occasions, encouraged the use of melodies from Italian opera for services, on the Wesleyan principle that the devil should not be allowed to have all the good tunes. As a result "the church filled like a theatre on Boxing Night and many converts were made". But Pope Pius intervened and there was a reversion to more austere music.

During Lent it was not the thing to go to the theatre in Dublin so there was a sparse attendance for a French Opera Bouffe company in Offenbach's *The Grand Duchesse*, in which the Can-can dance was introduced for the first time. Until one Sunday, that is, when from the pulpit the Cardinal denounced the dance which is so revealing of frilly underwear and promised penance for any of his flock who visited the theatre during the Lenten days. "The result," records Jimmy Glover, "was packed houses for the theatre and empty pews at the church."

In Czarist times in Russia, from the reign of Alexander III to 1898 it was illegal for theatrical representations in the Russian language to be given during Lent, a rule which led to actors being in penury at that period of the year. In 1898 there was a relaxation; during the second, third, fifth and sixth weeks drama and grand opera could be performed—but not comic opera.

In former times theatres in Britain were closed for the whole of Passion Week. The theatre is strong in superstition and there is the case of the Bath theatre where Holy Week performances took place for the first time in 1862. That was on the Wednesday. On the Friday (Good Friday) the house was burned down.

Patrick Drewry was not the first man intended for the priesthood who finished up on the stage. Albert Chevalier, famous for his interpretation of the song "My Old Dutch", followed the same deviationary course. Chevalier, who came to Northampton Corn Exchange in November, 1894, as part of a six-month tour embracing 108 towns, and also appeared at the Town Hall, returned to play Eccles in *Caste* at the Opera House in 1917. He had been intended by his parents for the priesthood and his taste for the stage had been a shock to them. He remained a lifelong student of theology.

But despite these youthful alternatives of Church and stage it must be rare, if not unique, for a leading actress to become Mother General of a community of nuns, or for a musichall artist to become a clergyman.

Isabel Bateman, sister of Mrs. Edward Compton, was a leading actress in the 1880s and 90s. The journal Truth described her as the cleverest of the Bateman children. In May, 1892, she appeared at Northampton Theatre Royal and Opera House, with a Friday benefit of a play written especially for her, *Clarissa Harlowe* by W. G. Wills, and returned in December, 1894. In 1898 she was appearing at the Court Theatre, London, in Pinero's *Trelawney of the Wells*. In autumn that year she was admitted a postulant at the Community of St. Mary the Virgin, Wantage. Twenty-two years later she was elected Mother-General of the Community.

The Northamptonshire parson who had dallied with a musichall career was the Rev. John Napleton, of Wymington Rectory, Higham Ferrers. His unlikely past was revealed in the Mercury in January, 1889, following the death of the Great Vance on stage at the Sun Music Hall, Knightsbridge, on Boxing Night. "Originally intended for the profession myself and being too poor to get on alone, my friend Vance helped me in every way he could." Napleton had an illness which so prostrated him that he hit the bottle, but Vance restrained him—"Not another drop shall you have!" Napleton recalled : "I have been a total abstainer now for years but thank God it was Vance that saved me from the drink curse."

With the background of Church–stage differences in mind, one can imagine the arguments which went on when it was proposed that the only way for the Church to reach the working man was to stage services in theatres. To some clergymen it was like being asked to preach in hell. And at least some stage people objected too.

Nottingham was in the forefront, services beginning at the Theatre Royal in November, 1860. The national stage newspaper The Era protested against "this unseemly mixture of sacred and secular associations". Using a theatre for services was as incongruous as if plays were given in churches, said the writer, who did not appear to know the origins of the drama.

Despite the opposition the idea caught on and more often than not there was a packed house, in contrast to week-nights! This was the case at the Northampton theatre in Marefair and services were also held at the Prince of Wales Musichall, on the opposite side of Horseshoe Street.

At one theatre the availability of scenery was not wasted. After her theatre book on Bristol had been published in 1974, Kathleen Barker came across information about its use for religious purposes. It was too late for her book but she kindly passed it to me. The Bristol Daily Post of January 3, 1870, reported that there was a crowded attendance for a service in the Old Theatre, King Street, the previous night. Dress circle and upper boxes were full half-an-hour before the service was due to begin. "The greater portion of the audience appeared to be of the class usually met with in places of worship" (in which case the purpose was not served) "but the front seats were packed with a number of undeniable street Arabs who required constant watching on the part of the more seriously disposed. On stage, seated in a semi-circle were gentlemen who had taken a considerable interest in the religious and moral welfare of the masses. The stage itself was suitably arranged, the background being a scene introducing an ecclesiastical structure." A letter published soon afterwards showed why the Arabs may have got restive. A sermon lasted an hour and ten minutes.

This era of Church and stage coming together has to me a parallel with the way in which members of the Salvation Army, bless their hearts, sally forth into public houses, copies of War Cry in one hand and collecting box in the other, making collections to further their cause—which if successful would assuredly lead to the closure of all licensed premises, including those in which the money is being collected.

In more recent times plays such as T. S. Eliot's *Murder in the Cathedral* have been acted in church. There have also been the Mystery Cycle plays.

But the most remarkable coming together of religion and stage has occurred since censorship was abandoned—in the shape of such productions as *Godspell* and *Jesus Christ Superstar*. Depiction of the Deity was previously forbidden.

THE INFLUENCE
of The Drink

"The Drink" has played a part in theatre history the importance of which has not always been realised, especially relating to the past century. And here I do not have in mind those instances in which actors have gone on stage under the influence or in which managers have refused to pay them because they were too drunk to act or to perform ancilliary duties such as bill-posting or scrubbing the stage floor. I have already dealt with a few examples of this aspect of tipsy Thespianism in Theatre Un-Royal and do not propose to repeat myself here. But other aspects of Alcohol and the Actor are relevant in assessing the manner in which the Drama has smelled in the nostrils of various sections of the community, notably the Church.

Drink was the third corner of the triangle of favourite hates of Canon Hull, the others, of course, being amusements in general (and the theatre in particular) and racing (or the betting associated with it). I suppose that his most unfavourite character would have been a betting man examining a race card while having a drink in the bar of a theatre.

But in the early days theatres had no bars of their own. This was something of a technicality, of course, if the theatre was a barn or other building attached to, or an assembly room actually in an inn, as was often the case. Some landlords would let the Thespians use their premises free or at reduced terms because of the custom they would bring on the liquid side. In other cases there was an inn or beer house in the vicinity—they used to be very thick on the ground—so that it might be possible to pop out and slake one's thirst or bring a bottle back during the many natural breaks in the performance. There was also the possibility of taking a container into the theatre.

A problem arising from the drink derived from the custom of half-price admission. Half-price was not a reduction for children, the elderly, or other sections of the community but meant that you paid half-price to see half of the performance—the latter half. The management let people in at a reduced rate—it was not actually half-price—half-way through the entertainment, usually before the last act of the main play and in time for the farce or afterpiece. At first sight this sounds ludicrous but it has a modern parallel in the switch-happy television viewer who watches half of one TV epic and then switches over to see half of another—which is equivalent to leaving one theatre at the interval and going into another.

Many of the half-timers would have spent at least part of the time when they might been gaining spiritual refreshment (assuming the play was Shakespeare or other elevated fare) in imbibing the spirituous variety in the nearest inn. Thus there could be a boisterous intake of patrons at about nine o'clock. The scene in one London theatre is described by Kingsley in Alton Locke : "We were passing by the door of the Victoria Theatre. It was just half-price time and the beggary and rascality of London were pouring in to their low amusement from the neighbouring gin palaces and thieves' cellars."

Then the theatres began trying to get a cut of the liquid trade for themselves, a move commented on by The Era in October, 1860 : "For some time now there has been antagonism between public houses and public entertainments and that antagonism was made more virulent by a change last year which we strenuously opposed. Theatres have been competing with public houses and public houses with theatres. We have always held that the two should be kept entirely distinct. When the theatres were partly converted into public houses the grounds of reasonable opposition by theatrical managers to the extension of concert room establishments were much weakened. Concert rooms in connection with public houses are now established in all quarters but it is a question whether they have militated against the interests of houses devoted to the drama."

It was often the case that the religious fraternity were not so much against a theatre or potential theatre as they were against the drink which might be sold inside it. Although the musichall was essentially of tavern origin, with the tightening up of the licensing laws in late Victorian times it could sometimes be less difficult to get permission to start a musichall or theatre than to get a licence to sell drinks on its premises—and this could be a vital factor in the commercial consideration.

In Northampton this clearly emerged in 1893 when Mr. James Gregory, who had operated the Birmingham Palace of Varieties for twenty-one years, sought permission to erect a £12,000 musichall seating 1,300 adjacent to the Rose and Crown Hotel, on the north side of Gold Street. In fact that is a mis-statement : to construct the building he needed no permission provided he observed the building rules. To get a drinks licence was the hurdle.

Understandably, the Nonconformists did not relish the prospect of a variety hall which would have doors opening near College Street Chapel. But as the Chief Constable, Mr. F. H. Mardlin, pointed out at the Brewster Sessions : "Recently one musichall has been established in this town" (this was the new Empire Palace of Varieties, previously the Plough Variety Hall, Bridge Street) "and there is a possibility of a second. As matters stand there is no public authority to say whether such places should exist or not and the rights of the police (in the absence of licences being issued) in the way of supervision and control are very meagre. I should like to make it clear that I have no objection to musichalls in themselves."

What the multitude of ministers and the Sunday School Union secretary could contest was the drinking licence. Success here achieved their object. The commercial importance of the bars—three were planned, in pit, circle and gallery with an extra one for temperance tastes—was such that when the alcoholic franchise was refused the musichall was not proceeded with.

At the hearing Mr. Gregory said that Northampton was the only town of its size which lacked a musichall (he appears to have ignored the Empire as being too much of a lightweight). In contrast, he pointed out, Liverpool had five theatres and ten musichalls; Birmingham had five of each; Portsmouth and Bristol had two theatres and three musichalls; Leicester had two of each; Walsall had two theatres and one musichall; while Derby and Southampton had one theatre and two musichalls.

The question of theatres and musichalls came in for legal discussion in 1901 when Frank Macnaghten, who had risen from the modest surroundings of the Empire, Northampton, to operate a chain of theatres in the north, was in Southwark County Court to contest the claim of some artists he had employed that he was in breach of their contract. The reason they could not appear at one of his houses, as promised, was that it was being turned from a musichall into a theatre. Judge Addison commented : "Then he was going against the tide. The tendency is to turn theatres into musichalls." Mr. Macnaghten's legal representative, who rejoiced in the name of Mr. Cannot, added : "It all depends upon the town for where the religious element is strong they won't swallow musichall but they will a theatre."

In 1901 Northampton acquired a more ambitious musichall, the Palace of Varieties, which was where the Prince of Wales had been, and three years later Mr. Goodwin Woodward, acting manager of this bar-less establishment, said that at interval time 75 per cent of his audience left for refreshment (no doubt at the Shakespeare public house). He was asking the audience to sign a petition for a bar to be permitted.

One of the earliest London managers to encounter the difficulties of mixing drink and drama was John Hollingshead, of the Gaiety Theatre, erected on the site of the unsuccessful Strand Musick Hall. The design was by C. J. Phipps, architect of the Northampton Opera House, and his brief had been to include a classy restaurant using the same entrance and with access from the theatre. Refusing a drinks licence for the restaurant, the authorities heeded arguments that Hollingshead's aim was to open an enormous public house in an area already well served. Hollingshead appealed to the Quarter Sessions and won. But he was beaten by the 1877 Licensing Act and had to build a wall between the two.

In 1910 a new theatre was planned in Northampton's Abington Street, much to the disgust of some of the residents who got up a petition. But, as the Northampton Mercury told them: "Unfortunately the Town Council has no power to do what the memorialists ask. If the plans submitted are in accordance with the building by-laws they must be approved. If they were disapproved for any of the reasons urged, or to advance public morals the High Court might grant a mandamus compelling the Council to pass the plans and permit the erection of the building."

In fact this house was built and forms the subject of my earlier book, Death of a Theatre, written and published just after it had been pulled down in 1960 and replaced by a supermarket. But though its promoters could carry on with building their theatre they were frustrated when it came to bars. This was tied to the question of securing a licence to present stage plays—legitimate drama, as opposed to musichall turns and revues.

Following opposition from a bevy of Free Church and other ministers and from Mr. Edward Compton, joint proprietor of the Northampton Opera House, the Town Council had a tied vote after a debate lasting three-and-a-half hours, so that the Mayor had the casting vote. He was Alderman Harvey Reeves who was later to play Pooh-Ba in The Mikado on the stage of the theatre which, by casting his vote, he condemned to be drink- and play-less for a decade. The theatre was not able to sell a drink until 1924—when the teetotal opposition mistook the date and failed to turn up to oppose the application.

POLITICIANS
found it Revolting

So much, then, for the degree to which the Drama has offended the nostrils of the Church and to which Alcohol has been an added irritant. The Stage has also been noxious to the nose of the Law itself.

Words mouthed by parsons and others may not have broken his bones but the letter and words of the law, emanating from politicians, have for centuries placed the Thespian in peril of arrest and confinement. The actor was ranked with rogues and vagabonds and the informer against him was sometimes offered a reward to remove from society a man who was regarded as a cancer, liable to spread amongst the people the diseases of idle amusement, novel thoughts, disrespect towards the wealthy and powerful who were their betters, chariness towards the politically corrupt, at worst a spreader of thoughts of revolution, a potential royal head chopper-offer. Not until 1824, a mere century and a half ago, did the actor cease legally to be a vagabond. Indeed, writing of the honoured Irving in 1895 the

Northampton Press noted that he was "one whom a brutal Act of Parliament stigmatises still as a rogue and a vagabond".

When Shakespeare retired to his native town as a comparatively young man, it was to a drama-less Stratford-upon-Avon. The aldermen had banned play-acting in 1603, which ordinance they renewed, as it happened, just as the Bard returned. Six years after his death some of his old colleagues, members of the King's Men with special licence "freely to use and exercise the arte and facultie of playing comedies, tragedies, histories, enterludes, morals, pastorelles, stage-plaies . . . and such like", returned to the town. Their welcome was of an inverse order : they were paid NOT to perform. In the accounts of the Borough Chamberlain is the entry :

To the King's Men for not playing in the hall 6s.

One early example in English dramatic history may be said to be the exception that proves the rule. Instead of a man of the Law prosecuting a man of the Playhouse a man of the law was himself prosecuted for saying some nasty things about the stage. His punishment was severe : he was made to stand in the pillory, lose both ears, pay a heavy fine and was imprisoned for life. This was the unfortunate William Prynne, an outer barrister of Lincolns Inn who had written a book, The Player's Scourge or Actor's Tragedy "wherein is largely evidenced by divers arguments, by the authorities of sundry texts of scripture . . . that stage plays are sinful. heathenish, lewd, ungodly spectacles and most pernicious corruptions; condemned in all eyes as intolerable mischiefs to churches, republics, to the manners, minds and souls of men; and that the profession of play poets, of stage players, together with the penning, acting, and frequenting of stage plays, are unlawful, infamous and unbecoming Christians". This was in 1633 when Charles I was King and Henrietta Maria Queen. Prynne was hauled before the Star Chamber and it was pointed out that the Queen, Lords of the Council, etc., were sometimes spectators of masques and plays and that in his "libel" Prynne had made use of infamous terms against the Queen. Thus it was a case of Lese Majesty rather than Lese Thespis.

As to which period of English history the drama was at its most nauseous to the legal proboscis there is no argument. It was during the subsequent period of Commonwealth when, oddly enough, they did chop off a royal head. In that era the drama was swept away as completely as it could be, along with the theatres, such as they were, and with the masques which had so delighted the Royal courts in the first forty years of the seventeenth century.

Puritanism was strong in Northamptonshire and the central church of All Saints was its focal point. During sermon or catechism none were allowed to "walk up or down abroad or otherwise occupie themselves vaynely". Journals of the House of Commons show that between May 12 and December 2, 1648, forty-three Puritan ministers were nominated to livings in the county.

The Puritans simply detested the stage. Furthermore, citing religious reasons, they declared that the times were not suitable for it. In 1642 a

Parliamentary order was made that: "Whereas the distress'd state of Ireland, steeped in her own blood, and the distress'd state of England, threatened with a cloud of blood, by a Civil Warre, call for all possible means to appease and avert the wrath of God appearing in these judgments ... and whereas publick sports do not well agree with publick calamities, nor publick stage-plays with the seasons of humiliation ... it is therefore thought fit and ordeined by the Lords and Commons in this Parliament assembled that while these sad causes and set times of humiliation do continue, publicke stage-playes shall cease and be forborne."

The following year a pamphlet appeared entitled The Actor's Remonstrance or Complaints For the Silencing of Their Profession. It protested that other recreations of "farre more harmful consequence" were permitted to continue, mentioning the bear gardens where the bears were baited by dogs watched by "the gentleman of the Stave and Taile, namely cutting coblers resorting thither ... making with their sweat and crowding, a farre worse stink than the ill-formed beast they persecute".

It was of no avail. In February, 1647, an Act was passed "That all stage galleries, seats and boxes should be pulled down by warrant of two Justices, that all actors of plays for the time to come being convicted should be publicly whipped and all spectators should for every offence pay 5s."

The threat of whipping was not an idle one. Actors were whipped. As Eleanor Trotter notes in her book, XVIIth Century Life in the Country Parish, at Richmond, Yorkshire, in January, 1656, eight men were sentenced to be "Whipt being on their own confession convict for being common players of interludes and rogues by the statute and to have certificates and to be sent from Constable to Constable to the places of their abodes". There were also warrants against constables in the district who had known of the actors' activities but had done nothing about it. At Helmsley, Yorkshire, in January, 1658, players were ordered to be "Stript from the middle upwards and whipt in the Market Place".

Persecution of the players was not a new thing and by no means a Puritan patent. It was the law of Henry VIII which said that vagabonds were to be whipped and sent back to their native land with a "testimonial" which would ensure their chastisement and correction. For a further offence they were to lose part of the "grisel of the right ear". By the time of Edward VI it was worse—branding with the letter "V" in the breast with a hot iron and being reduced to the condition of a slave. By a statute of 1572 they were to be "grievously whipped and burnt through the gristel of the right ear"; if caught vagabonding a second time to be treated as felons; while for a third offence there was the surest punishment of all— hanging.

An actor was liable to be treated as a vagabond, if not a rogue. There was some distinction between the two. The vagabond was a wanderer "such as unlicensed players of interludes who might be expected to corrupt the morals". The term included "all persons being whole and mighty in body and able to labour, having not land or master, not using lawful merchandise, craft or mystery". It embraced all the entertainers who wandered about amusing the inhabitants—bearwards, fencers, common players of interludes, jugglers, pedlars, tinkers and chapmen. The Elizabethan Act banned "common players of interludes, other than players of interludes belonging to anie Baron of this realm or anie other honourable person of greater degree" and the punishment was "to be stripped naked from the middle upwards and be openly whipped till his or her bodie be bloudie".

The only way to avoid the peril of arrest and/or whipping was to get a licence from two Justices of the Peace and the difficulty of this varied from county to county. Frowned upon by the Church, harried by the Law, treated with immense condescension even by those who enjoyed his performances, the actor was indeed a low form of humanity.

To a certain extent the pendulum swung the other way when Charles II came to the throne and restored the stage. The way in which he made the theatres a happy hunting ground for his sexual activities was not likely, however, to increase the public estimate of the worth of the drama, certainly not in the eyes of the Church critics. And his system of Patent Theatres was restrictive.

It is not, perhaps, a coincidence that it was in two cathedral cities that civic action was taken against the players. In 1706 Salisbury banned plays and in 1715 Winchester followed suit: "It is this day order'd and unanimously agreed that whereas complaint has been made of the disorders committed by the players of interludes within this city, and that it tends to the corruption of youth, and that some of the scholars of the School of the College of St. Mary's have laid out of the college on this occasion, that the said players be forthwith commanded and forbidden not to act or play any more comedies or tragedies within this city, and that they and every one of them do forthwith depart out of this city upon peril of the law."

Feelings against the stage were nowhere more plainly expressed than at Bristol. The 1704 "presentment" of the Grand Jury there reflects perfectly the degree to which playhouses smelled in their nostrils. As causes of looseness they cited "music-houses and other lewd and disorderly houses, the exercise of unlawful games, the extravagant number of ale-houses, tippling or idly walking on the Lord's Day, profane cursing and swearing, acting of plays or interludes". The Jury was apprehensive that the recent permission given to the public stage had led some to hope that it would be tolerated always, "which (if it should be) will exceedingly eclipse the good order and government of this city, corrupt and debauch our youth, and utterly ruin many apprentices and servants, already so unruly and licentious, that they are with great difficulty kept under any reasonable order or government by their masters". Playhouses were attended with "all manner of profaneness, lewdness, murthers, debauching and ruining youth of both sexes, infusing principles of idleness and extragavance into all people who resort to them". It was not sufficient, moreover, to keep them within modest bounds—"All wise men are convinced that there are no methods of hindering or preventing their mischiefs but by totally suppressing them."

The target for all this was the Power Company who returned the following year with promises of reform which were neatly put in a prologue to the opening production of *Timon of Athens*:

We therefore your assistance must implore,
Whilst we the honour of the Stage Restore;
Our plays from all their fulsome rubbish clear,
Bring banish'd virtue back and fix it here

If you but smile upon our bold design,
Once more you'll see the charming goddess shine
Here on her throne she shall a monarch sit,
Dress'd in the gay embellishment of wit.
And we disclaiming vice in every play,
Like faithful subjects her commands obey.

No lewd expressions shall here pass for wit
No blasphemy shall fright the trembling pit
No modish curses lard a trifling scene
No roaring here swear, and nothing mean.

To chuse such plays shall be our constant care
As won't offend the nicest Vestal's ear.
Such as shall yield both profit and delight
Such as you'll see presented here tonight
We'll give offence to neither Church or State
Burlesque no text, buffoon no magistrate,
Laugh at no law; but with such caution move
We will (if possible) deserve your love.
So strictly we'll observe dramatic rules
To lash designing knaves and banter fools
Whilst all brave actions to preferment rise
And merit with applause, obtain the prize.
Even Collier shall confess we'ave well begun
The happy change, and own his books outdone.

Note the reference to the danger of the utter ruination of apprentices and servants. Masters have often placed restrictive covenants on their servants, banning them alike from playhouse and public house. In the time of the Stuarts the London City Corporation instructed the Guilds "to charge all Freemen with the responsibility of keeping their servants from repairing to any play whether in the city or the suburbs". Until fairly recently one of the time-honoured phrases in the indentures of every apprentice to a trade enjoined that he should not resort to taverns or playhouses.

But if it was the Puritans who made a determined seventeenth-century attempt to put the drama out for the count and who virtually succeeded for a couple of decades, it was the Politicians who made an eighteenth-century effort at almost total smotheration, in which they were very much less successful.

The means they employed to deodorise the drama was a powerful disinfectant indeed, the infamous Act of 1737, the aim of which was to outlaw the drama apart from the two Patented theatres in London and the few elsewhere. The provinces were to be drama-free if Walpole had his way.

A **BILL** *for Restraining the Number of Houses for Playing of Interludes, and for the better Regulating Common Players of Interludes.*

Hereas his Majesty King *Charles* the Second, did, by Letters Patent, bearing Date the twenty-fifth Day of *April*, in the Year of his Reign, give and grant unto *Thomas Killigrew*, his Heirs and Assigns, full Power, Licence and Authority of erecting one Theatre or Play-house, and of keeping Players and other Persons for acting Tragedies, Comedies, Plays, Operas, and other Entertainments of the Stage, with several Powers and Provisoes therein mentioned.

And whereas his said Majesty, did by other Letters Patent, bearing Date the fifteenth Day of *January*, in the fourteenth Year of his Reign, give and grant unto Sir *William Davenant*, his Heirs and Assigns, the like full Power, Licence and Authority of erecting one Theatre or Play-house, and of keeping Players and other Persons for acting Tragedies, Comedies, Plays, Operas, and other Entertainments of the Stage, with the like Powers and Provisoes; by both which Letters Patents aforesaid, it is declared and enjoined, that all Companies of Players

A other

THE FIRST page of the Act of 1737 aimed at suppressing the drama in theatres not holding the Royal Patent.

It was the effectiveness of the drama as a form of political and social commentary which led to the legislation. The Prime Minister had been offended greatly, as Prime Ministers tend to be offended greatly, by some perfectly justifiable remarks made about his manner of political life. Had they been written by a journalist or political opponent it would have been bad enough, but he might have stomached it though liking it none the more and resolving to put up the newspaper duty at the earliest possible moment. But to hear the criticism cleverly and pointedly mouthed by some popinjay of an actor on a public stage, using words supplied by some upstart dramatist . . . this was insufferable.

In the case of Press criticism the powers that were could tax the journals so that the words of the critic did not get too widely disseminated. The newspaper tax meant that papers had a very limited circulation; in any case only a minority of the population could read. But they could nearly all hear. . . and smell.

Walpole went along to John Gay's *The Beggar's Opera* and heard pointed references, albeit oblique, to his chicanery. At the first night at Lincolns Inn Fields on January 28, 1728, many an eye was turned to his box at the lines :

> *When you censure the age*
> *Be courteous and sage*
> *Lest the courtiers offended should be*
> *If you mention vice of bribe*
> *Tis so pat to the tribe*
> *Each cries that was levelled at me.*

This was sung by an actor named Hall who had a stomach as vast as Walpole's. From the central character, Macheath :

> *Since laws were made for every degree*
> *To curb vice in others as well as in me*
> *I wonder we've not better company*
> *Upon Tyburn Tree.*

> *But gold from law can take out the sting*
> *And if rich men like us were to swing*
> *T'would thin the world such numbers to string*
> *Upon Tyburn Tree.*

Gay himself, an embittered loser in the South Sea Bubble scandal, was quite clear on the rights of the dramatist. After *Polly*, his sequel to *The Beggar's Opera*, was banned for performance he published it with great success and included in the introduction this slap in the face of authority : "The stage, sir, hath the privilege of the pulpit, to attack vice however dignified or distinguished; and preachers and poets should not be too well bred upon these occasions; nobody can overdo it when he attacks the vice and not the person."

When we see *The Beggar's Opera* today—and I have recently seen an excellent amateur performance by Northampton Theatre Guild—it is not always easy to remember that at the time this brilliant work was first staged the hanging of the many for all sorts of misdemeanours, major and minor, was actually going on. That when an expectant but condemned mother "pleaded her belly", as is mentioned in the text, it was a reprieve only until she had had the child; then she would be brought back to the court and sentenced again, and hanged, leaving the child motherless. So much for the age of benevolence.

The Beggar's Opera did not bring immediate suppression. The first attempt at legislation in 1734 did not succeed. Tony Aston, country theatre manager, protested that it would be a great loss to the country gentlemen to be deprived of their playhouses. The country was regularly entertained at great expense with good plays and wagon-loads of scenes and adapted habits. He forecast an outcry and that "if all the country actors must promiscuously suffer by this Act I question if there is enough wood in England to hang them".

After Henry Fielding's *The Historical Register* the following year, a less concealed attack on corruption, a further attempt at suppression was made and this time the Bill was passed. In 1737 Walpole's infamous Act virtually outlawed all legitimate drama outside the Patent theatres. On the oath of a credible witness an actor was liable to be fined and his property distrained upon; if he had no property, which was more than likely, he was to be put in gaol with hard labour for up to six months. If the fine was paid, half went to the informer and the rest to the poor.

This penal Act might have been expected to put down the drama, to write "finis" to country acting, to have dropped a final curtain on the barnstormers and other echelons of the provincial drama but England being what it is and Englishmen being what they are, this did not happen. The Act was about as effective as the Industrial Relations Act in the 1970s (though in saying that I express no personal opinions as to its merits or the motives of those who in this case stifled a law). If Englishmen do not like what Parliament has told them to do they ignore the instructions as far as possible. To take a parallel in the American sphere the Act was about as effective as Prohibition was in banning booze from the United States in the 1920s.

One reason for this, as Tony Aston had forecast, was that the country gentlemen, magistrates among them, and other members of the quality, simply did not wish to be deprived of their theatrical amusements; so that, in the absence of any informers, they turned a blind eye in court and continued to turn two appreciative eyes stagewards.

The remarkable thing about the ensuing half-century is, indeed, the amount of acting that did go on, considering that it was almost wholly illegal. In many places there was no visible effect whatsoever. In others the type or form of the entertainment was modified in a semblance of conformity with the Statute. Perhaps the most perceptible changes it brought about were in London, oddly enough, where, as the theatres were operating so near the seat of Government, the law could not so blatantly be ignored.

There were, however, cases where the Act was brought into full and powerful effect. Actors were fined and thrown into gaol, theatres were closed, and in at least one instance—at Bath—a theatre was demolished. Usually this was the result of "information" although the person doing the informing was likely to make himself unpopular. Usually the Methodists were blamed.

In 1754 another theatre at Bath had to be closed for a time and in 1773 there was trouble at Bristol where four performers were fined £50 each. At Salisbury Assizes two theatrical managers named Collins and Davies were fined £100 for playing in the city. These were vast sums in those days.

At Nottingham in 1755 the manager and his entire company were clapped into gaol. This was the fate of that great character Jemmy Whitley who had erected a small theatre in the city on land bought from Alderman Fellowes. The alderman showed no favours to his customer for it was during his Mayoralty that Whitley and Co. were committed to the House of Correction for "presuming to perform without leave or licence".

There appears to have been a further misunderstanding with the authorities for in 1764 an advertisement in the Nottingham Journal stated : "The differences which unfortunately happened in this town occasioned by theatrical amusements, and an opposition of sentiments, it is now hoped are happily subsided. Mr. Whitley, on his part, being sincerely desirous of living in perfect HARMONY with everyone; he therefore wishes for a continuance of the public's favours and begs leave to inform the town that during the company's short stay at Nottingham this season he proposes a benefit night for the poor, the cash to be immediately laid out in coals or otherwise and impartially distributed GRATIS among the necessitous, the ensuing winter by the churchwardens." The performance announced in the advertisement was in the nature of "a concert of vocal and instrumental musick", with a play presented gratis in between. This was, as we shall see, a legal dodge.

Whitley's well-aimed charity was virtually an attempt to bribe his way into local good books. Even this sort of thing could be misconstrued as the Elringtons found out at Manchester in 1753. Having gained leave to appear in the city the company thought they would enhance their esteem by giving the proceeds of a performance in the theatre, then brand new, to the almost equally new Manchester Infirmary. They plastered the city with bills only to find themselves hauled before an indignant bench of magistrates who declared themselves insulted by the implication that the Infirmary needed the charity of "rogues and vagabonds". They were ordered to get out within twenty-four hours. The company was that of Richard Elrington whose wife was the former Betty Martin, who was such a deceiver as to give rise to the expression "All my eye and Betty Martin".

At Northampton and in the county there appears to be no actual evidence of dramatic persecution. Northampton did have an official flogger, who wore a uniform when on duty, and the records at Towcester mention several purchases of whips but the only two instances I have come across of whippings on Northampton Market Square for acting were not of the theatrical variety. In September, 1751, Christopher Donnelly, an Irishman, was "publickly whipp'd on our Market Hill as an imposter in asking charity under the pretence of having lost the use of one of his arms which upon examination was found to be as sound as the other". In July, 1752, a man was arrested at Boughton Green Fair, near Northampton, as an imposter after pretending to be dumb and lodged in the County Gaol. This dumb actor was also sentenced to be whipped, on two Saturdays.

In neighbouring Warwickshire that year the Justices ordered all constables to be very diligent in apprehending all rogues, vagabonds and other disorderly persons and if age or circumstances permitted to have them publickly whipt, or sent to the House of Correction and afterwards conveyed by a pass to their legal settlement. Here a bondage of domicile is implied, as well as of labour.

In London the case of John Palmer was a classic example of the attitude to theatres outside the magic circle of the Patents. Previously an actor at Drury Lane and the Haymarket he attempted to set up a theatre of his own, the Royalty, of which he laid the foundation stone on Boxing Day, 1785. He appears to have been under the impression that the theatre would have a proper legal standing because of a letter of approval from the Governor of the nearby Tower of London. When its legality was challenged by the Drury Lane proprietors he resorted to the dodge of devoting the proceeds of the opening night to the London Hospital and took the opportunity to make a speech, which had been written by Arthur Murphy. Here are excerpts :

> *The magistrates soon saw, in Virtue's cause*
> *The stage a supplement to public laws . . .*
> *No more the stroller with his mimic art*
> *Rumbled about each village in his cart . . .*
> *Their vagrant life the actors then gave o'er*
> *Deemed Beggars, Rogues and Vagabonds no more.*
> *We bid this night another dome aspire*
> *And hope—while your protection quells each fear*
> *The Muse will find a safe asylum here*
> *Yet some there are who would our scheme annoy*
> *'Tis a monopoly they would enjoy*
> *The Haymarket, Covent Garden and Old Drury*
> *Send forth their edicts full of sound and fury*
> *Three jarring states are leagued in jealous fit*
> *And they—whom wit maintains—wage war on wit.*

After the opening night the house was closed for a few nights and when it attempted to reopen several of the company were arrested and put into gaol as vagrants. A petition to Parliament was summarily dismissed and Palmer had to return to Drury Lane. In 1789, while appearing at the Circus in *The Bastille*, he was himself arrested. His subsequent seasons in the provinces brought him to Northampton in 1796.

In The Itinerant, published in 1808, S. W. Ryley tells of a company that was carried miles to gaol in Newcastle "with all the ignominy and insult attached to criminals".

Cork was the scene of an eighteenth-century episode concerning Actors and Gaol which reads more like a figment of the imagination of Charles Dickens than real life. But this was Ireland. An actor named Frederick Glover, who was also a "surgeon", was a spectator at the hanging of Patrick Redmond, a tailor, on Gallows Green, Cork, on Wednesday, September 10, 1766. After the tailor had been suspended a short while it came on to rain and the officials departed rather earlier than usual. Friends cut down the "executed" man and carried the "body" to a nearby cabin called Resurrection House. Glover stepped forward and revived the man by "massage and fumigation" (an early example of the kiss of life technique?). Up sat Paddy and helped himself to a whisky. Being an Irishman he acted like a stage Irishman : instead of quietly disappearing and hoping his executioners would not hear of their error he helped himself to a lot more whisky and presented himself at the theatre, where Glover was on stage in a part that called for him to acknowledge a debt. Waving a shillelagh Redmond forced his way through the audience and scrambled on to the stage shouting his thanks : "Good Christians and honest people, whatever debt Mr. Glover is talking about 'tis nothing at all to what I owe him for sure he saved my life!" A sheriff happened to be patronising the theatre but the tailor managed to get away and later took up a post in Dublin which acknowledged his debt . . . as a tailor serving the theatrical fraternity there.

But Irish episodes apart—and Redmond was not hanged for acting—in considering the effect of the Act it is important to remember that it cannot be evaluated merely by listing or adding up the number of the performers who landed up in gaol or being fined. Liberty is more than being out of prison. The inhabitants of a totalitarian state do not all spend their entire lives in a cell; the great majority never spend a single minute there. But it is the fact of the existence of an oppressive code or secret police to enforce it which constitutes their confinement. Most actors went through the illegal years without being directly affected by the Act either financially or physically; but the very fact that the Act was Law, making them criminals in theory, must have conditioned their self-respect, attitudes and actions. Not to mention the inhibitions, real or imagined, upon the dramatists.

It seems that if a Mayor or magistrate gave his blessing to performances, it was in a negative manner. The actor Thomas Snagg said in his recollections that the manner of "taking the town" was by application to the Mayor or magistrates whose answer, if in approval, was usually : "If I find your conduct regular and orderly I shall not take notice of it." As there were specific acts against strolling players a Justice could not give valid permission. Adding to the paradox was the fact that in some towns the theatre belonged to the Corporation and in others the Town Hall was let to the players.

THE DODGES
around The Law

On the whole the persecution was intermittent and unpredictable and many were the devices employed to circumvent the letter of the law. If it was illegal to stage plays for reward why not present the drama gratis . . . and charge for the music in which it was sandwiched? Or turn your theatre into a snuff factory and offer that commodity with a guarantee that it would "raise the spirits"? Or invite one's audience to take a cup of chocolate (paid for) and watch a group of actors being "rehearsed" (without charge). These were among the many dodges, some of which were effective in satisfying a magistrate's conscience.

The first in the field of dramatic subterfuge appears to have been Giffard, friend of David Garrick, who had bought and rebuilt the Goodmans Field Theatre. Giffard believed that the Duke of Grafton, Lord Chamberlain, would relent and when he did not, reopened without a licence, advertising concerts for which tickets had to be bought, with a play given free during the interval. For three years he got away with it in this manner.

Roger Kemble, head of one of the most renowned of our theatrical families, did not need any artifice when performing at Northampton but he did need to employ one at Worcester where, in 1767, he followed the Giffard pattern.

At Bedford too, among many other towns, one finds the drama provided free in a paid-for sandwich. Performances at the New Theatre, in the George Yard, in 1780 were announced as concerts of vocal and instrumental music—"between the parts of the concert will be performed (gratis) a comedy call'd *The Wonder, A Woman Keeps a Secret*, also a pantomime interlude".

The snuff merchant was Theophilus Cibber who, in 1756, opened the Lincolns Inn Fields Theatre, of doubtful legality, as a snuff warehouse, "late called the theatre on the hill". He advertised that "Cibber and Co., snuff merchants, sell at their warehouse on Richmond Hill most cephalic snuff, which, taken in moderate quantities, will not fail to raise the spirits, clear the brain, throw off ill humours, exhilarate the mind, give joy to the heart and improve the understanding". At the same premises, he added, he had opened a histrionic academy for the instruction of young persons in the art of acting and proposes for the better improvement of such pupils, and frequently with his assistance, to give public rehearsals without hire, gain or reward.

One manager had to have a leg amputated before he could get a licence. This was Samuel Foote who, visiting Lord Mexborough in 1766, was given, unbeknown to himself, a fractious horse to ride, the noble Lord thinking that this leg-pull would amuse the other guests. Foote, who was manager of the Little Theatre in the Haymarket, where only burlettas and other lesser forms of entertainment might be given, was thrown by the horse and had to have a leg off. The conscience-stricken nobleman made representations to the

King to give the theatre a licence and this was done, though only for between
May 14 and September 14 each year, in between the seasons of the
patented theatres.

It was the same Mr. Foote who had a few years earlier announced in
the General Advertiser that his friends were invited to "drink a glass of
chocolate with him" promising that he would endeavour to make the afternoon as diverting as possible—Sir Dilbury Diddle would be there and Lady
Betty Frisk had promised. These were, of course, characters from plays.
Having bought their tickets at George's Coffee House in Temple Bar the
audience went along to the Haymarket where the curtain went up and Foote
announced that while the chocolate was being made they might as well
watch him training some actresses.

Another way of legitimising a bastard piece of drama was to sing a few
songs during it and this was one of the reasons why Shakespeare's works, as
elsewhere related, appeared in some pretty odd guises. *Macbeth* might be
illegal if performed as the author intended but could beat the law if
punctuated by songs. Then it became a "burletta", the definition of which,
according to Planché, was that it contained at least five songs in each
act.

In his book The Georgian Theatre, Arnold Hare examines the account
book of a small and lowly itinerant company and comments : "We notice
that small as their resources were and whatever had to be skimped 'musick'
was always hired. It may be no more than a cracked fiddle with a drunken
player whom nobody listened to but if he kept the players out of court he
served his purpose." A case of Musical Licence?

The point is reinforced by the actor-manager Henry Lee in his memoirs :
"At the Minor Theatres the Actors were supposed to be amenable to the
laws if they spoke properly and plainly; but they escaped all penalty if
accompanied by a Jew's harp, a hurdy-gurdy, or a penny whistle, a brass
drum or a brass pot lid or any other agreeable musical instrument."

And what of *The Beggar's Opera,* which had helped to bring on repression? Dr. Johnson's opinion was that it was not likely to do much good, nor
be productive of much evil as highwaymen and housebreakers seldom
frequented the playhouse "nor is it possible for anyone to imagine that he
may rob with safety because he sees Macheath reprieved upon the stage".
Yet every night at that moment cheers would ring out from the gallery.
At least some of the common people were glad to see wrong triumph over
right.

The degree to which any form of literature or other art form can affect
the morals of a community is an endless topic for debate, as is also the effect
of punishment by way of example. As I write these lines Pierrepoint, the
ex-executioner, has just written a book giving his opinion that all his hang-
ings were pointless and did no good at all.

In April, 1782, a woman from Northamptonshire literally died of laughing as a result of a visit to *The Beggar's Opera* at Drury Lane. The lady
whose funny bone was fatally touched was a Mrs. Fitzherbert, relict (widow)
of the Rev. Mr. Fitzherbert of Northamptonshire. When the actor Bannister
appeared in the role of Polly, the whole audience went into fits of laughter

but Mrs. Fitzherbert's fit proved to be just that. "The actor's whimsical appearance had a fatal effect ... she could not suppress the laughter that seized her and before the end of the second act was obliged to leave the theatre ... not being able to banish the figure from her memory she was thrown into hysterics which continued without intermission until the next morning, when she expired."

But *The Beggar's Opera* was still not a laughing matter with the authorities in London. Authority once leaned so heavily upon the piece as to get the ending altered. Though Macheath was not hanged he was seen on the hulks, suffering retribution. This was produced at Covent Garden in October, 1777.

Garrick had stood out against magisterial requests not to perform *The Beggar's Opera* despite the claim of Sir John Fielding that it was never played without increasing the number of thieves about the Metropolis.

When George Colman wanted to present the play at Covent Garden he was discouraged by the magistrates who sent him a letter to inform him that "on *The Beggar's Opera* being given out to play some time ago at Drury Lane Theatre they requested the managers of that theatre not to exhibit the opera, deeming it productive of mischief to society as in their opinion it most undoubtedly increases the number of thieves; and the managers obligingly returned for answer that night it was too late to stop it but for the future they would not play it if the other house did not. Under these circumstances, from a sense of duty and the principles of humanity the magistrates make the same request to Mr. Colman and the managers of His Majesty's Theatre, Covent Garden; the same opera being advertised to be played there this night."

The Bench got a dusty answer : "Mr. Colman presents his best respects to the magistrates with whose note he has been honoured. He has not yet had an opportunity of submitting it to the other managers but for his own part cannot help differing in the opinion of the magistrates thinking that the theatre is one of the very few houses in the neighbourhood that does not contribute to increase the number of thieves."

Relief came to some extent in 1788 when a new law was made empowering magistrates to license theatrical representations in the provinces for sixty days at a time, though no second licence was to be granted until eight months had elapsed after the first nor to any place within the same jurisdiction within six months.

Meantime the number of legitimate theatres had increased by the granting of Royal patents, such as Bath and Norwich (1768), York and Hull (1769), Liverpool (1771), Manchester (1775), Chester (1777), Bristol and Newcastle (1778).

The 1788 Act was criticised by the aforementioned Henry Lee who said that it was so briefly worded that nobody could understand it—"I have talked with scores of magistrates on the subject and I have never met one that did not say that it was imperfect ... the two fathers of the Act (Lord Radnor and Mr. Hussey) differed in their interpretation of their own law."

Particularly in London, where the Patents of Drury Lane and Covent Garden were jealously guarded, the need for subterfuge continued.

8—TDTS * *

Even when full emancipation did arrive with the Act of 1843—which was to the theatre what the Reform Bill had been to the electoral system—it proved to be a mixed blessing. The Act removed the restriction on the length of season and thus stock companies could stay in one theatre for the entire season or year. This was in itself a death-blow to many of the old circuits. Increasing use of the railways in turn led to the replacement of the stock company by the touring one which might perform the same play night after night, months, even years, on end, instead of having varied roles and repertoire. No doubt the standard of production went up but the old local loyalties and sense of "belonging" were lost. In due course the wheel was to turn full circle and local loyalties came into their own again with the advent of the repertory theatre movement.

HOW ACTORS
got into Gaol and helped others get out

Another prison peril for the actor was one he shared with other impecunious members of the community; he could be put in gaol for debt and not infrequently was.

We need to go back only 250 years to find a time when the individual could be gaoled for owing any trivial sum without the alleged creditor even having to swear an affidavit. Matters were regularised but only slightly ameliorated by the Frivolous Arrests Act of 1725, a reform referred to in *The Beggar's Opera*. A century later the Imprisonment for Debt Act provided that no one could be summarily arrested for debts of less than £20. Imprisonment for debt was finally abolished by the Debtors' Act of 1869. Though even today you can still go to prison for failing to pay; but only after a court has examined your means and ordered you to pay a reasonable sum.

As dramatists, actors and managers have often been hard-up there are few theatre history books covering the pre-1869 period which do not contain some references to prison, though as we shall see, they do not always concern a Thespian being sent to gaol.

I have found no record of actors being clapped into gaol at Northampton, either for debt or for acting, but on at least one occasion it would have been an exceptionally short trip from stage to cell. The drama and the law could scarcely have been in closer proximity than when the Town Hall was at the corner of Abington Street and Wood Hill. It stood there for several centuries and in 1584 the authorities decided that shops under it should be converted into a gaol; as such the premises served for two centuries. They were in this use, therefore, when as the Borough Records show, the Town Hall was let to Mr. Coysh for acting plays in 1705. It seems somewhat of a dramatic situation that the actor playing up above could well land up in the cells below. Another theatre in close proximity to a gaol was at Colchester where, in 1810, the minute books of the Norwich Theatre Circuit which held the lease, said the theatre was in a state of delapidation and was inconvenient "the whole house having but one access and that through one of the courts of the town hall and part of the gaol".

Among the accounts of actors being "inside" there was Charles Bannister who, when strolling in the Eastern Counties at 15s. a week in 1758, was "full of jokes, very popular, perpetually in debt and frequently in gaol". The low comedian James Spiller was often in arrears especially over the bar and was on one occasion seized by the bailiffs just as he was going on stage as a country squire, with hounds. He persuaded the officers of the law to lead the animals on while himself making a strategic exit and escape.

It was not always the lowly members of the profession who found themselves arrested. When he was at the bottom rung of the dramatic ladder, John Philip Kemble was put behind bars at Worcester because he failed to pay for a new suit : this was while he was strolling on his own, when his father disowned him following his running away from Douai Academy; at the time he was stealing turnips from roadside fields in order to survive. But when he had scaled the ladder and was managing the Theatre Royal, Drury Lane, for Richard Brinsley Sheridan, the dramatist politician and proprietor of the theatre, between 1788 and 1796, John Philip Kemble was still not inviolate, though it was one of Sheridan's debts for which he was arrested this time.

Sheridan himself was the subject of the most dramatic arrest. Just before he was about to be put into his coffin, after lying in state, a stranger rushed in and formally arrested the corpse on behalf of a money-lender. Lord Sidmouth and George Canning paid the money due.

The talented but haughty actor William Charles Macready—whose term for the stage was "the pariah profession"—gained some of his early experience and skill in the managerial side of the stage simply because his father was either dodging his creditors or had failed to dodge them and was "inside", awaiting a better turn in the family fortunes.

McCready (Senior) was one of the managers who succeeded at the Birmingham theatre but several others failed including Mr. Watson, of Cheltenham, who was imprisoned in Warwick Gaol for debt; Mr. Wightman, who practically lived in the theatre, emerging only on Sundays because the sheriff could not arrest him on the Sabbath : Mr. Armistead, from Liverpool, who went to gaol and, when his case came up at Warwick Assizes, was released only on condition that he relinquished all claim to the theatre; and a manager who should have gone to gaol but didn't, Mr. Fraser, who engaged Paganini for three nights and absconded with the takings on the third.

I have not come across any record of the great comedian Charles Mathews, who visited Northampton in 1815, 1821 and 1833, ever being incarcerated, but his son of the same name was, following his tempestuous and adventurous marriage to Madame Vestris in July, 1838. It was their season at Covent Garden which put this couple into depths of debt from which they never fully emerged. Mathews went bankrupt and was imprisoned in the Queen's Bench prison. Later he fled to France to escape his financial problems, came back and took the Lyceum, only to go bankrupt once more. While playing at Preston in 1856 he was again arrested for debt and thrown into Lancaster Gaol from which he was released just in time to be with his dying wife in London.

I know of three cases of benefit night appeals being made from behind bars. The first is related by Kathleen Barker in her Bristol theatre book and occurred in 1733. Two managers named Kennedy and Booth came to the city and set up in opposition to the established theatre next door. They were informed against and four of the company were fined £50 each. Despite this setback they carried on advertising and performing and returned the following year. This season "petered out in apparent disaster" and, as Miss Barker tells us: "They appear to have had to organise their benefits from prison." In Northamptonshire the pair turned up in April, 1770, at the Moot Hall, Daventry, a predecessor of the present building.

Secondly there was J. Carleton, who managed seasons at Northampton in 1772 and 1773 and was in gaol at Nottingham on the last night of Jemmy Whitley's 1778 season there which had been set aside as a benefit for the Carletons. "As Mr. Carleton's melancholy situation prevents him from waiting personally on the public . . ." ran his newspaper advertisement. Tickets could be got from him at the gaol.

Finally, there was Mr. Penn of the Manchester Company who was in prison for debt in 1789 and was kept going by gifts from his manager and fellow actors. A bill stated that he now had to trust to the benefit—"the only chance now left to him to procure (that blessing so dear to every species of humanity) his—*LIBERTY* !"

The Birthday Honours knighthood of 1895 bestowed by Queen Victoria on Henry Irving is generally regarded as the first stage title but there was at least one earlier one and he was once accommodated in one of Her Majesty's Prisons. Irving did not use the title in cast lists or on playbills but the previous knight did, as a gimmick. His "Sir" was not an honour but an inheritance. Sir William Don was the only son of the sixth baronet of Newtondon, Berwickshire, whom he succeeded in 1829. He took to the stage not because of any towering talent or irresistible inclination but was driven there by the massive debts he had piled up during a three-year career as an officer in the 5th Dragoon Guards. The Newtondon estate had to be sold, producing £85,000, but still he was in the red. After some acting in the north of England Sir William went to the United States, probably as much to escape his pecuniary pursuers as to forward his stage career. Returning after five years he found there was still more than £7,000 owing. At Bristol with his actress wife, Lady Emily (Saunders), he had played a fairly successful season and was leaving by cab to catch a train when he was arrested and spent the next fortnight in Bristol Debtors' Prison. Released on bail he played at Birmingham, then returning to Bristol for a benefit performance at which the stoney broke baronet, thin and lanky, gave this advice to the audience : "Keep out of debt, dear young gentlemen. Take this long monumental warning before you."

Three years later Sir William and Lady Emily went to Australia where he played female characters in burlesque. He died at Hobart Town, Tasmania, aged thirty-seven, after playing Queen Elizabeth in a burlesque of *Kenilworth*. Returning to England Lady Emily was briefly lessee of the Theatre Royal, Nottingham, where the couple had previously appeared but later sang in musichalls. Quite a come-down for a Lady.

I interpolate here two examples of titled actors from the later period when a debt could no longer directly land one in prison. The first was a twice bankrupt dancing earl, the second an impecunious viscount in the Gaiety chorus.

The dancing earl was the Earl of Yarmouth, eldest son of the Marquis of Hertford, who wrote musical comedy and appeared in Tasmania as a skirt dancer. In June, 1900, a bankruptcy order then in existence against him was annulled when he managed to pay 10s. in the pound. Ten years later he faced another receiving order in respect of a £406 money lending debt. In between he had appeared in America and achieved some notoriety through marrying Alice Thaw, whose brother Harry three years later, in 1906, murdered Stanford White in New York Theatre. The marriage was dissolved in 1908.

The impecunious viscount was Viscount Dangan, eldest son of the Earl Cowey, who left the 5th Lancers because he was "fed up" with the Army. Needing to earn a living, he became a paint room labourer at 25s. a week and later joined the Gaiety chorus and appeared in *A Message from Mars*. May, 1913, found him rehearsing with Arthur Bourchier there and engaged to a fellow member Pearl Aufrere, who had appeared in *Hello Ragtime*.

Being in gaol for debt was worse than being there for contempt of court. Whereas, after a time, a contempt is usually regarded as purged and release follows, in the case of debt the "offence" was not purged by time, only by repayment of the debt, or forgiveness by the creditor. The Restoration dramatist Wycherley languished seven years in a debtors' prison. He had had an affair with one of Charles II's lady loves, the Duchess of Cleveland, and subsequently married the Countess of Drogheda. Neither of these moves pleased the monarch so that when Wycherley fell into debt Charles refused to assist him. Subsequently his debts were paid by James II.

While "inside" the debtor would in some respects be worse off than a criminal : in others better. For instance, he would be better off in the seventeenth, and eighteenth and early nineteenth centuries than the male-factor because for that unworthy the affair was likely to end, if not in the rare acquittal, on the gallows tree or in transportation abroad for a term of years, with execution kept in reserve should he have the temerity to return prematurely. Debtors like John Philip Kemble might be incarcerated for failing to pay for a suit but as the law was before the 1820s had they stolen the self-same article they would have been hanged !

The debtor would be better off too in not being encumbered with chains and fetters. These were no lightweight matter. At Northampton County Gaol on an icy day in December, 1796, there were no prayers : "The reason was the severity of the frost. The alleys in the gaolyard were as glib as glass. The gaoler was afraid that the prisoners, in coming from their cells to the chapel, would slip down and break their legs, especially those loaded with chains." Also the chapel was upstairs and it was painful for prisoners thus loaded to make their way to the appointment with the Deity.

Whereas the criminal would receive some definite food ration, however small or lacking in quality, the debtor might get nothing at all from the authorities and have to rely on what was sent in to him or on the doubtful charity of the criminals. Actually getting food into a prison appears to have presented no problems in Northampton when the Town Gaol was in Abington Street. It had windows to the street and victuals and drinks could be passed in. In any case, visitors had almost free access and could take in beer and gin quite freely; by night time a prisoner might be roaring drunk.

But whatever the relative advantages of being a criminal or a debtor, being "inside" at all was a very dodgy business in the earlier centuries.

One of the earlier gaols in Northampton was the Castle, where Thomas à Becket, Archbishop of Canterbury, had stood trial in 1146. Between 1332 and 1333 the deaths of eleven prisoners in the castle within sixteen months were attributed by a coroner's jury to cold, hunger, thirst and privation. At Oxford Castle in 1577 gaol fever was so rife that at the Assizes held there all 300 present perished within forty-eight hours, including the judge and the sheriff. In the eighteenth century Lord Montagu's report on conditions said that the fever killed more people than the executioner, and this included debtor prisoners.

The Northampton Castle was demolished in 1662 and the County Gaol was subsequently in part of the Bell Inn, George Row. After the Dreadful Fire of Northampton had wiped out most of the town in 1675, the County Hall was built on the site of the Bell and next door to it was a house erected for Sir William Haselwood, which later became the gaol. Next to this was the County Infirmary, later the bank and home of Mr. H. B. Whitworth, who was for a time one of the proprietors of the Theatre, Marefair, Northampton. Later still the Whitworth property became the home of Northampton Club, in which use it remains to this day.

The great reformer in this sphere was John Howard of Bedford who went round the county reporting on the conditions he found, remarking especially on the plight of the debtor. On a visit to Northampton in 1776 he noted that it was the only prison in England which lacked both of two vital facilities—an exercise yard and a water supply.

At Coventry City and County Gaol there was no proper separation of debtors : at Leicester County Gaol the Debtors' Free Ward (where they did not have to pay for a bed) was "still a dungeon"; at Derby County Gaol debtors were two in a bed if they paid 2s. a week, mixed in with felons if they paid 6d.; there are many references to a total lack of sanitary facilities—no sewers at Lincoln, for instance, in 1788. As regards the lack of water supply this was no doubt deplorable but water supplies were not always pure and it could be safer to drink beer. A licence to sell wine and beer was one of the perks of John Scofield when he was reappointed gaoler of Northampton County Gaol in 1785.

One result of John Howard's travels was an attempt to stop the drink trade in the prisons. But even after Scofield had been given a salary in place of this source of income he was obliged, out of the £200 he was paid, to "give every prisoner three pints of small beer daily". Outside Nottingham County Gaol in 1787 there appeared a notice with the Fred Karno touch : "No ale or liquor sold within the prison."

Scofield, who had taken office originally in 1773 following his lack of success at the Riding School, had one duty which may appear quite extraordinary—to sell tickets for the Northampton theatre, as will emerge.

The main result of John Howard's reforms as far as Northampton was concerned was the erection of new gaols. In 1792 the new Town Gaol was opened in Fish Street, not far from the St. Giles Street theatre. Until the opening of St. Andrew's Hospital (which is today the country's leading private mental hospital) as the Northampton Lunatic Asylum in 1838 lunatics were also kept in the Fish Street (or Fish Lane) premises, chained to the floor and lying on a bed of straw. Even when the asylum did open, as a result of Masonic endeavour, enlightenment was only partial—patients were taken there chained and manacled. Those were the days of Bedlam. Later the St. Andrew's Hospital had its own "pretty theatre" and in later Victorian times a remarkable amount of theatrical activity went on there including visits by leading amateur companies from London.

Northampton's present theatre might easily have been erected on part of a gaol site. The new County Gaol had been erected in 1792 at the rear of the old one in George Row and on the model lines suggested by Howard. When extensions were required in the 1820s the authorities tried to purchase Whitworth's house but the price he asked, £19,200, proved too much so they extended in the opposite direction, taking in the houses and gardens of Mr. Hughes and Mr. Gates. It was on part of this extension area, when the gaol was made redundant in 1880, that there was a plan to build a new theatre for Northampton, to replace the modest one in Marefair. This would have been on the west side of Guildhall Road. In fact the theatre which was erected in 1884, and which is now Northampton Repertory Theatre, was placed on the opposite side.

As I mentioned earlier not all the theatre book mentions of gaols are about Thespians being imprisoned. Because of their intimacy with the problems of the empty pocket, the remittance which has been promised but is somehow delayed, actors and managers had a fellow feeling of sympathy for those detained for mere lack of ready money. There are many instances of debtor prisoners being assisted.

In September, 1728, the Bath Company, which had appeared in Northampton the previous year, gave a performance in Bristol for the relief of poor insolvent debtors in Newgate Prison. In 1750 David Garrick gave a benefit at Drury Lane in aid of the Marshalsea prisoners.

Languishing in Northampton Town Gaol in 1759 was a man named Thomas Greenhough. He must have been in despair for he had been there

for four years. If there is a record of the precise sum he owed, to whom he
owed it, and to whom he was therefore also indebted for his long imprisonment, I have not found it. But clearly the sum was such as could be raised
by one night's performance at the theatre.

For to his rescue came the Durravan Company, then on their first season
in the town. On Friday, November 23, 1759, they performed a tragedy
The Distress'd Mother for the benefit of Mr. Greenhough "in order to
release him from a miserable confinement in the Town Gaol of Northampton where he has been imprison'd upwards of four years for debt—and 'tis
humbly hoped that all charitable well dispos'd persons will lend their assistance to so humane a benefaction. The profits arising from this night's
performance will be put into the hands of Mr. Mayor for the purpose above
mentioned, of whom tickets may be had or at Mr. Tyer's in The Drapery."
The advertisement also expressed the wish that the "publick on this occasion
will not be offended at the whole house being laid at 2s. each person". The
practice of "laying" appears to have involved removing the divisions between
various parts of the house. Sometimes the pit would be laid into boxes, and
so forth.

In the Mercury the following week the released debtor expressed his
thanks : "Thomas Greenhough with a heart full of gratitude humbly begs
leave to return his sincere thanks to all his worthy benefactors who by their
generous contributions were pleased to release him from prison on Friday
last."

During the Kemble period at Northampton there are two instances of
assistance for debtors. On December 7, 1778, "Mr. Kemble truly sensible
of the kind reception he has met with in Northampton apprehends that he
cannot acknowledge the favours he has received in a more acceptable way
than by performing this play for the benefit of several poor debtors who
have large families and are at this time confined in Northampton County
Gaol. Tickets to be had at the usual places and of Mr. Scofield at the
County Gaol." The attractions for which the gaoler served as a de facto
box office keeper were *The School for Scandal, The Examination of Dr.
Last before the College of Physicians* and *Midas*.

Charity for the confined was not restricted to theatrical performances,
nor to debtors. There are a number of mentions in the newspaper at this
period of gifts of coal and food; such as : "The prisoners in general of the
County Gaol beg leave to return their humble thanks for two legs of mutton
and five twelvepenny loaves from persons unknown." The following week
two pieces of beef were acknowledged.

Almost the last act by the Kembles in Northampton was to lend their
aid again to the debtor prisoners, this time those in the Town Gaol. On a
Wednesday, in November, 1781, Shakespeare's *Richard II* was given, the
Mercury reporting : "The benevolence of the design, with the uncommon
merit of Mr. Taylor, who kindly undertook the part of King Richard
brought together a very polite and crowded audience and we hear there was
upwards of £24 collected at the door."

Mr. Taylor, who was evidently a local amateur, spoke an Epilogue :

Again I've ventured on this little stage
And took my part with Shakespeare's noble page
Again I'm honoured with your kind applause
Child as I am in dramatic laws
Oh! Whilst I strive to please with honest art
Your frequent plaudits warmed my grateful heart
No more a tyrant but a suppliant now
To you my lawful sovereigns I bow
Pleased with subjection, hoping to obey
Stern Richard though, abhorred I cast away
It was not fame nor bold ambition's flight
Nor youthful ardour brought me here tonight
Some gentle souls by generous motives swayed
Sent me a summons; I with joy obeyed
Go, said the mandate, strive with all thy power
To sooth the prisoners' solitary hours
Ere winter comes with all its dismal train
Of chilling blasts, of frost and searching rain
Collect the willing aid which pity lends
And show that poverty itself has friends
Ah! whilst I look, with transport, all around
In every eye benevolence is found
Hail mercy! Sweetest attribute divine
To ease the wounded heart is only thine
Oh! Let our ardent wish this night prevail
To chase the horrors of this gloomy gaol
Sure in this house—this generous house—I see
Substantial help, if not full liberty.

Roger Kemble's illustrious daughter, Sarah Siddons, many times showed her concern for the gaoled debtor. Prevented by her impending departure for a season elsewhere from giving a benefit for the prisoners in the Dublin Marshalsea Prison she instead "sent a sum of money to the conductor of the above prison".

In Limerick, Ireland, a company of amateurs was formed in 1785, in the absence of professional entertainment. As they were not out to make money, or even a living, for themselves, they gave performances in aid of various charities, leasing the Theatre Royal from Mr. Daly. A performance by this Limerick Theatrical Society on March 15 that year was "for the relief of fellow creatures in distress, many of whom are detained in a loathsome prison for their fees". Four years later a group of young gentlemen in the same town performed for good causes including "the relief of confined debtors who now labour under the greatest distress for want of common necessaries at this inclement season".

For many years Cork had an organisation called the Society for the Relief and Discharge of Persons Confined for Small Debts. Towards the end of the theatrical season each year it was allowed the proceeds from a benefit night and a 1791 report stated that forty persons with debts totalling £390 had been restored to their families at a cost of £60. A case of cut-price releases. At Cork in 1837 the Mayor and Sheriff ordered a charity play to be acted "for the benefit and relief of poor insolvent debtors". In the case of the sheriff it would appear that he arrested the impecunious with one hand and released them with the other!

At Northampton there were others, beside the actors, who remembered the plight of the debtors. In 1713 Rebecca Hussey gave £768 12s. 11d., the income from which was to pay the debts and procure the discharge of poor debtors committed by County Court judges. Lady Lucan, an aunt of Earl Spencer, gave £100 in October, 1818, the interest to be paid to the poor debtors. A little more unusual was the Hall's Charity created by John Hall, of Northampton, in his will, dated April 28, 1821, bequeathing £100 to be invested and the income applied to providing a Christmas Day dinner for felons in Northampton County Gaol. In the 1850s this money was diverted to prisoners leaving gaol or juveniles sent to Reformatory after the Rev. F. Litchfield had protested that it was not right that people in gaol at Christmas should feed better than some of the honest ones outside!

You could also be gaoled for debt in the U.S.A. In the 1840s F. C. Wemyss, Scottish-born manager of the Philadelphia, Baltimore and Pittsburg theatres, was arrested a number of times. "Arrest for debt followed arrest : execution followed execution, until to keep my person out of gaol I was compelled to apply for the benefit of the Insolvency Laws." These events seemed to bear out the worst fears of Wemyss's rich uncle and guardian who, when he showed a desire to go on the stage, warned him that it represented "the lowest dregs of humanity" and implored him to "resume your proper sphere in society, otherwise habits of idleness inimical to all exertions will insensibly be formed". In the early 1820s Wemyss appeared with the Elliston company at the Marefair theatre in Northampton.

VILLAINS
in real life too

Having commisserated with the dramatic fraternity for their misfortunes with regard to prisons, and praised them for their charity with regard to prisoners, it is only right to mention that, as with all other sections of the community, there have been Thespians in gaol who deserved to be there. And that there were others who deserved gaol but managed to avoid it.

Every profession and calling has its share of downright villains on the one hand and likeable rogues on the other; outright thieves and cunning charmers who leave a trail of debt as they go their honeytongued way. By the very nature of its art, the stage has probably had more than its quota of men and women making an illicit living by one form or other of false pretences. After all, acting the part convincingly is half the battle for the "deaf" or "blind" beggar, or the man whose monthly cheque has mysteriously failed to turn up. Likewise, there are few professions of a more itinerant nature, with the attendant temptation to depart before paying one's bill.

Most managers would see that they paid all their dues and demands before leaving a town at the end of a season, if only to keep their slate clean for the next visit. The actor who envisaged changing companies might sometimes be less honest.

When announcing their departure some managers would make a point of inviting creditors to send in their accounts. Francis Raymond, who managed the Northampton theatre in the late 1820s, advertised that application should be made to Mrs. Raymond by a certain time and date. Other managers also allowed their wives to look after the exchequer, as Miss Rosenfeld instances in her Strolling Players. Though Dennis Herbert, the Lincoln manager, was accustomed to drink ninety-three half-pints of beer in a day, he luckily had a provident wife who kept hold of the cash and paid his tradesmen's bills punctually every morning after play night. On the other hand Miss Rosenfeld mentions a manager named Mossop who "was in the habit of never announcing his last night and stealing out of town with his bills unpaid".

There is not room for a who's who of the stage's real life villains, only to mention one or two of varying degrees of criminality or culpability.

Perhaps the best-known dramatist who was put inside was the quick-tempered author of the Masque at Althorp mentioned in our Royal Curtain Raiser. While an actor in London with Henlowe's Company Ben Jonson had lived a Bohemian life and was extremely quarrelsome. Fighting a duel with a fellow actor, Gabriel Spencer, he killed the man and went to gaol for a year. He had previously been imprisoned for completing *Isle of Dogs*, a play left unfinished by Thomas Nashe and which was denounced by the Privy Council as seditious and slanderous.

Less well-known but according to one witness the most villainous of English playwrights was William Dimond, son of William Wyatt Dimond of the Bath Theatre, who wrote two dozen popular plays including *The Foundling of the Forest*. J. C. Bunn wrote about him in January, 1838: "Heard of the death of William Dimond which took place at Paris more than three months ago and has been kept secret by his friends who, though they rejoiced at his decease, were ashamed of his existence and ergo kept silent. His enormities are said to have broken his mother's heart and to have been the cause of his father cutting his throat. He has been in many gaols and tried in many courts under many names for heinous crimes, out of all of which he escaped by sheer miracles. His deeds at Bath, the early and great scene of his profligacy, would fill a volume."

Having quoted him, however, it must be added that Bunn does not appear to be too reliable a witness. When I mentioned this case to Kathleen Barker she pointed out that Dimond senior had died on January 2, 1812, ... of a cerebral haemorrhage. She added: "William junior was certainly not a very nice piece of work but Mrs. Dimond did not die until June, 1823, so her heart took a long time to break!"

At Bristol's Theatre Royal there was one lessee whose whole tenure was a charade, as Miss Barker relates. Behind "Bristol Theatres Ltd." was an irrepressible and quite unscrupulous theatrical confidence trickster, Cecil Hamilton Baines (real name William Francis Jackson) who had twice been bankrupt and sentenced on several occasions for fraudulent misrepresentation.

The story of Baines and the Bottles is typical of the more extravagant flights of imagination in the field of theatre publicity. During a period when interest in the theatre was at a low level Baines phoned the editor of the local newspaper and said he had found some very ancient bottles of port, which, he thought, might have been laid down in 1766, when the theatre was opened. A young reporter was shown the vintage, covered with grime and cobwebs. Elegant ladies and gentlemen thronged the theatre and, during the interval begged to see the bottles. With feigned reluctance Baines allowed himself to be persuaded to sell the stuff in tiny measures at half-a-crown. The customers held the precious liquid under their noses, went in raptures over the bouquet, sipped it with reverence, declared they had never tasted anything like it before. It was in fact Australian port, costing 3s. 6d. a bottle and not more than a year or two old. Thus the theatre survived another crisis but in time the inevitable happened and Baines was bankrupted again, in 1922.

Here in Northampton by no means all his bills were paid by Errol Flynn, when he departed after a 1933–4 spell with Northampton Repertory Company.

Which brings me as near as I dare advance in time in the field of shysters of the stage. The field of libel and slander is full of mines and I have no wish to explode any.

SLANDERS
on The Stage

Slanders on the stage itself have had to be endured, however, in guide books and other accounts of various towns. In his history and antiquities of Derby, published in 1826, Robert Simpson gave a potted history : "The Theatre which is situated in Bold Lane was erected in 1773 at the sole expence of Mr. James Whitley. Prior to the erection of this building a room in the Iron-Gate was used for the purpose of histrionic exhibitions. "To this unexceptionable factual statement he added this astonishing gratuitous insult : "Happy will it be when these nurseries of vice and immorality no longer exist . . . the profaneness and blasphemy with which most of our tragedies abound; and the ribaldry, lewdness and obscenity of our comedies sufficiently indicate the malignant influence they will naturally have upon the morals of a people who are fond of such amusements."

NEW THEATRE,
NORTHAMPTON.

IMPORTANT NOTICE TO ARTISTES

The Management wish to draw the special attention of all Artistes to the following Rules and Regulations.

1. **The Management cannot accept responsibility for loss or damage to Artistes' property due to fire, theft or other cause. Artistes are strongly advised to lock their dressing room doors and not to leave articles of value about.**

2. SMOKING on the stage or in the dressing rooms is STRICTLY PROHIBITED.

3. Artistes are requested to furnish the Hallkeeper with their addresses immediately on arrival.

4. Persons not employed at the theatre may not be brought behind the scenes or to dressing rooms unless written permission is obtained from the Manager.

5. All keys must be given up to the Hallkeeper before departure.

6. Variety artistes must adhere strictly to the time allotted for their act and under no circumstances exceed it.

7. **Any Artiste giving expression to any words or gestures of a vulgar, offensive or obscene nature shall be liable to instant dismissal and forfeiture of salary for the current week. Comedy material based on effeminacy is expressly prohibited.**
   Artistes are warned that this rule is rigidly enforced by the Authorities and the Management. The Management's decision on this rule is final and binding on the artiste.

8. ELECTRIC LIGHTS MUST BE SWITCHED OFF BEFORE LEAVING ROOM.

S. H. NEWSOME, Managing Director.

THE AUTHOR rescued this notice from a dressing room at the New Theatre, Northampton, just before it was demolished in 1960. Note especially Regulation 7—what an astonishing change in attitudes toward effeminacy in entertainment there has been in the decade-and-a-half since then.

While on the Isle of Wight for a few days away from the chores of theatre research and writing, a rainy day drove me from the beach and deckchair reminiscences of a honeymoon of twenty years earlier into Ventnor Public Library where I came across a book about the island written a century ago by T. Redding Ware. Writing in 1869 he singled out the theatre at Ryde for a singularly virulent attack : "The town even boasts a theatre, the usual wretched, bankrupt, out-at-elbows and disreputable temple one finds in nine out of ten seaside resorts. "After describing how Mrs. Jordan, mistress of the Duke of Clarence (afterwards William IV) made her farewell appearance and how Edmund Kean was hissed there Mr. Ware added : "Possibly it would be quite judicious conduct on the part of the inhabitants of seaside towns to buy up the theatres and sell them for rubbish : such action would make the towns quite respectable." This serves as a lead-in to his comment that "The theatre of the Isle of Wight is the Theatre of Nature —what need of a canvas garden when every square yard of the island is a series of lessons in botany? What need of a pasteboard castle where there is wonderful Carisbrooke to wander over? The Isle is its own theatre and

"ALL THE WORLD'S A STAGE", a farce by Isaac Jackman first seen at Drury Lane in 1777, was produced several times at Northampton. This illustration of Act II Scene 2 is from a Dick's edition of Victorian times. The play deals with "the phrenzy for spouting" in stately homes which occurred both upstairs and downstairs—in the shape of amateur acting alike by lords and ladies, butlers and cooks. (*By courtesy of Harry Greatorex*)

laughs at its poor little rival perched on the hill and pushing forward its bold face and haggard walls like some old coquette who will not understand that she is passé."

Tom Robertson's use of his stage background in his classic play *Caste* is well known because the play was popular for many years and is still revived from time to time. Less well-known are the remarks he put into the mouths of some of his characters in *M.P.* a play which has dated rather more. One line declares that "the stage is considered quite one of the learned professions nowadays" but another defines an actor as "an inflated simpleton who only desires to exhibit himself for the gratification of his own petty vanity".

Even some theatre critics shared in the low opinion of stage folk, as far as their private life was concerned. One of the old guard of dramatic criticism was Clement Scott of the Daily Telegraph who in 1899 went into print with a statement implying that no girl could become an actress and remain an honest woman. Leading actor-managers of the West End made a joint protest to the editor and Scott was sacked.

THE ACID TEST
The Officer and the Actress

But apart from the attitudes of the Church and Law, historians and guide book authors, dramatists and drama critics, what was the general demeanour of "ordinary" people, both high and low, to the stage and the drama?

Even some people who, like bishops, would not have been seen dead in a theatre, practised drama in domestic surroundings. During the latter part of the eighteenth century there was a growing fashion for family performances of plays in stately homes and country houses. When Isaac Jackman selected the theme for his farce, *All the World's A Stage*, first presented at Drury Lane in April, 1777, the London Chronicle said it was aimed at "tne prevalent phrenzy for spouting which has not only shown itself in the parlours of private houses but even descended into the kitchen and stables, the very footmen and grooms becoming Romeos and Alexanders while cooks and scullions have left their fire-sides and dripping-pans to love like Juliet and die like Statira". A principal role was that of Diggory, a stage-struck butler. Garrick honoured the piece by writing a prologue which, said the Morning Post, was "descriptive of the passion for acting so prevalent at present thro' the private families of the kingdom".

The fashion continued into the nineteenth century and was in some measure a detriment to the professional theatre. In December, 1864, there was a crowded, distinguished audience for the first performance by Northampton Amateur Dramatic Club, which took place at the theatre, Marefair. The Mercury commented : "For many years, as everyone knows, the drama has led a somewhat forlorn life. The theatre has not been fashionable" ... "people who shun dramatic representations offered by a regular stage and the conveniences of boxes, pit and gallery flock to witness pretty much the same sort of thing on a makeshift, miniature stage at the end of a long room, under the title of drawing room entertainments, monopylogues and other avoidances of the legitimate name." The tide, it added, however, was beginning to turn. Which it was. The smell was dying down.

Proposing the health of Henry Irving at an on-stage dinner at the Lyceum, London, to mark the hundredth performance of his company in *The Merchant of Venice*, Lord Houghton said that the general improvement in the status of the profession was so marked that "families of condition are ready to allow their children to go on the stage". Actors and actresses of humble origin found themselves competing with genteel folk who were prepared to play for even less than the lowly going rates of pay. Stage-struck middle class daughters put advertisements in The Times, such as this one of February, 1878 : "A young lady of good voice, figure and stage appearance, wishes to meet with a lady or gentleman who can introduce her on the stage." She added, oddly enough : "No managers need apply."

Whether or not it might be possible for the daughter of a respectable family to go on the stage one thing she could not do was to attend the theatre as a member of the audience without an escort. Even the convention-defying young woman who was to become an eccentric Countess of Cardigan would not do that. She did not object to being courted by the Earl who had led the Charge of the Light Brigade in the Crimean War, despite the fact that his wife, from whom he was separated, was still alive, nor yet by the even more scandalous fact that she was known to be dying. The future Countess was then Miss de Horsey and when her father, who was a Member of Parliament, excused himself from accompanying her to the theatre by saying that he had a prior engagement she persuaded the Earl to take her instead, it being unthinkable to go alone, as she recalled in her sensational memoirs, which so scandalised society. The amusing sequel was that when the pair arrived at the theatre they found that her father had preceded them and was sitting there with two women "not of their circle". Father was angry when she got home but was not in a position to upbraid her too severely. After the marriage in 1858 Earl and Countess lived at Deene Park, Northants, until his death ten years later, when he fell from a horse. After a second marriage and widowhood she returned to Deene to end her days there in 1915, at the age of ninety, taking up permanent abode in the coffin which she had had for many years, trying it for size and comfort from time to time.

At the time of Queen Victoria's Diamond Jubilee in 1897 a number of Britain's leading figures were asked what they considered to be the most striking characteristic of the sixty glorious years. The leading actor was Sir Henry Irving who referred to scientific progress but added : "I am glad to think that the reign is equally distinguished by the growth of tolerance, the disappearance of many prejudices, and the marked abatement of others— not only in religion but in the attitude of society towards artistic callings— notably my own. In short 'the arts' have grown respectable, happily

without losing any of their native vigour." From the managers Mr. George
Alexander, of the St. James Theatre, London, was selected, and he spoke
of the "great broadening of the national mind in the matter of the circumstances of the stage. The reproach of the stage—I speak of the legitimate
stage—is dead; and this in great measure is due to the grace and favour of
the First Lady of the Realm."

Along with the theatre in general, the profession of acting has today
almost entirely lost its smell in the nose of Church, Law and public, apart
from such people as Mrs. Whitehouse of the Purity Campaign. And this
oddly enough despite a larger number of bared breasts and bums, not only
in the peep-shows of the nude revues which closed the variety theatres in
the 1950s but also in long-running serious drama and musicals in the West
End and almost anything goes since the end of censorship in 1968.

My purpose here is not to moralise, merely to record, so I will refrain
from saying anything either censorious or salacious. But if I chose to comment in greater pornographic detail on what has been going on in the
sixties and seventies I could, in today's climate, do so. Freedom, if such
it be, has extended to the written word as well as that spoken on stage.

It seems incredible that this is less than two decades after Phyllis Dixey,
after appearing at the New Theatre, was hauled before Northampton
magistrates for allowing her tits to be glimpsed on the move, or some similar
earth-shaking misdemeanour. Though she did get off.

I suppose that the Acid Test of one's attitude towards any particular
profession or calling is whether one would be prepared or proud to have
one of them as a member of the family.

Henry Mackenzie came from a long line of highly respectable Puritans.
So when he decided to go on to the stage, rather than shame them with
association with someone "on the boards" he changed his name to Compton,
which be borrowed from the maiden name of one of his grandmothers,
Susannah Compton, of Northamptonshire. As Henry Compton he became
one of the leading actors of his Victorian day. He married an actress
Emmeline Montague and one of their two sons was Edward, who carried
on the adopted name and calling, founding the Compton Comedy Company
in 1881 at Southport, and spending the remaining thirty-seven years of his
life touring the provinces until his terminal cancer and death in 1918. His
company was the first to appear at Northampton Theatre Royal and Opera
House when it opened in May, 1884, and from 1903 until his death, he
was joint owner of that theatre, with Milton Bode of Reading.

The Acid Test involves not only the question of whether Mrs. Worthington should be prepared to allow her daughter to go on the stage but also
whether she should allow her son or daughter to marry a member of what
Macready called the Pariah Profession.

On the stage of the Theatre, Marefair, Northampton, in 1827 Miss Maria
Foote sang "a number of her peculiar dancing songs", as Maria Darlington
in *A Rowland for an Oliver* and paid a return visit the following year. But
when she entered the house again in October, 1836, it was as the Countess
of Harrington, the marriage to the Earl having taken place four years
earlier.

9—TDTS * *

The "caste" barrier was by no means impenetrable. When T. W. Robertson wrote his famous "turning point" play in 1867, called *Caste*, his class distinction plot involved the marriage of a stage dancer and a hero who was not only the son of a Marquise, but also an officer in the British Army. There was a significance here which is not always realised. For while a gentleman could sometimes marry an actress and have her accepted as his Lady, Countess, Duchess or Marchioness, if he was a serving officer, as well as a gentleman, acceptance was much less likely. Especially if he was in the Guards.

There were officers who married actresses without dismissal. In January, 1912, a member of my old regiment, the Buffs, Major Edward Finch Hatton, D.S.O., married Miss Dagmar Wiehe, "the well-known actress". The groom was, moreover, the son of the former Rector of Weldon, Northants, while his mother was a cousin of the Earl of Winchilsea. But his actress bride had the presumably saving grace of herself being the daughter of an Army officer, Col. F. G. A. Wiehe, of Sandgate, Kent.

Some words uttered by the real-life colonel of the Scots Guards in February, 1908, might well have been written for him by Robertson. A promising young Lieutenant in the Royal Scots Guards had married an actress and as a direct result was obliged to give up his army career. The officer was twenty-two-year-old Lt. Basil Loder, grandson of Sir Robert Loder, of Whittlebury, and a nephew of the Loders of Maidwell Hall, Northants. His bride was Miss Barbara Deane, a close friend of Seymour Hicks, the actor (later Sir Seymour Hicks) and his wife Ellaline Terriss, who had been appearing with Miss Terriss in *The Gay Gordons* at the Aldwych Theatre, London.

Interviewed on the subject Lt.-Col. F. W. Romilly stated with great candour the principles involved : "It is quite true that Lt. Basil Loder has resigned but he resigned quite voluntarily. Having married an actress he would, of course, retire from the regiment. An officer of the Guards cannot marry an actress and remain in the regiment. If a person of one rank marries a person of another rank . . . well! He knew that if he married an actress he must resign . . . you see his wife could not be presented at Court. I am very sorry to lose Lt. Loder. He was a young officer who was doing very well."

The 5th Marquess of Northampton, who served as an M.P. before succeeding to the title in 1897, was a Radical and Progressive but in 1913 he found it altogether too radical and progressive when his son, Earl Compton, came home to one of the family seats—Castle Ashby, Northants, or Compton Wynyates, Warwickshire—and announced that he intended to marry an actress.

The lady of the footlights with whom the twenty-eight-year-old Guards officer had fallen deeply in love was Daisy Markham. Born in India in 1886, the daughter of Charles and Lydia Markham, she first appeared on the stage in Manchester in 1904 as Celia in *As You Like It* and was afterwards seen in London and New York in *The Case of The Rebellious Susan, Mrs. Gorringe's Necklace, Leah Kleschna, Raffles, Sally Bishop* and in *The Glad Eye*, as Suzanne Polignac, which had ended its run at the Globe Theatre

London, on January 30, 1913. Daisy had been married before, which was probably another complicating factor : it was described as a "boy and girl affair" with a stockbroker's clerk called Harold Moss whom she had divorced in January, 1906.

Earl Compton, who was a Lieutenant in the Royal Horse Guards, desperately wanted to marry the girl but when his father told him it was absolutely out of the question and demanded a promise that he would not marry her, the Earl caved in. In effect it turned out to be that type of promise often used on the stage, the death bed vow. At least, by the time William Bingham Compton had broken the news to his intended bride and she had resolved to sue him for breach of promise, his father had died, being among twenty-five peers who died within a period of six months. It was therefore as the 6th Marquess that the defendant attended the Kings Bench Court in London.

King's Counsel were briefed on both sides for what was to be the shortest of hearings. When the court opened there was a rush for seats and it was a packed "audience", consisting mainly of actors and actresses, for this sensational real-life performance. The gangways were jammed when the Judge, Mr. Justice Buckhill, stepped through the doorway behind the judicial dais. Seeing the mob he gave a start of disapproval and ordered the gangways to be cleared. When nothing happened he announced that he would not start until they were clear—"Go up in the gallery", he told the audience. Still no one moved and the ushers had to eject the surplus one by one.

The reason for the brevity of the proceedings was that the Marquess, whose conduct did him credit, had agreed to settle, but did not object to the reading in court of a letter he had written to his beloved Daisy. Again, it read just as if Tom Robertson were the author. Had he indeed written it for one of his plays, some producers of today would have dismissed the document as hopeless melodrama and hammed the scene for laughs. Here are excerpts : "My dearest Daisy, I am just writing you a line as I am wretchedly miserable. I want to assure you that I am trying to do the right thing . . . but Daisy, the ways of the world are hard . . . my father talked to me on Friday, Daisy, you don't know how these so-called ladies will treat you. I really could not bear to see you suffer with your sweet sensitive nature . . . it would be torture to me. If only I could escape from my position." As the Judge commented, the letter showed a "deep and sincere affection" for the plaintiff.

If this was not sensational enough, then came the settlement—£50,000, a most generous one and a record sum in breach of promise cases. One of the previous largest had been the £10,000 given to Miss Finney, a Savoy actress whose stage name was Miss Fortescue, by Viscount Garmoyle, son of Earl Cairns. This too had been a case in which the father's intervention had prevented a marriage; it was also settled by agreement.

Daisy also seems to emerge with credit from the sad though profitable affair. As the new Marquess left the courtroom her eyes lovingly followed him until he passed through the doors, out of her sight and out of her life. She told a newspaper : "I didn't want the money : I love him and only wanted to marry him." Lawyers were said to have worked out the actual sum without reference to her.

What makes the episode so illuminating is that the old Marquis was no backward despot, but a forward looking man, an ornament of the Radical Party, according to the Mercury obituary; in this matter, however, he appears despotic and backward.

The new Marquess subsequently married three times. The first, with a daughter of the 5th Marquess of Bath, ended in divorce in 1942, the year in which his second bride was Miss Virginia Lucie Heaton, a daughter of Captain David Remington Heaton, D.S.O., of Crownhill, Devon. Miss Heaton, who was a Land Girl on the Castle Ashby estate at the time, provided a family and the succession. After sixteen years he divorced her and she married a naval captain. The Marquess married for the third time in 1958.

Yet the case was exceptional. For though acting was so far down the social scale it had not been at all uncommon for a Lord to marry a stage lady : though it was much more rare for a Lady to marry an actor, presumably because it was so much easier for the stage-door johnny or members of the audience actually on stage, as in former times, to make overtures to an actress than it was for a Lady admirer in the auditorium to make contact with the Thespian she admired, or vice-versa : the drawbacks of the feminine standing in law was also a factor here.

Immediately after the case of Markham v. Compton (that is how it appeared in the court lists) a woman columnist in the Express newspaper who wrote under the pen-name of "Madge" commented : "In spite of what the young Marquess wrote to Miss Markham there is very little for such a girl to fear from the women with whom she would associate after marrying into the peerage. On the contrary they would be received with pleased interest as something gay, novel, brilliant and agreeable. There is a cult in high society for clever actresses and beautiful Gaiety girls. They offer variety in the midst of the monotony of fashionable life."

"Madge" presented a well-documented case, mentioning fifteen instances of actresses marrying into High Life, including : Miss Louisa Farebrother and the late Duke of Cambridge; Miss Connie Gilchrist and the Earl of Orkney; Miss Belle Bilton and Lord Dunlo, afterwards Lord Cloncarty; Miss Rachelle Estelle Berridge and the Earl of Clonmell; Miss Rosie Boote and the Marquess of Headfort : Miss Dolly Tester and the Marquess of Ailesbury; Miss May Yohe and Lord Francis Hope, brother and heir of the Duke of Newcastle (in fact he had divorced her in 1902); Miss Sylvia Storey and Earl Poulett; Miss Camille Clifford and the Hon. Lyndhurst Bruce, elder son of Lord Aberdare; Miss Denise Orme and the Hon. J. B. Yarde-Buller, later Lord Churston; Miss Eva Carrington and the late Lord de Clifford; Miss Ellis Jeffreys and the Hon. Frederick Curzon, brother of Lord Howe; Miss Zena Dare and the Hon. Maurice Brett, second son of Lord Esher; Miss Francis Donelly and Lord Burton; and Miss Olive May and Lord Victor Paget, brother of the Marquess of Anglesey.

As regards those "beautiful Gaiety Girls" mentioned by the columnist one finds four ex-actress Peeresses attending a dinner at the Hotel Cecil,

London, in October, 1913, to mark the tenth anniversary of the opening of the new Gaiety Theatre. They were the Countess of Orkney, the Marchioness of Headfort, the Countess Poulett and Lady Churston.

Clearly, of all the "lower orders" of humanity the actress would have the least difficulty in carrying off at least the superfluities of an elevated station in life: not only were they by definition used to being the objects of interest but they would have played the lady in make-believe on the stage. In carriage, dress, deportment and dignity they were schooled to it.

The Marquess who figured in the 1913 case is now one of the grand old men of Northamptonshire. At ninety he is only seven years short of the span reached by that grand ducal old man of the county, the 7th Duke of Grafton, of Wakefield Lawn, who was ninety-seven when he died in 1918. I hope my recollection of this early incident will not embarrass his lordship. It has been included not to titillate but because it could scarcely be conscientiously left out of a Northamptonshire book under the present title... *"You don't know how these so-called ladies will treat you..."*

Embarrassment must certainly have been caused to the venerable Duke in earlier life when his eldest son and heir chose to marry a musichall artiste. It was before the Duke's succession to the title when his son, the Hon. Henry James Fitzroy, married the vivacious Katie Walsh at Worcester on May 29, 1871, and settled £10,000 on her; and it may have been a reason why the Duke did not step in to rescue his son from appearance in the Bankruptcy Court some years later.

Not only was it a disastrous marriage for the bridegroom who was to become Lord Euston, and was for many years to be Provincial Grand Master of the Freemasons of the Northants and Hunts Province, but it resulted in one of the most complicated matrimonial cases ever to come before an English court.

Any marital bliss the couple experienced was short-lived and after several temporary separations they parted for good. But Katie had been married before, to a commercial traveller named George Manby Smith in 1863. That marriage had not been successful either and she entered into a state of widowhood when the name of George M. Smith appeared on the list of deaths (along with that of the bibulous actor Gustavus Vaughan Brooke) when the S.S. London went down in the Bay of Biscay on its way to Australia with a load of 200 immigrants in 1865.*

After the parting Lord Euston had obtained a post in Australia and while there he heard that the George Smith who had married Katie was not dead after all but living in Australia. He brought back to England the alleged husband and set him up as principal witness in a nullity suit against Katie, who immediately admitted that this was indeed the man she had "married". But, on her behalf, cross-examination of Smith and then of the sister and brother of a woman he had previously married elicited that his first wife had not been dead when he "married" Katie, though she was by now. So the Earl lost his case and Katie remained Countess of Euston until her death at Fulham in November, 1903, at the age of fifty-one. There were

* Not 1886 as stated in Theatre Un-Royal

no children to dispute the inheritance when the Earl died in 1912, before he could become the 8th Duke of Grafton.

Happiness apart, there were some peers and titled folk with whom marriage was not the doorway to respectability. One of the fifteen actress brides mentioned by "Madge", Miss Dorothy Hasely (Dolly Tester), of Brighton, became Marchioness of Ailesbury. But the man she married had at twenty-one, a year before the ceremony, owed £200,000, loved theatricals and used to carry acting over into real life by going round dressed as a costermonger with donkey and cart. At twenty-four he inherited the title not only of Marquess of Ailesbury but also of Earl Cardigan, Earl Bruce, Baron Brudenell and Baron Bruce. He dissipated the fine Savernake estate in Wiltshire, said to be the finest woodland outside the New Forest; was warned off the Turf, and died in his thirty-first year in a cottage at Brixton, the pensioner of moneylenders, in 1894. Even the financier who insured his life for £100,000, reckoning on an early demise, is said to have lost on the speculation.

One of the first places where the death of the Marquess was reported was the London Bankruptcy Court.

ACT
THE
SECOND

KEMBLE & WHITLEY

...relating how Mr. Roger Kemble tried in vain to follow the good advice later given by Mr. Noel Coward; giving an account of Strolling with Mr. Shatford; telling how Mr. Jemmy Whitley, who made his mark at Stamford, had the odd habit of riding in a hearse, and how his final such journey prevented him leading his company at Northampton; describing a dogs' dance in a warehouse theatre; and how the dramatic succession passed in turn to Mr. Pero and Mr. Beynon.

"Mr. Kemble flatters himself that the performers will not only appear respectable ON *the stage but will prove themselves an ornament to the profession* OFF . . ."

"Don't put your daughter on the stage, Mrs Worthington, don't put your daughter on the stage . . ."
Song by Noel Coward

ROGER KEMBLE

Scene One

SANS SARAH—
THE KEMBLES

It's called NORTHampton. But is it in fact North? Or is it South? Or for that matter is it East or is it West? Northampton is an odd sort of place. It has never been quite sure where it is: and folk in other parts of the country have not known of it at all. Placed as it is, almost bang in the very middle of England, and therefore as far from the sea as you can get, I don't suppose it can deny being in the Midlands.

It's a town which until fairly recently was almost totally unknown once you got more than a hundred miles away. When as a Northamptonian you made that longish journey to the seaside and mentioned where you came from the locals would ask, "Northampton? Where's that?" Or the more knowledgable, assuming you had travelled south, east or west, might respond, "Northampton, let's see, that's up north isn't it?" Although I've never heard a northerner say it was down south.

Northampton has equally been in a sort of no-man's land with regard to the pattern of theatrical companies. Whenever a circuit company took Northampton under its wing it was nearly always a temporary affair, the one great exception being the Jackman era of 1839–62, which is a little ahead of our time and a terminal case anyway, as the circuit system was then coming to the end of its days.

Northampton was usually the greatest distance that a company had to travel away from its old beaten track. The Lincoln Company had to make quite a detour from its stamping grounds in Lincolnshire to come to Northampton for its first visit in 1799. The Durravans almost certainly travelled no further south or east than Northampton and were more at home in Leicester or Lichfield. The Kembles used to stroll about in the area nearer the Welsh border, though coming as far as Coventry, before they ventured into the outpost of Northampton. Among the many towns they visited, the Nottingham and Derby Company rarely got any further away from home in a south-easterly direction than Northampton.

Northampton's artistic tastes have had a reputation for being unreliable and uncertain, not to say Philistine, and playing in the town was probably never one of the most looked forward to dates on the calendar of the various companies.

It appears to be by chance, however, that the town missed performances by the two great names of the next two companies in the Northampton dramatic parade. In the case of the company of Roger Kemble it was Sarah Kemble (or Siddons) that they missed, one of the most illustrious names in theatrical history. In the case of the Nottingham and Derby Company it was for another reason that the town did not witness the drolleries of the company's creator, James Augustus (Jemmy) Whitley, today an unknown to the general public but in my view deserving at least as much Thespian credit as the great Sarah.

Announcing his first season in Northampton in the Mercury on July 4, 1774, Roger Kemble said he had "long wished for an opportunity of entertaining them with his company" and assured them, in a significant phrase, that the theatre would be "fitted up in the best manner the place will admit of". As regards the company, it was more than merely a question of talent: "Mr. Kemble flatters himself that his performers will not only appear respectable ON the stage but will prove themselves an ornament to the profession OFF."

Among the "respectable" actors and actresses were Mrs. Kemble, Messrs. Sidney, Hinde, Vaughan, Ledwith, Donnell, Smith, Morris and Brown, Mrs. Adams, Mrs. Donnell, Mrs. Sidney, Mrs. Osborne and Master Smith.

There is no mention in the first of the three Kemble seasons of any other members of the family, although there were over half a dozen of them at this time. There were Sarah, John Philip, Stephen, Frances, Elizabeth, Anne, and Henry, who was a babe in arms, having been born the previous December at Leominster. We would have expected to find at least some of the older ones taking part at Northampton. But the motto of Roger Kemble, who had been running the company since 1753, appears to have been

NORTHAMPTON,

☞ THEATRE.---*Mr. Kemble presents his most respectful Duty to the Nobility and Gentry of Northampton, and it's Environs; begs Leave to inform them, that he has, at a very great Expence, fitted up the THEATRE in St.-Giles's-Street, in a very elegant Manner; where he intends exhibiting most of the new Pieces now extant; and, as his Stay will be but short, humbly hopes they will encourage a respectable Set of People, mostly from the Theatres Royal, who will spare no Pains to render the Evening's Entertainment agreeable.----And on Monday Evening, August 10, will be presented the Tragedy of*

VENICE PRESERV'D;
Or, A PLOT DISCOVER'D.
With the FARCE of
ALL THE WORLD's A STAGE.

N. B. *The Days of Playing are Mondays, Wednesdays, and Fridays.*

"A respectable set of people, mostly from the Theatres Royal, who will spare no pains to render the evening's entertainment agreeable . . ." Roger Kemble describing his own company at Northampton in August, 1778. (*Northampton Mercury*)

"Don't put your children on the stage". A Roman Catholic, he had married Sarah, the Anglican daughter of John Ward, whose company he had joined and later took over: Ward died eight months before the company's first season at Northampton. Kemble had positively decided that none of his children should follow in their parents' footsteps. Not for any more Kembles, he had vowed, the rickety rigours of a profession always on the move from one set of tatty lodgings and theatre to another, income always uncertain, status always doubtful. Despite his own involvement the drama smelled strongly in his paternal nostrils.

It was a policy that was to be a success only by its total failure. Sarah (Siddons) was to gain the reputation of being the greatest tragic actress in the history of the English stage, able to move an audience to tears as few had done before and few have done since. John Philip was to become a notable manager of the Theatre Royal, Drury Lane, as well as a celebrated performer. Stephen, while not covering himself with an equal measure of glory, was to become a memorable Falstaff because his huge girth enabled him to look the part without padding. Fanny became an actress but, despite packed houses in London to see the sister of Sarah, was nervous and unsuccessful and subsequently married a dramatic critic, Francis Twiss, left the stage and opened a school for girls at Bath. Elizabeth had two seasons at Drury Lane before returning to the provinces and marrying Charles Edward Whitlock, manager of the Theatre Royal, Newcastle upon Tyne, and emigrating to America where, with less competition in the firmament, she became a star.

It was not for want of trying that father Kemble failed to keep his daughters and sons off the stage. He tried to persuade Sarah to marry out of the profession, against her desires, John Philip he tried to turn into a priest; Stephen was apprenticed to an apothecary; Fanny was put to millinery; while Elizabeth was to be a dressmaker.

Sarah was the oldest. Born on July 5, 1755, in an inn called The Shoulder of Mutton at Brecknock, Wales; she first appeared on the stage when about four to recite a poem called "The Fable of the Boys and Frogs", beginning as Kathleen Mackenzie recalls in her book The Great Sarah:

> *'Tis death to us, though sport to you*
> *Unthinking cruel boys.*

In 1767 there were as many as five Kembles in a performance by Mr. Kemble's Company of Comedians at the King's Head, Worcester. The play was *Charles I* and to avoid the restrictions of the Law it was nominally performed free, sandwiched between the halves of a "musical concert for which tickets may be had at the usual places". Mr. Roger Kemble played General Fairfax, Mrs. Kemble was Lady Fairfax, Master J. Kemble was James, Duke of York, Miss F. Kemble was Duke of Gloucester, while Miss Kemble (Sarah, no doubt) was Princess Elizabeth. It must have been the youngest ever casting for the Duke of Gloucester for Miss F. (Frances) was seven at the time. Playing the Duke of Richmond was Mr. William Siddons, whose father was a publican in Walsall, and who had intended his son to be a barber.

As the Kemble parents saw an affection developing between young Sarah and William Siddons they were not at all pleased. Especially father. The more so when a more eligible candidate appeared in the person of a Mr. Evans, owner of a small country estate near Brecon.

Meanwhile Sarah had been sent to school at Thornlea House, Worcester, where she was not happy because the parents of the other girls were of more elevated status than that of theatrical manager; although the girls were impressed by Sarah's knowledge of Shakespeare. If the play demanded it she would be kept from school, which happened three times during the Worcester season, when she played Edward the boy King in *Richard III*, in *Love in a Village* and *The Tempest* (the Dryden version). When the company moved on Sarah left school and shortly afterwards her brother John, aged ten, went as a boarder to Sedgerley Park School.

As regards Sarah's romance, the crunch came when William Siddons proposed and she accepted, without even asking her father. Kemble senior was hopping mad and sacked his daughter's would-be-husband. This episode made him realise that he must do something more positive to drive his children away from the boards. First his daughters. Sarah was posted off to a position with a country family, the Greatheeds of Guys Cliffe, Warwickshire. For Fanny (twelve) there was an apprenticeship to a milliner in Worcester, while for Elizabeth (eleven) it was a dress-making life in Leominster.

Parents' plans for their children probably worked out in more cases in the eighteenth century than they do today but this was certainly not so with the Kembles.

Sarah yearned for the stage. When she accompanied Lady Mary Greatheed on a visit to her mother the Dowager Duchess of Ancaster, she recited to the servants in their hall. Fanny hated being a trainee milliner and Elizabeth detested making dresses.

John Philip, the oldest son, born on February 1, 1757, at Prescot, near Liverpool, was posted off from Sedgerley Park to Douai, France, to learn the mysteries of that brother profession of the stage, the priesthood. After some time, equally rebellious as his sisters, he ran away. Charles Lee Lewes states that the company was at Northampton at the time but if it was the winter of 1775, it does not appear so. After tramping about to find the company John Philip got the shortest possible shrift from the father who had made considerable sacrifices to send him to the university which was the nearest available for a Roman Catholic (to whom Oxford and Cambridge were barred in those intolerant days). Father told him he was a fool and to get out of the theatre, or words to that effect.

After two years at the country house Sarah persuaded her parents on two matters in which they had opposed her. She was allowed to come back to the family company; and she was given their blessing to marry William Siddons. The company were at Coventry when she rejoined them and soon afterwards, with William also back, the pair walked to Holy Trinity Church, on November 26, 1773, to be married.

We might therefore expect to find both William and Sarah among the company for that first Northampton season, beginning in July, 1774. But by then the lovebirds had flown. After a winter of bad business in Leominster and Wolverhampton (where the Mayor had declared that "Neither player, puppy nor monkey" should perform, but had been forced to relent by popular demand) the Siddons decided that they would do best for all concerned by leaving. Also, Sarah was in the family way.

So by the time Mr. and Mrs. Kemble brought the company to Northampton the Siddons had begun a summer season at Cheltenham. Their son, Henry, was born at Wolverhampton on October 4, 1774, and as Kathleen Mackenzie says "was bundled about from town to town, nursed at the back of draughty stages, and put to sleep in dressing rooms that were no more than curtained off recesses in the wings, and it did him no more harm than it had done her". Equally undeterred he formed the intention to follow in his parents' footsteps.

The black sheep of the family, incidentally, was Anne who grew up to drink heavily and love notoriety. One of her off-stage acts of theatre was to take poison (a calculatedly insufficient dose to solve the family's problem).

For the 1774 season at Northampton Mr. Kemble took a house "near St. Giles Square" and tickets could be obtained there and "at the inns".

As we have seen the drama was strictly speaking illegal at this time, outside the few theatres smiled upon by the monarch and made truly Royal, and therefore managers were called upon to do a difficult feat of balancing when performing any piece which might cause offence to one political school of thought or other.

A fortnight after the first advertisement Kemble announced the "celebrated tragedy, never acted here, *The Royal Martyr* or *The Death of King Charles I*" With the French nation leading up to chopping off the heads of their Royalty, following the English example, a degree of nicety had to be observed, to avoid upsetting either Royalists or anti-Royalists. Kemble's well-chosen words were as follows: "As this very affecting tragedy is founded on so late a period of English history little need be said by way of explanation. Suffice it to be observed that the language is allowed by the most competent judges to be elegant and harmonious; the nice impartiality of the author in drawing his characters and the caution observed to avoid giving offence to any have gained him the esteem of every lover of science, candour and truth."

Another Royal death was depicted a few days later with *The Albion Queens* or *The Death of Mary Queen of Scots*. After Act II Mr. Brown gave "A Countryman's Trip to Portsmouth", describing the Royal Naval Review; after Act III came a song by Mr. Chambers; and after Act IV Mr. Chambers again obliged, this time with "Oh What a Charming Thing's a Battle".

The affairs of Royalty and nobility had an even greater fascination than usual and another choice was "The celebrated tragedy written by the Earl of Chesterfield and Mr. Jones" called *The Unhappy Favourite* or *The Earl of Essex* containing "the fall of this noble peer in its true light, the author being furnished with the papers of the intrigues of that court by the nobleman who patronised it and whose abilities are so well-known to the learned".

In August came *Henry II* which had brought crowded houses to the
Theatre Royal, Covent Garden, the previous winter. "To render it still
more pleasing Mr. Kemble (who ardently wishes to give satisfaction to the
ladies and gentlemen of Northampton) has had a new scene of Rosamund's
bower painted with every other decoration proper to the play." He added
this poetic propaganda :

> *Ye generous who feel for each other's woes*
> *Ye fair whose tears for injur'd virtue flow*
> *Tonight your Bard from your own annals shows*
> *A dreadful story of domestic woes.*
> *From fact he draws his picture from the life*
> *The faithless husband and the much wrong'd wife*
> *Doom'd all the train of bosom pangs to prove*
> *Pangs which must always wait on lawless love.*

There were more of those characters with names redolent of their
qualities : in *The School for Wives* performed by desire of Mrs. Raynsford
of Brixworth, on August 22, Mr. Smith was "Ghastly", Mr. Donnell was
"Spruce", Mr. Brown was "Captain Savage" and Mrs. Donnell was "Mrs.
Tempest"; in the farce *Lethe* or *Aesop in the Shades* Mrs. Kemble was
"Mrs. Riot"; in the farce *The Ghost or Dead Man Alive* there were
Captain Constant (Mr. Hinde), Trusty (Mr. Donnell) and Clinch (Mr.
Ledwith).

On Monday, August 29, came "a new pantomime entertainment in
grotesque characters *The Witches' Revels* or *The Transmutation, Adventure,
Death and Restoration of Harlequin* with scenery, machinery, and all other
decoration proper to the piece. To conclude with a dance by the characters
and a grand cascade of falling water. The extraordinary expense renders it
impossible to take less than full price."

Later in the season in *Neck or Nothing* or *Harlequin's Leap from the Moon*
Mr. Brown "surpassed the famous Sieur Boaz by leaping through a hogshead
of fire six feet high which he has done with universal applause in most of
the capital cities and towns of England". There were also "many other
feats of activity too numerous to mention".

On Tuesday, October 24, the accent was again on spectacle with *Merope
with the Royal Shepherd* in which Act 1 featured "a burning altar for the
sacrifice of Dorilas before the tomb of his father Cresphontes and husband
to Merope with solemn incantations" and in Act IV "will be discovered an
Hymeneal temple in which the tyrant Pelphonte is slain by Dorilas with
the Axe of Sacrifice". This was "founded on facts in Grecian history altered
and translated from the French of the celebrated Mr. Voltaire by Aaron
Hill".

Royal English spectacle again on Wednesday, November 2, with *Henry
VIII* with the Coronation of Anne Boleyn and the ceremony of the
Champion in Westminster Hall. The robes, dresses, insignia, decorations
and paraphernalia in the Coronation procession were "as reproduced at
the Theatres Royal in London, Dublin and Edinburgh for a series of nights
in every season with uncommon applause".

Before the farce which followed Mr. Saunders was to give what appears to be an early example of the act of a stand-up comic: "He will entertain his friends with a satirical, humorous and descriptive lecture on rum codgers, dry shavers, comical quists, geniuses and genos." It being the benefit for him and his wife he was also down to give an address.

When Milton's *Comus* was staged in October, 1774, for the benefit of Mr. Smith, prompter, and Master Smith the latter delivered an epilogue in the character of a recruiting officer. The play featured "an elegant banquet with the revels of Comus".

Other benefits that season were for Mr. Hinde and Mrs. Adams; Mr. and Mrs. Sidney; Mr. Chambers and Mr. Gamble, musician; and Mr. and Mrs. Kemble. The Smiths were at Mr. Cliffe's in Abington Street; the Sidneys were at the Black Lion Inn, St. Giles Street (still standing today); Mrs. Adams was at Mr. Dyer's china shop on the Market Hill; Mr. and Mrs. Kemble invited you to knock on the door of their house near St. Giles Square.

Each age of plays naturally draws upon the familiarities of its age. Many dramas were set in or included references to windmills, of which there were at this period over a hundred in Northamptonshire, so that they were as familiar on the horizon as church towers and spires were then and are now and as blocks of flats and electricity pylons are today. Not that today's playwrights seem to be inspired by pylons. Not surprising perhaps? In the 1774 presentation of the comic opera *Maid of the Mill* Kemble himself took the lead role of Fairfield the Miller. *The Fashionable Footman* was another reflection of the times. Other plays presented were *The Wonder! A Woman Keeps a Secret, The Fashionable Lover, The Country Lasses.*

Mr. and Mrs. Kemble played Macbeth and Lady Macbeth in *Macbeth* which was at the request of Mr. William Hanbury, of Kelmarsh, who had his own private theatre in this Northamptonshire village where, a fortnight later, he staged two newly written pieces, *The Princess of Parma* and *The Election.* According to the Mercury the village audience consisted of "the nobility and gentry of the county together with strangers of distinction, rank and character". There was a band of music including several London performers and they played for a ball afterwards.

A surprising recruit on the last night but one, Friday, November 11, was Mr. Barrett who was for many decades organist of All Saints Church. The bill included *The Country Lasses, The Recruiting Sergeant* and *The Deserter,* a musical drama in which the songs were accompanied by a full band. Musical items were also interspersed in *The Country Lasses* and at the end of Act IV Mr. Barrett played a harpsichord solo. His turning out for the stage that night is probably accounted for by that remarkable cameraderie that exists between musicians of all stratas—the evening was a benefit and a joint beneficiary was "Mr. Gamble, musician".

The first night of the season had also been that of the first local performance of Sheridan's *School for Scandal* which was at the request of the officers of the 3rd Regiment of Dragoons. They again commanded the last night, when the choice was *The Merry Wives of Windsor* and Mr. Kemble spoke a farewell "epilogue on every-body, to be spoken by some-body, in the character of no-body".

It was four years before the Kembles returned and this time Miss E. Kemble and Miss Kemble were among the company. Miss Kemble's portrayals included Miss Titup in *The Beaux Stratagem*. Mrs. Kemble spoke a comic epilogue describing the different humours of husbands, Spanish, Italian, French, Dutch and "Honest John Bull the Englishman". Again, almost a variety act. Described as being a respectable set of persons mostly from the Theatres Royal, the company also included Messrs Thomson, White, Davis, Glocester, Warner, Cumberland, Masterman, Johnson, Mrs. Filden, Mrs. White, and Mrs Masterman. Quite a few changes, it will be seen.

The season which had begun on Monday, August 10, 1778, with *Venice Preserv'd* or *A Plot Discovered* and Isaac Jackman's *All the World's A Stage* ended in December with a night when there was an additional and unusual point of sale for tickets—the County Gaol. "Mr. Kemble, truly sensible of the kind reception he has met with in Northampton apprehends he cannot acknowledge the favours he has received in a more acceptable way than by performing this play for the benefit of several poor debtors who have large families and are at this time confined in Northampton County Gaol." The main choice for the evening, as mentioned in the Interlude, was *The School for Scandal*.

Three years later, after a season in Coventry, Kemble was back in town for what was to be his last appearance here. In a season lasting from March to November his bill of fare included *The Flitch of Bacon* or *The Humours of Dunmow Priory* and *Percy* or *The Fall of Douglas* in which the parts of Percy and Douglas were played by two young gentlemen of Northampton for their amusement and at the end of the second act "a song of Masonry by Brother Davis, properly cloathed" was included.

The auditorium must have been as colourful as the stage on the night of a bespeak by the Northampton Hunt when the members attended in uniform. Other patrons were Sir Robert Gunning, Bart., and the Gentlemen of the Coffee Room.

The company now included Messrs. Masterman, Southgate, Glocester, Davis, Smith, Phillips, Chamberlain, and Baker, Miss Kemble, Miss Truwhitt, Miss Powell and Miss Vaughan.

The season, and the Kemble era, concluded with another benefit night for the gaoled debtors, this time for those in the Town Gaol, when a local amateur Mr. Taylor took the part of Richard III and spoke a most pertinent epilogue, which is quoted in the Interlude.

As for Mr. Kemble he went on to become perhaps the first and last actor to make a London debut at the age of sixty-seven. This was on August 26, 1788, when he took the title role in *The Miller of Mansfield* at the Haymarket Theatre in a benefit for his son Stephen.

MANAGERS and managers' wives would usually ride but the "strolling actor" would frequently do just that—stroll from place to place. This conception of the company wagon arriving at the Riding School, Northampton, is by R. C. Chatburn, who drew it for the dustcover. This chapter includes Henry Lee's account of his first theatrical stroll, from Newport Pagnell to Huntingdon.

Scene Two

STROLLING WITH SHATFORD

In about 1777 a lad named Henry Lee, aged about twelve, saw what he described as a showy funeral passing on the turnpike road through his native town of Bingham in Nottinghamshire. It was on its way from a place near Grantham to Nottingham. Hearse and horses, with their black feathers on their heads, earnestly engaged his attention. After a halt of an hour and a half at the Marquis of Granby, one of the inns of Bingham, the hearse went on its way, the driver promising to call back the next day.

Young Henry contrived to be on the spot and when the vehicle arrived was surprised to hear the driver call to the ostler to bring some steps.

"Well," asked the innkeeper, "have you left the corpse?" "Yes, but I am bringing back another corpse," replied the driver, who told the ostler to put the steps up to the hearse door. Needless to say, this caused some surprise. Many years later Henry Lee wrote in his memoirs : "The door was opened and we saw a man lying at full length on his back in his travelling dress and with his boots on. We all stared, looking much amazed and indeed quite astonished at seeing a corpse in a hearse without a coffin and equipped with a large pair of jack boots. Under him was a greatcoat."

Surprise increased when the corpse was heard snoring. After a few shouts from the driver the man who was sleeping like the dead awoke and descended. He had taken off his wig, and his white pocket handkerchief was round his head, adding to the bizarreness of his appearance.

Thus did young Henry Lee, a provincial theatre manager of the future, meet for the first time one of the most eccentric and successful provincial theatre managers of the eighteenth century.

James Augustus Whitley, better known as "Jemmy", had seen the hearse at one of the inns in Nottingham, where his company had just ended its season, and bargained with the driver to take him to Grantham. He had walked to the Trent Bridge before boarding the hearse. Henry noted "The goggle of his eye and rubicundity of his jolly carbuncled face". After an hour in the inn Jemmy and the driver climbed back to their respective accommodation on the hearse and continued their journey.

As Henry Lee tells the story first hand there is no reason to doubt its basic truth, though he may have elaborated a bit. And it may well be that Whitley made a custom of travelling dead weight. But there is a very similar story of Whitley arriving in a hearse at Stamford where he was driven sound asleep into the yard of the George Inn and a crowd was collected before he was awakened. On this occasion he is said to have sneaked off, denying his identity, but this does not seem credible in view of his nature. Indeed the theory I have formed is that Whitley may have used hearse trips as a form of publicity. An eighteenth-century forerunner, in fact, of Fred Karno and his mock escaped convicts dashing around town when *Jailbirds* was being staged.

The theory seems to be supported by Charles Lee Lewes who says in his memoirs that Whitley was a past master at publicity—"There is good reason to believe that the true art of theatrical puffing originated among our provincial actors. Whitley might be reckoned, with respect to his excellence in this art, to be one of the first of itinerant puffers. So great was his skill that old Ward, grandfather of Mrs. Sarah Siddons, often lamented his incapacity for inventing such sublime advertisements as came from his sworn foe and formidable competitor."

Whether it was parsimony or publicity which was in Jemmy's mind in his hearsal, it may well have been this strange encounter with him which clinched young Lee's decision to go on the stage.

Theatrical managers, as he was to find for himself, usually managed to secure some form of conveyance to get themselves from town to town, from season to season. They may have journeyed on a wagon, along with the scenery and properties and wardrobe. They may have ridden on horseback; Thomas Shaftoe Robertson, manager of the Lincoln Company, relates how at the age of only a few weeks he travelled from Alford to Boston in a hand-basket carried by his mother, riding behind his father.

In his Memoirs of an Unfortunate Son of Thespis, E. C. Everard wrote: "I saw an open waggon with a woman and two or three children; at the top some old boxes with what appeared to be scenes and a green curtain; and to confirm and crown the whole, a drum at the head; a picture of the paraphernalia of a poor strolling company."

The meanest of the seventeenth-century companies had traipsed with only a few belongings on their back plus their share of the scenery or wardrobe; the women sometimes had to carry their share. Some even carried the poles and canvas for their theatre "booth".

Those prosperous enough to travel by stagecoach were liable to be involved in accidents. One case I have come across concerned the members of Mr. Mudie's company and occurred soon after their single season at Northampton in 1808. After moving on to Banbury they interrupted their season to play at Ascot during the races but on the way back to Banbury the coach in which a party of them were travelling had an accident in Oxford and some were injured. Mr. McGibbon had a wheel go over one of his legs.

Stars would perforce travel the long distances between some of their engagements by stagecoach. George Frederick Cooke, noted Thespian and imbiber of brandy, described how in June, 1806, he "left the Castle and Falcon in Aldersgate, London, in the Manchester coach, about two in the afternoon, supped at Northampton, breakfasted early the next morning at

Leicester, dined at Buxton and arrived at Manchester early the same evening".

But the strolling player himself, the rank and file member of the company, was appropriately named. For him it was shank's pony, even into the nineteenth century. William Robertson, Henry Compton, and Mr. Chippendale had thirty miles to walk and when one of them found himself minus a shoe the three of them took it in turns to hobble. The incident was recalled by Dame Madge Kendal, youngest of Robertson's twenty-two children. "There was only one thing to be done and to the credit of the profession they did it—and took it in turns to walk with a single shoe."

Henry Lee gives a fascinating account of his own first "stroll" after his very first season, with the company of James Shatford at the Swan Inn, Newport Pagnell, Bucks. The three week season had begun on July 24, 1787, and when it ended Mr. and Mrs. Shatford left for the next place, Huntingdon, in a post-chaise with an actress as passenger, leaving their young recruit to fend for himself. (What a member of Equity would say to this procedure in the present day, one dreads to think.)

"Mr. Shatford had given me three parts to study namely Courtall in *The Belle's Stratagem*, Charles Weston in *I'll Tell You What*, and Horatio in the tragedy of *Hamlet*. I proceeded for at least 20 miles without once thinking of eating or drinking, so much was my mind occupied with what I had already done, what I was studying to do, and the prospect of the brilliant stage prospects before me. Thus I walked on briskly, reading, spouting and singing until sunset.

"I bought as I passed through a village two halfpenny loaves (they were as big as penny ones now); seeing a girl milking her cows in a field by the roadside I asked her for a little milk; she said I was welcome to take whatever I chose. I took her at her word, drank some milk and snatched a kiss with it. I saw a country boy approaching : I shook hands with the girl, took another kiss and departed. The little adventure raised my spirits and infused, as it were, quicksilver into my heels. I found myself nearly perfect in all my parts—so much so that with the aid of the pale light which the moon afforded I was able to repeat the whole of them literally, and without omitting a syllable.

"I stayed about half-an-hour over a cup of tea at Bedford, but again I trudged on gaily and merrily as before; the redness of the eastern sky gave goodly token of the approaching morning. I soon perceived symptoms of a town some distance before me and on inquiry found it was Huntingdon."

At the inn he found no one yet astir and slept an hour in a hayloft. Shatford came down to breakfast looking "as if still exhausted with the fatigue of riding in a post-chaise so many miles the previous day."

Their next calls were at St. Ives and Bedford, where they remained until Christmas and lent some scenery, which Lee was deputed to accompany, for private performances at the seat of the Earl of Upper Ossory near Ampthill. After Bedford came Woburn where they were "honoured by the patronage of the different branches of the Russell Family" (i.e. the Duke of Bedford's family). They also performed at Buckingham and at Abingdon in Berkshire.

THEATRE, in *Towcester*.

On *Monday* Evening, *May* 14th, will be performed,

A Celebrated TRAGEDY, call'd

The GAMESTER.

(The great End of the Drama is here fully anfwered, and this Depravity of the human Heart, exhibited in its moft glaring and fatal Colours; who can behold the amiable Wife of Beverly, ftruggling amidft furrounding Miferies, and yielding her laft remaining Treafure (her Jewels) an eafy Prey to the Diffimulation of a falfe Friend, and not pant to give her Affiftance ? or, pouring the Balfam of Peace to the wounded Mind of Beverley, and forget the tender Duties of the Wife to the Hufband. The animated and difinterefted Friendfhip of Lewfon, is a fine Contraft to tha Duplicity of Stukely ? The Cataftrophe fhews the dreadful Effects of this infernal Practice, which, as our Author beautifully obferves,   " Turns all our Comforts to bitterest Pangs, and all our Smiles to Tears.")

Mr. Beverley,   Mr. SHATFORD.
Lewfon;   Mr. DORMER. | Jarvis, Mr. CRAVEN.
Bates,   Mr. HUDSON. | Dawfon, Mr. CURTIS.
And Stukely, Mr. MARRIOTT.
Charlotte, Mrs. CRAVEN.
Lucy, Mrs. DORMER.
And Mrs. Beverley, Mrs. SHATFORD.

End of the Play, An INTERLUDE, taken from the Devil upon Two Sticks, call'd

Dr. LAST's Examination before the College of Phyficians.

The Devil, Mr. CRAVEN.
Secretary, Mr. HUDSON.
Dr. Camphire, Mr. MARRIOTT. | Dr. Calomel, Mr. HOLMES.
And Dr. Laft, Mr. CURTIS.

To which will be added, An ENTERTAINMENT, call'd

The FLITCH of BACON:

Or, Matrimonial Prize of *Dunmow-Priory*.

With all the Original AIRS, DUETS, &c.

The Fable of this Piece is taken from the Story of the fame Name in the Spectator—The Charter is retained to this Day, as it is . . . fince the Flitch of Bacon was claimed by a Nobleman and his Lady. In Order to obtain the Prize, a young Couple muft fwear they have lived a full Year together without once repenting.
Mark but this, and we'll anfure you
To be ever bleft and wife;
'Tis the Charm that will fecure you,
Dunmow's Matrimonial Prize.

Greville, Mr. CURTIS.
Major Benbow, Mr. MARRIOTT.
Tipple, Mr. SHATFORD. | Juftice Benbow, Mr. PEOVER.
Daub, Mr. CRAVEN. | Ned, Mr. HITCHCOCK.
And Wilfon, Mr. HUDSON.
Eliza, Mrs. FERGUSON.

PIT 2s.   GALLERY 1s.——To begin exactly at Half paft Six o'Clock.
Tickets to be had of Mr. *Shatford*, at Mifs *Chinner*'s.

NORTHAMPTONSHIRE seasons of Mr. Shatford's Company in 1786. At Towcester the "Theatre" is not identified (though some interesting observations are made on "the great End of the Drama") . . .

FOR THE
Benefit of Mr. CURTIS, and Mrs. TAYLOR.

THEATRE, Swan Inn Wellingborough.

On   Evening, the   of *December*, 1786,
Will be presented, A COMEDY, (never performed here) called,

DUPLICITY;
Or, The Generous Gamester.

Sir Harry Portland,	Mr. SHATFORD,
Sir Hornet Armstrong,	Mr. MARRIOTT,
Vandervelt,	Mr. CRAVEN,
Squire Turnbull,	Mr. PEOVER,
Trim'd (alias Lack-a-Day)	Mr. CURTIS,
George,	Mr.

And Osborne, (the Generous Gamester) Mr. DORMER.

Clara,	Mrs. SHATFORD,
Milissa,	Mrs.
Mrs. Tripp,	Mrs.
And Miss Turnbull,	Mrs. CRAVEN.

Between the Acts, several Favorite Songs, by Mr. CURTIS, and Mrs. FURGUSON,

Particularly Mr. EDWIN's celebrated COMIC SONG, of Bow-Wow-Wow, and a Favorite
New Hunting Song by Mr. CURTIS,

To which will be added an ENTERTAINMENT, called,

All the World's a Stage;
Or, The Butler in Buskins.

Sir Gilbert Pumpkin,   Mr. CRAVEN,
Charles Stanley, Mr. SHATFORD, —— Harry Stukely, Mr. DORMER,
Wat, Mr. PEOVER, —— Simon, Mr. DAVENPORT,
And Diggory, (the Butler)   Mr. CURTIS,
Miss Bridget, Mrs. CRAVEN, —— And Kitty, Mrs. SHATFORD.

PIT 2s. GALLERY 1s. —— To begin exactly at half past Six o'Clock.

Days of performing — Mondays, Wednesdays, and Fridays.

☞ Tickets to be had at the Swan Inn, of Mr. Curtis, at the Horse and Jockey,
and of Mrs. Taylor.

. . . while at Wellingborough the Swan Inn is named in a playbill which is interesting
because the day and date of playing have been omitted by the printer and are to be
written in. (*Both Northamptonshire County Library at Northampton*)

Lee describes an incident in the earlier life of Shatford when he was excessively thin and belonged to the Cheltenham company of Mr. Watson : "My old friend Shatford, who was a remarkably bulky man during the later part of his life, was when I first knew him in Northamptonshire [Lee appears to have thought Newport Pagnell was in Northants] very slender and had been known much thinner. Mr. Watson was himself a clever man but not a match for Shatford in ready wit."

When the Cheltenham Company played *Hamlet* the manager took the title role and Shatford, of the lean and hungry look, doubled the roles of Horatio and the Player King. "Hamlet, it will be remembered, gives instructions to the player as to the manner how some of the speeches are to be spoken. Watson felt a little piqued by Shatford soon convincing the audience that he could speak a good deal better than what the Prince could, who was then instructing him." This made the manager try to raise a laugh against Shatford. "Hamlet goes on asking : 'How are theatricals supported in the city of Denmark?' Watson took Shatford to the front of the stage and turned him round, 'Why my young friend, I fear theatricals are not so much encouraged now as they were formerly, when I knew the city. Say is that the case? You look very thin and more like a skeleton than a well-fed actor. 'No my good lord,' replied Shatford bowing. 'Lately our business has been excellent; but we have got a sad rogue of a manager, who keeps nearly all the money to himself and more than half starves his performers.' "

Collapse of overbearing manager. This was by the way, a sharing company, the performers not being on salaries but drawing a share after expenses had been paid, the manager taking an extra four shares for his property. Managers were known to fiddle under this system.

With his own company Shatford is stated in other books to have operated in Berkshire, Bedfordshire and Huntingdonshire. To these can be added Buckinghamshire, as already mentioned—and Northamptonshire, for despite Lee's error the company did play in the county. Northampton Public Library has playbills of them at Wellingborough and Towcester.

Shatford steps vividly to life from the Lee memoirs as a man of practical talent, but with unaccountable whims. "He had at all times an utter dislike to umbrellas; would maintain that none but effeminate coxcombs used them; and would get wet to the skin sooner than hoist one over his head. During the early part of his life he was obliged to dress according to the fashion; generally wore very good clothes but seldom properly put on or consistent with one another. He would dress himself in such apparel as might happen to fall in his way."

Here I have some sympathy with Shatford for on more than one occasion, deep in thought about some problem of theatrical history as I have walked to work from St. George's Avenue I have got half-way across Northampton Racecourse to find myself looking down at one brown shoe and the other black. Not to mention odd shoes of the same colour, or odd socks.

Shatford wore "shirts with large frills and deep ruffles at the hands even after such things had gone out of fashion". Here again I sympathise. By the time I have got around to buying narrow bottomed trousers the mode has swung to bell bottoms; by the time I get adjusted to narrow lapels on my jackets the fashions are reaching out to either shoulder.

As regards Shatford, "You might see him about ten in the morning at breakfast, but oftener at 11 or 12. Perhaps he would read the newspapers and write half-a-dozen letters while under the hands of the barber. As soon as this process was over, his shoulders covered with pomatum and powder he would put on perhaps a handsome cocked hat with a silver loop and gold tassels and then tie round his neck one of Mrs. Shatford's coarse blue coloured handkerchiefs, then, with spangled waistcoat, satin small clothes, white or peach blossom silk stockings he'd draw over them his top boots or slip on his red morocco slippers and off he'd march to the theatre or more probably into the shop of some poulterer or pastry cooks to purchase seasonable rarities for himself and friends at dinner, not forgetting good wine, excellent spirits, and choice fruits for the dessert."

There is no hint of poverty in this picture, drawn largely from the later period when the pair were partners at various theatres in Wessex, starting in 1790. Shatford's maxim that "The man who keeps his accounts regularly and accurately will never be ruined" is of doubtful validity but he seems to have prospered.

When Lee was set on by Shatford in July, 1787, the year after the Northamptonshire playbills, Shatford was already married, for Mrs. Shatford appears on all five surviving playbills.

At the "Theatre in Towcester" on Monday, May 14, 1786, tickets could be had of Mr. Shatford at Miss Chinner's for *The Gamester* and *The Flitch of Bacon*. They cost 2s. for the pit and 1s. for the gallery. Probably the theatre was an inn room.

This was certainly the case at Wellingborough for the four bills there are headed "Theatre, Swan Inn, Wellingborough". Monday, Wednesday and Friday were the days of performing but the bills for *Duplicity* and *All the World's a Stage*; *Chapter of Accidents* and *Rosina*; *Othello* and *Barnaby Rudge* are not dated. The only dated bill is for *Hamlet* and *Harlequin's Invasion* which were performed on Wednesday, November 8. Evidence of the degree to which the nobility and gentry could prescribe the theatrical fare comes in a footnote: "Any Lady or Gentleman who chuse to honor the company by bespeaking a play will be waited on with a catalogue, in which are most of the admired new pieces, by sending to Mr. Shatford, at the Swan." In a season lasting into December, members of the company were Messrs. Peover, Craven, Curtis, Marriott, Pilgrim, Dormer and Mrs. Craven, Mrs. Peover, Mrs. Shatford, Mrs. Taylor and Mrs. Furguson.

The only other eighteenth-century reference to theatre at Wellingborough which I have come across is of a benefit night for Mr. Collins on Monday, January 18, 1779, when there was an early start at 6 p.m. for a marathon entertainment consisting of *The Provok'd Husband*, *The Devil upon Two Sticks* and *Love a La Mode*. This was advertised in the Mercury. The explanation of such isolated announcements seems often to be that they are for benefit nights and were paid for by the players concerned.

Mr. and Mrs. Curtis were still with Shatford in the Wessex Company and by then, like the manager, Mrs. Curtis had increased to considerable proportions. One part in which her casting was not ideal was that of Ariel in *The Tempest* for which she was in fact chosen on account of her good singing voice. As altered by Dryden the play ends with a view of the sea, with Neptune and Amphitrite near the front of the stage and Ariel in the clouds singing :

Where the bee sucks there lurk I
In a cowslip's bell I lie.

"Bell? In a bell!" said an Irishman sitting in the pit one night. "Lurk in a bell! Then by jingo it must have been the Great Tom of Lincoln for no other bell could half cover you."

Mr. Curtis was another "character". Just as Shatford abhorred umbrellas Curtis abjured braces for his trousers. Nor would he wear a belt and consequently, according to Lee, "adopted a unique method of locomotion by shuffling and hitching".

Shatford's principal calls in Wessex were at Salisbury, Lymington, Blandford, Newport (Isle of Wight), Dorchester, and Jersey, on the way to which they were once chased by a French privateer, and there was also one season as far afield as Gibraltar. He built theatres at Devizes and Lymington (1792), Dorchester (1793), Jersey (1794) and Blandford (1805) some, no doubt, in concert with Lee. After Shatford's death at Newport in 1809, at the age of fifty-five, his widow kept the company going for some years.

However, we have got rather off circuit from Northampton. Back there in the centre of England from these extremities the question arises as to why Shatford came as near to Northampton as Wellingborough (eleven miles away) and Towcester (eight miles away) without playing in the county town. No Northampton theatre performances whatsoever are reflected in the 1786 file of the Mercury so those companies which were in the habit of advertising were not here. It could well be that Shatford was a non-advertising manager and did play in Northampton that year in between Towcester and Wellingborough. But this is pure speculation and we must now get on to discuss another absence.

By Meffrs. W H I T L E Y and H E R B E R T's Company,
At the NEW THEATRE in the KING's ARMS Yard, L I N C O L N,
On WEDNESDAY Evening the 6th of SEPTEMBER, 1775, will be Prefented,

A NEW T R A G E D Y, call'd,

M A T I L D A.

(Written by Dr. F R A N K L I N, the celebrated
Tranflator of SOPHOCLES.)

MORCAR, Mr. C O O K E.
S I W A R D, Mr. T A N K E R V I L L E.
O S W A L D, Mr. M A D D O C K S.
E D W I N, Mr. T H O R N T O N.
OFFICERS, GUARDS, &c. by the Reft of the COMPANY.

B E R T H A, Mrs. M A D D O C K S.
M A T I L D A, Mifs G L A S S I N G T O N.

To which will be added, a C O M I C O P E R A, call'd,

The W A T E R M A N.

B U N D L E, Mr. A D C O C K.
R O B I N, Mr. M A D D O C K S.
T U G, (the Waterman) Mr. T H O R N T O N.

Mrs. B U N D L E, Mrs. R E A D.
W I L H E L M I N A, Mrs. W A T S O N.

To begin as foon as the R A C E is over.
Boxes, (during the RACE-WEEK) 3s. — Pit, 2s. 6d. — Gallery, 1s.

TICKETS to be had at the Angel, and White Hart, above-Hill; the King's Arms, Rain-Deer,
and of Mr. W O O D, Printer hereof, below-Hill.

JOINT COMPANY—Because he was short of cash Mr. Herbert, manager of
the Lincoln Company, entered into a partnership arrangement with Jemmy
Whitley. Thus at Lincoln "Mr. Herbert's Company of Comedians" appeared
at the theatre in Drury Lane. Then "Whitley and Herbert's Company of
Comedians" performed at the New Theatre in the King's Arms Yard on a
number of occasions in 1775 while in 1776 the company was referred to as
"Herbert and Whitley's". The following year it again became "Mr. Herbert's
Company" and was similarly billed in 1779 and 1780. (*Lincolnshire County
Library at Lincoln*)

Scene Three

SANS JEMMY—
NOTTM. & DERBY

The reason why James Augustus (Jemmy) Whitley did not lead his company on their first season in Northampton in 1784 is a much less complicated one than the set of reasons why some of the Kemble family had not been here a decade earlier. Jemmy the Joker had travelled in a hearse for the last time : he had died in 1781.

It was because a solicitor was in gaol for debt in Dublin that Jemmy had first gone on the stage. Whitley was in the lawyer's service and visited him to arrange his work. On one of these calls Jemmy met an actor who was also "visiting", Joe Elrington, and got an introduction to the Smock Alley Theatre in the city, writing out parts, with later recruitment as prompter's call boy. From this small start he became one of the leading English provincial managers of the eighteenth century.

Someday someone will piece together the story of this whimsical Irishman : at present it lies scattered in jigsaw pieces in the memoirs of various actors and managers and the histories of various theatres (the best collection of Whitleyana appears in the history of the Manchester theatres by J. L. Hodgkinson and Rex Pogson). I feel most strongly that all that is available should be assembled between the covers of one book. Whether or not posterity demands it, Jemmy deserves it. His story is at least as important in the development of eighteenth-century theatre as that of celebrities such as Sarah Siddons. The bicentenary of Jemmy's death, September 13, 1981, would provide an ideal opportunity for a volume to appear under some such title as Jemmy Whitley, Theatre Manager Extraordinary.

The full calendar of towns where Whitley and his companies played may never be accurately compiled but the Thespian Dictionary of 1802 said that he had "the most extensive Midland Circuit ever known in England. The Worcester, Wolverhampton, Derby, Nottingham, Bedford and Stamford theatres were his." I know of him or his companies being also at Wakefield, Manchester, Cambridge, Leeds and Newark and towns on the Lincoln circuit but our coverage must be largely restricted to Stamford.

According to James Winston there were two places where Whitley's ghost walked, Worcester and Stamford. Well, if his shade is likely to turn up anywhere it will be at Stamford for there the theatre he helped to erect and cherish may soon be reborn. Another reason is that he would probably like to have a final, spiritual, row with his wife, Cassandra, who is buried in the town.

It is not surprising that Stamford is one of the places where the shell of a Whitley theatre survives and is about to be re-inhabited as a theatre. Indeed, perhaps this could only happen at Stamford, that superb stone fortress against change, improvement so-called, and development. In many another town it would long have been torn down and replaced by a super-market, department store, bookmakers, building society branch office or other mirror of the soul of the nation in the twentieth century. That it still stands at Stamford is partly due to the fact that the land on which it stands was leasehold and under the wise control of successive noblemen named Exeter, who have meantime dwelt in nearby Burghley House; and more recently also to the fact that Stamford is one of those conservation areas which the planners, a little conscience-stricken at what they have done elsewhere in permitting or actively promoting the demolition of old theatres, coaching inns, and similar obstructions in the path of progress and making more pence per square foot, have set up as architectural museums where the curious may repair to see how they built in the bad old days before concrete and steel ruled the architect.

Making inquiries at Stamford Town Hall, during the last days when the town had the dignity of being a borough authority before local government "improvements" I was presented with a copy of Frank Hance's excellent booklet on the twin subjects of the theatre and the races, invited to look at the splendid collection of playbills, and referred to the offices of the Stam-ford Mercury. The booklet quotes Harrod's Antiquities of 1875 which said that the theatre had been erected a century before that date in place of an earlier theatre and "the site of the Old Theatre is unknown".

After taking a few notes from the playbills I went to the Mercury archives and found an almost inexhaustible mine of information, such as the Northampton Mercury had provided. Anyone wishing to research the Stamford scene over a period of two-and-a-half centuries will find the files readily open. They are in a room over the Trustee Savings Bank. Downstairs cashiers deal guardedly with the trivia of pounds and new pence : upstairs is freely available the priceless record of life in this Lincolnshire town perched on the Welland river, near the border with Northamptonshire.

As far as Whitley is concerned, for the very early years, and in a cursory examination, I drew a blank, a problem being that there are gaps in the files. I did, however, find one 1746 reference to entertainment at Stamford : at the Guildhall "during the time of the Mid-Lent Fair several curious pieces of machinery, particularly The Battle of Culloden won by England's Reliever; likewise very fine dancing on the rope and several other curiosities performed by an ingenious balance-master".

It may seem extremely odd that the earliest mention of a Stamford per-formance by Whitley appears to be in a Manchester newspaper. The Manchester Mercury reprinted an Epilogue of thanks to the ladies and gentlemen, spoken by Mrs. Stanford in Mr. Whitley's Company of Comedians at the theatre in Stamford in Lincolnshire on April 21, 1752. Why print a report of an event in the Stamford Theatre in the Manchester

Press? This was seemingly an example of Jemmy's cuteness. He had heard that a new theatre was to be opened in the city and was making himself known. If it was indeed a sprat it was a fairly hefty mackerel which he reeled in for he was to play eleven lengthy seasons there between 1760 and 1774 before losing the battle to secure the Royal seal of approval for a Patent theatre at Manchester.

At Stamford it seems that Whitley played at least once a year, during the Mid-Lent Fair or at the Races in June.

In April, 1766, the Whitley Company of Comedians appeared at "our theatre near All Saints Church" when their plays included *Love in a Village*, *The Beaux Stratagem* and the pantomime *The Enchanters of Harlequin Necromancy*. They were back in March, 1767, for a season lasting at least until May, with *Midas*, *The Clandestine Marriage*, *Love in a Village*, *Thomas and Sally* and *The Country Lasses* or *The Customs of the Manor* among their offerings.

Another company had apparently operated at Stamford at least more than once and perhaps for some time, judging by an announcement on November 26 that year that "On Friday night will be acted here by Mr. Goodhall's Company of Comedians for the benefit of Mrs. Granger, a widow, and five children, *The Distressed Mother* being the last time of their performing in this place".

At Stamford, seemingly, Whitley was the battle victor for in 1766 the 9th Earl of Exeter leased to him and William Clarke, mason, for ninety-nine years at £6 per annum a piece of land in St. Mary's Street, 110 ft. 8 in. by 43 ft. 6 in., with the stipulation that they were to build a theatre. Permission was given to pull down the existing building on the land. By the time the theatre was complete in 1768 it had cost £806, and was "to the manner and style of the London theatres, the compleatest playhouse of its size in the United Kingdom".

Love in a Village was the opening production in March, 1768, and while it was being given there was some competition at "the old playhouse in the Corn Market at the Nag's Head" where the Sadlers Wells Company of Performers were performing "for the fair week only and positively no longer on account of going to Grantham Fair". There was dancing on a stiff rope by a boy of seven, lofty tumbling by Signior Carlino, singing by Mr. Rugg and Signior Colpi, on the slack rope, and his children.

At the theatre nothing further was mentioned in the Press until April 14 when it was said that *The Tempest* had been performed the previous Friday and would be given again the following evening. The Earl of Exeter commanded the comedy *The Foundling* and the farce *The Lottery* on Friday, May 27, for the benefit of Mrs. Granger and other commands that year were by Lady Mary Noel and Master Edwards. What appears to be the final night, June 24, was for the poor.

It might have been expected that the provision of more splendid accommodation would have meant longer seasons but towards the end of the 1768 run we find an announcement that future seasons would be shorter. With more seats available, perhaps the company could do all the business they wanted in fewer weeks.

The year after the theatre's opening Mrs. Whitley died and was buried in St. John's Church, Stamford, where a marble monument was erected : "On the tenth of February, 1769, was entombed Cassandra, wife of James Whitley, gent., who amply possessed all the good qualities that accomplish the best of women :

> *The silver moon shall wither in her prime*
> *The golden sun himself shall yield to time*
> *The stars grow dim but chastity and truth*
> *Shall ever flourish in immortal youth."*

Ever ready to extend his theatrical domains, Jemmy teamed up with Mr. Nathaniel Herbert who by now was in control of Herbert's (or the Lincoln) Company, the result being that Messrs. Whitley and Herbert's Company of Comedians appeared in various towns on the Lincoln Circuit (though Mr. Herbert's Company continued to be billed at Spalding Races) and at Stamford, now firmly Whitley territory. Being short of cash is said to have been Herbert's motive. Precisely what the arrangement was is not clear. In 1775 at Stamford we find both the Whitley and Herbert Company (in March) and the Whitley Company (in October). I have not been able to make anything like an exhaustive search into this interesting episode but have, among other billings, found the Whitley and Herbert Company at Stamford in June, 1774, and at Peterborough in July, 1774, but Herbert's Company at Spalding in June that year. In some cases the billing of the joint company is reversed to Herbert and Whitley, as at Newark in 1775 and at Lincoln in 1776. Whether this led to a row between the joint managers is not apparent.

When the joint company played at Stamford in March, 1774, the cast for *The West Indian* included Mr. Herbert as Mayor O'Flaherty, Mr. Robertson as Fulmer and Mrs. Robertson as Lucy. Others were Messrs. Whitfield, Cooke, Parker, Donnell, Light, Moore, and Kane, Mrs. Donnell, Mrs. Light, Mrs. Cooke and Mrs. Monk.

Mr. James Shaftoe Robertson had been deputed by Whitley as his manager, to look after his interest in the company and he later bought Whitley's share.

Three actresses of the joint company were injured in a road accident during the Peterborough season in July, 1775. Mrs. Read, Mrs. Light and Mrs. Maddocks were returning in a single-horse chaise from a village near the city when the horse took fright and "running with great violence against a corner of the street Mrs. Read had the flesh torn off her foot and her leg very much bruised. Mrs. Light and Mrs. Maddocks were also much hurt but luckily no bones were broke."

Like so many people Jemmy left making his last testament until rather late. Not until August 4, a mere six weeks before his death on September 13, 1781, did he will his theatres to Andrew Joseph Gosli Carrighan of Stamford and Elizabeth (nee Whitley) his wife; an annuity to his other daughter Judith Whitley; and to John Anderson O'Bryan rights of employment "so long as my Nottingham Circuit shall be continued". Carrighan, or Gosli, as he was usually known, had been a dancer at Covent Garden but had for some years run a dancing school at Stamford. As regards O'Bryan (or O'Brien) as late as 1808 he and his wife were still being given benefits by the then managers of the circuit, Robertson and Manly. An announcement then referred to O'Brien's forty years' service.

The Stamford theatre ceased to operate as such in 1871, becoming the Stamford Chess, Billiards and News Club, in which guise it continued until the 1939–45 War. Since then it has had sporadic lettings for auction sales, meetings, exhibitions, film shows, dog training and as a badminton club. All traces of the interior of the Georgian theatre have disappeared leaving a large room with a flat floor.

In 1971 the present Marquess of Exeter generously offered to lease not only the former theatre but also the adjacent assembly rooms, erected in 1727, and land adjoining, to Stamford Arts Centre for a nominal rent. An appeal was launched for money to help turn it into an arts centre for the district. The local authority and the Arts Council have contributed and work has begun on improving some of the facilities and a feasibility study has been completed for creating a 250-seat intimate theatre in the shell of that which was Jemmy's.

Four months before his death Whitley's Company made its first appearance in Northamptonshire of which I have found trace. This was at Kettering, the Northampton Mercury carrying a curious form of publicity on April 30, 1781. It was a letter, addressed to Mr. Printer: "Though no frequenter of public diversions for some years, curiosity led me to attend the performance of *The School for Scandal* with the farce of *Bon Ton* on Monday evening last by a set of players at a small though convenient theatre at Kettering. Every actor seemed to vie with each other in the support of their different characters and I can without exaggeration pronounce them equal to any set in the country. A very numerous and polite audience attended this exhibition and never did so large and respectable a company leave a place of public entertainment with more universal satisfaction depicted on every countenance. As an encourager of merit I am happy to hear the nobility and gentry both in the town and neighbourhood are determined to support a community so very respectable. Lady Robinson honoured them with her patronage on Wednesday and I am well assured Lady Cullen has bespoke the play of *The School for Wives* with the farce of *Florizel and Perdita* for Monday, April 30, instant which I make no doubt will be well attended and the example of these worthy ladies followed by many principal families in the circumjacent towns.—A.B."

Where the theatre was is a mystery. That month, it may be noted, the Kembles were at Northampton.

The following week a conventional advertisement stated that "*The Chapter of Accidents* will be presented by desire of Col. Maunsell, with the farce of *The Camp* with a perspective view of the Grand Camp at Cox-Heath in which the Army will appear in their uniforms and go through their manual exercises with the utmost punctuality". *The School for Scandal* was at the desire of John Robinson and his Lady. Tickets could be had at the George and the White Hart.

A performance on May 28 for the benefit of Mr. and Mrs. O'Brien was

of *The Belle's Stratagem* with "new scenes, clothes, masks etc. fabricated
by a neighbouring gentleman (pro hae vice) Poet Laureate to Mr. Whitley's
Company of Comedians in Kettering." The O'Briens said it was at great
expense that they had procured a copy of the play and that there would
therefore be no second price.

When the company visited the town again in 1783 Mr. O'Brien, who
was acting as manager for the Goslis, referred to opening "a temporary
but compact theatre for a month". During their short stay he would perform
"all the fashionable and approved pieces with every strength of performance, machinery, etc., and humbly hopes to meet with the countenance
and support he has hitherto experienced from the Nobility and Gentry in
and around Kettering".

This time they were billed as the Nottingham, Derby and Stamford
Company and had a member called Everard, a name currently familiar in
Britain as that of an imaginary character in the act of "camp" comedian
Larry Grayson. Everard's principal billings at Kettering were for dancing
in between the play and the farce. When the Rt. Hon. Lady Cullen
patronised the comedy *Which is the Man?* and the comic opera *The Son
in Law* on Friday, May 9, Everard danced a hornpipe and a reel.

With Lord Cullen her ladyship also attended *The Clandestine Marriage*
and other bespeaks were by Sir George and Lady Robinson, of *The
Suspicious Husband,* and Mr. and Mrs. Robinson, of Cransley, of *The
School for Scandal.*

On May 26, "the last night but three", there was a quadruple benefit for
Mr. and Mrs. Richardson, Mr. Peters and Mrs. Dunn. Other company
members included Messrs. Leister and Southgate. The season ended early
in June.

An interesting phrase occurs in one of the announcements during the
company's two-month season—the first, it appears—at Northampton in
1784. Advertising *The School for Scandal* on April 12 they stated that the
performance would begin "precisely at 7 to whatever company is in the
house". The implication is that there had been times in the town when a
small audience might be sent home.

Every theatre manager hopes to fill his house (apart perhaps from one
or two present-day subsidised theatres which care not about the attendance
so long as the producer and/or cast approves of the plays). But his most
nagging worry must be : what if *nobody* turns up?

Of course, it rarely happens. I hesitate to say that it has never happened
for if I do I am sure to be deluged with letters and phone calls from
bankrupt theatre managers and entrepreneurs to cite time and place. There
was once an audience of one, which rapidly dwindled to none. Tom
Robertson described a two-man show with fellow playwright. H. J. Byron,
at which there was only one in the house. When the audience heard the
first line of Byron's opening monologue dealing with the Origins of Man
he took the cue. The line was : "In the beginning there was only one
man . . ." "Yes", said the audience," and I am that d----d fool" and walked
out asking for his money back, explaining that he had come to see a troupe
of Chinese jugglers and was in the wrong room.

During the terminal years of the Northampton New Theatre in the 1950s a mere handful watched John Gielgud, Pamela Brown, Peter Bull, Richard Burton, Claire Bloom, Esme Percy, Harcourt Williams, Eliot Makeham and Nora Nicholson perform Christopher's Fry's superb play, *The Lady's Not for Burning*. The people of Northampton just did not want to know and stayed away in droves. At the same theatre the Robert Brothers Circus, men, women, horses, and elephants went through their entire routine for a mere handful.

The tradition seems to be that the show must go on, even if only one person turns up and he has a free ticket for displaying a bill. It was not always so. There have been times in theatrical history when a company would size up the audience at curtain-up time or a little after, decide it was not worth their while to proceed, and give the few their money back, or cajole them to accept a ticket for tomorrow. Theophilus Cibber called to mind "one filthy foggy dismal dreary night when one of the Theatres Royal debated till very late whether they should play or no, to a most scant company; and the other Theatre Royal forbore to light the candles which the thin appearance they had would hardly enable them to pay for and so courteously dismissed the very few who through foul weather had come to see them". But in 1704, advertisements in the Daily Courant for *The Libertine* and *Don Quixote* gave the assurance : "We shall not dismiss, let the audience be what it will."

Ireland rarely fails to provide a suitable illustration of any chosen facet of theatrical procedure. In this case it is credited to "the manager of a small theatre in Ireland" where, there being but three in the house, he addressed them : "Ladies and Gentlemen, as there is nobody here, I'll dismiss you all; the performance of this night will not be performed; but the performance of this night will be repeated here tomorrow evening."

A member of the "performance guaranteed" company at Northampton in 1784 was Mr. Pero, who stayed at Mr. Dongworth's in Bearward Street. He was later to take charge but at this stage Mr. O'Brien was still acting as manager and showed himself anxious to please. In mid-April he announced that "as many ladies and gentlemen have complained there is not enough box room, the manager begs leave to inform them there are three front boxes which are fitted up as neat as possible", and on the last night but two, in May, it was announced that as several ladies and gentlemen had complained of the extreme heat several ventilators had been fitted.

That night the main piece was *Lady Jane Grey* or *The Innocent Usurper* complete with replica of the scaffold, officers, executioner, etc., for the beheading of Lady Jane Grey. In between the acts, presumably with the law in mind, were popped some songs, which must have shattered the illusion. It sounds an odd business until we remember that there is a modern parallel, in the sachrinous advertisements which pop up at critical points in programmes thrilling, romantic or informative on the television, whether halfway through a wrestling match, film epic, or Royal saga. In between the sad account of the Queen of a few days the Northampton audience of

The Laſt NIGHT of PLAYING.
BY DESIRE OF
Captain and Mrs. Naſon.

FOR THE BENEFIT OF

Mr. BEYNON.

By His Majeſty's Servants.
NEW THEATRE STRATFORD.

On WEDNESDAY Evening JUNE 24, 1795, will be Preſented
the admired and Favorite COMEDY, of The

Wheel of Fortune,

Written by RICHARD CUMBERLAND Eſqr. Author of the Weſt Indian, the
Jew, &c. &c. and Performed upwards of Thirty Nights this Seaſon at the Theatre
Royal Drury Lane, with diſtinguiſhed Marks of Approbation and unbounded
Applauſe.

Penruddock, Mr. B R I S T O W
Tempeſt, Mr. R I C H A R D S O N.
Sir David Daw, Mr. S M I T H
Woodville Mr. M A X W E L L.
Henry Woodville, Mr. W A L L A K E R.
Sydenham Mr S I N N E T.
Jenkins, Mr. S A U N D E R S.
Attendant. Mr. B E Y N O N
Servants, Meſſrs. M A R K S, R E E D, Miſs. N O R R I S. and Miſs S M I T H.
And 'Weazel, Mr. C H A M B E R L A I N.

Mrs Woodville, Mrs. N O R R I S.
Dame Dunkley, Mrs. R I C H A R D S O N.
Maid of the Lodging, Mrs. V E R N S B E R G
And, Emily Tempeſt, Mrs. B E Y N O N.

In the Courſe of the Evening The Song of Sweet Echo
from the Maſque of Comus, by Mrs. VERNSBERG.

A MUSICAL DIALOGUE, called

A TOUCH at the TIMES.

Phelim O'Carrol, Mr. S M I T H. Moll Flaggon, Mr. R I C H A R D S O N.
To which will be added a FARCE (never performed here) called The

FARM HOUSE,
Or, the Country LASSES,

As Altered by I. P. KEMBLE, Eſq. &c. performed at the Theatre Royal Drury Lane.
Modely, Mr. W A L L A K E R.
Freehold, Mr. R I C H A R D S O N.
Shakſilegure,, Mr. S M I T H.
Sir John Engliſh, Mr. M A X W E L L.
Firſt Conſtable, Mr. M A R K S.—Second Conſtable Mr. S A U N D E R S
Country Men by the Reſt of the Company.
And Heartwell Mr. B R I S T O W.

Flora Mrs. N O R R I S.
And Aura, Mrs. B E Y N O N.

To begin preciſely at a Quarter before Seven o'Clock.—PIT, 2s.—GALLERY, 1s.
TICKETS to be had of Mr. Walford, Printer, and of Mr. BEYNON. at Mrs.
BLACKS, Confeƈtioner.

☞ Mr. BEYNON with all Reſpeƈt informs the Ladies and Gentlemen of STRATFORD and its
Vicinity, and the Publick in general, he has ſeleƈted the admired Comedy of THE WHEEL OF FOR-
TUNE and THE FARM HOUSE, which he hopes will meet their Approbation, ſhould he be ſo fortunate
to obtain their kind Patronage on this Occaſion, it will add to thoſe Favors already conferr'd, and be
ever ſtampt upon his Mind with the warm Seal of Gratitude.

THE BEYNON COMPANY which performed at Northampton in
the mid-1790s included Stratford-upon-Avon in its tour. This 1795
playbill describes the company as "His Majesty's Servants".
(*Shakespeare Centre, Stratford-upon-Avon*)

1784 heard Mr. Waylett recite "The Picture of a Playhouse" and Mr. Thompson sing "The Moment Aurora Peeps into My Room".

The desire to please was further evinced in an announcement that plays stated would be given "unless any other plays should be desired".

The O'Briens again used the ploy that they had obtained a copy of a play "at considerable expense". This time it was *The Poor Soldier* which was "justly allowed the most fashionable and approved piece now performing in London". It was a benefit night for the couple who were staying a fair distance from the theatre, at "Mr. Teeton's, taylor, the bottom of Gold Street, where places for the boxes may be taken".

The Way to Keep Him was performed on Thursday, May 14, "by desire of the Independent Electors of Northampton as assembled at dinner at the George on Friday, May 14". Between the play and farce (not named) there was a song by Mr. Hudson in the character of an Independent Elector, with full chorus by the gentlemen of the company.

For a brief period in 1787 Northampton had another fit-up theatre. It was in Mr. Joshua Stevenson's large warehouse in Church Lane, alongside the ancient round church of the Holy Sepulchre, built by Simon de Senlis, following his return from the Crusades. There Signior Scaliogni presented his famous Dancing Dogs whose visit to York two years earlier was noted by Tate Wilkinson: "Early in February, 1785, Signior Scaliogni with his Dancing Dogs from Sadlers Wells performed seven or eight nights at York Theatre and brought full houses . . . they entertained me and I laughed immoderately."

At Northampton, for reasons unstated, the Signior could not procure the theatre and therefore fitted up the warehouse. This is the only recorded instance of its use. Performances were on Monday, Wednesday and Friday, with a special morning performance one Tuesday at 11, lasting until 2. Boxes were 2s., pit 1s. and gallery 6d. Tickets could be had from the Signior at the Black Boy Inn.

The warehouse did not prove entirely satisfactory. An advertisement stated that "as several ladies found the boxes inconvenient by being too low they are respectfully informed that they are now being raised considerably above the pit". To prevent disappointment those who took boxes were requested to send their servants to keep the places.

The entertainment was far from being a mere canine caper. There was the comic performance of Mr. Herman and the celebrated Miss V. E. Nells from the Theatre Royal, Haymarket, and the surprising exhibitions of the inimitable Mr. Saunders from Sadlers Wells, Paris, and last from Edinburgh. This was the ambitious opening show on Monday, June 4: "Part I A new burlesque tragic opera called Trolloppina in Tears. Part II Slack Wire. Part III a Pantomime Entertainment call'd Harlequin Les Ombres. Part IV General Jacko and the astonishing performance of the Dancing Dogs, the parts of which will be express'd in handbills."

In earlier times companies often clothed themselves in the borrowed respectability afforded by a title; Mr. Power's Company were "The Servants of the Duke of Grafton". The idea was to avoid the possibility of being classified as rogues and vagabonds. The next stage of development was represented by "Mr. Power's Company", the manager, usually quite a "character" (or he would not have risen to be a manager), giving his name to the company. Thus it might be "Mr. Herbert's Company" or "Mr. Whitley's Company of Comedians". While Jemmy Whitley was alive that is how his company was known. Almost as soon as he was dead instead of becoming "Mr. and Mrs. Gosli's Company" (he left it to his son-in-law and daughter) it was changed to the Nottingham and Derby Company, this being also elaborated to Nottingham, Derby and Stamford Company. Likewise the Herbert Company in later management came to be known as the Lincoln Company.

Sometimes there was a mixture of the two as in the case of "Mr. Pero's Nottingham and Derby Company" after Mr. William Pero had in turn taken over from his in-laws, the Goslis, (who had, anyway remained "sleeping"). This was the billing for the season beginning at Northampton on Friday, July 27, 1789, and continuing to Monday, October 15.

Pero was another manager who crops up in the memoirs of Tate Wilkinson : "I took a trip to see a play at Sheffield where a Mr. Pero had taken possession of the theatric throne in October, 1785. I saw a Mr. Southgate act the part of Acres and Billy Bristle and was highly pleased."

That month they also performed a pantomime interlude called *Harlequin's Frolics* in which Harlequin jumped through a hogshead of real fire, to which was added the comic opera of *Robin Hood of Sherwood Forest*.

The Clandestine Marriage was performed on Monday, August 20, "to which will be added (by permission of the author the Rev. Mr. Knapp of Stamford, who has obligingly presented Mr. Pero with a copy of the original manuscript) the celebrated farce of *Hunt the Slipper* (as performed at the Theatre Royal in the Haymarket with the most universal applause.)" On September 1, Lord and Lady Cathcart commanded Sheridan's *The Rivals*. On September 10, came the old favourite *The Beggar's Opera* along with *The Scheming Lieutenant*, the new farce by R. B. Sheridan "never performed here".

Tickets could be obtained from Mr. Pero in the Riding or Mr. Lacy, bookseller. The company included Mr. James (from the Theatre Royal, Norwich), Messrs. Newport, Dunn, Cross, Mapples and Mason, Mrs. Mason, Mrs. Ferguson and Miss Byron (from the Theatre Royal, Edinburgh).

The final night was an extra quadruple benefit for four performers who had "failed in their former attempts", Mrs. White, Mrs. Ferguson, Mr. Marriott and Mr. Ferguson who "humbly hope this will be a sufficient apology for their troubling the public on this occasion; they beg leave to assure them that they should not have preferred to have done it had they not been encouraged to it by the solicitations of some of their particular friends".

A measure of freedom for the theatre came with the Act of 1788 and it is not perhaps a coincidence that the year following saw Pero call his company "His Majesty's Servants" for the first time and also saw him build a theatre at Retford, Nottinghamshire. This was constructed in the centre of Carhillgate on land purchased from Sir Thomas Wollaston White,

STAMFORD THEATRE was built over two centuries ago (in 1768 by Alderman Clarke and James Whitley, comedian) and has been used for other purposes for the past century. Now it is proposed to make it a theatre again, as part of Stamford Arts Centre. In the drawings below, from a leaflet issued by the Arts Centre committee, are seen the three buildings involved: the Assembly Rooms built in 1725 for Aske Kirke, dancing master, a house built in 1806 and the theatre. The new theatre is envisaged to seat about 250. Performers at the old theatre included Macready, Edmund Kean, Sheridan Knowles and Mr. and Mrs. Charles Kean.

BLACK LION INN, St. Giles Street, where members of the Kemble Company lodged in the 1770s, is still there. (*Northampton and County Independent*)

NEW THEATRE, Abington Street, which was unable to sell drinks for over a decade after its opening in 1912.

HENRY COMPTON, father of Edward Compton, changed his name from Mackenzie to avoid embarrassing his Puritanical family.

JOHN DRYDEN, Northamptonshire dramatist and Poet Laureate, in his niche in the façade of the Abington Street Public Library, erected at the expense of American millionaire Andrew Carnegie.

Monday, May 9th, 1892, at 7-45, for Six Nights only,

Engagement of the Distinguished Actress, Miss

ISABEL BATEMAN

SUPPORTED BY

Mr Edward Compton's Specially Organised Company.

Monday and Thursday, May 9th and 12th,

The Great Princess's Play, in Five Acts, by Special arrangement with
Mr. WILSON BARRETT—

JANE SHORE

Richard, Duke of Gloucester, afterwards Richard III.	..	Mr. HENRY VIBART
Prince Edward ⎱ Sons of ⎰	..	LITTLE CISSIE
The Duke of York ⎰ King Edward IV. ⎱ ..	..	LITTLE BERTIE
Henry Shore, a Goldsmith ..	.. ..	Mr. G. R. PEACH
Lord Cootes ⎱ Courtiers ⎰	..	Mr. HAWLEY FRANCKS
Catesby ⎰ ⎱ ..	..	Mr. ROBERT GREVILLE
John Grist, a Baker ..	.. ..	.. Mr. EDWARD PRICE
Walter Ludlow ⎱ Tradesmen ⎰	..	.. Mr. E. L. FORD
Humphrey Dynecourt ⎰ ⎱ ..	..	..Mr. W. H. WILLIAMS
Hardingley, Head Servant at the Palace ..	..	Mr. H. LANGFORD
Old Peter, a Pensioner of Jane Shore ..	..	.. Mr. THOS. HARDY
First Ruffian ⎱ Creatures of the ⎰	..	Mr. F. W. FREEMAN
Second Ruffian ⎰ Duke of Gloucester ⎱	..	Mr. A. S. HOMEWOOD
Elizabeth Woodville, Queen of England ..	..	Miss ADA MELLON
Lady Cootes ⎱ Ladies ⎰	.. ..	..Miss ETHEL HOLMES
Lady Melles ⎰ of the Court ⎱ ..	..	Miss Amy CROWE
Dame Ford, Housekeeper to Henry Shore	.. ..	Mrs. F. R. VERE
Mrs. Grist, John Grist's Wife ..	..	..Miss FRANCES RAYMOND
Dame Margery, a Pensioner of Jane Shore	.. ..	Miss J. WATSON
	AND	
Jane Shore	.. ..	Miss ISABEL BATEMAN

Ladies, Lords, Soldiers, Citizens, &c.

Act 1—Scene -   -   The Palace of Westminster

Act 2—Scene   -   -   The Home of Henry Shore

Act 3—Scene 1   -   The Old Cross, Whytefryars
Scene 2   Jane Shore's former Apartments in the Palace.
Scene 3   -   -   Westminster Abbey

Act 4—Scene   -   Old Cheapside on a Winter's Night

Act 5—Scene   -   The Home of Henry Shore

Acting Manager ..	.. ..	.. Mr. WILMOT HARRISON
Stage Manager	.. ..	Mr. HAWLEY FRANCKS

For Miss ISABEL BATEMAN

ISABEL BATEMAN, the leading actress who became Mother General of a community of nuns. The sister of Mrs. Edward Compton, she is pictured at eighteen, in 1873; and at seventy-five in 1930. The cast list is from her appearance at Northampton Theatre Royal and Opera House in 1892, six years before she became a postulant of the Community of St. Mary the Virgin, Wantage.

IF THIS BOOK serves no other purpose it will have been worthwhile in recording the likeness of the doyen of theatre historians, Professor Allardyce Nicoll, who is pictured above (right) in the garden of his home, Winds Acre, Colwall, at the foot of the Malvern Hills. Photographs of the leading chronicler of the British theatre are rare simply because he hates having them taken—"I have always sought to resist the reproduction of photographs of myself—I've no idea why, but I presume everyone has some quirk or other." But after having most kindly agreed to be Patron-in-Chief of "The Mackenzies Called Compton", the fourth and final book in the Northampton Theatre History Series, against all the odds he also agreed to submit to the camera. "You are indeed most persuasive," he told the author of the series, Lou Warwick (left). Since purchasing the property as a primitive cottage in 1933 he has converted and extended it, something he might not be allowed to do today because it is in the Malvern Conservancy Area. Professor Allardyce Nicoll (the unusual Christian name was taken from his mother's maiden name) was the Director of the Shakespeare Institute, Stratford-upon-Avon, from 1951–61 and is a Life Trustee of the Shakespeare Birthplace Trust and honorary president of the Society for Theatre Research. Appropriately one of his very first theatrical memories is of a visit to a Glasgow theatre to see the Compton Comedy Company in "The Gentleman in Grey", by Compton Mackenzie, son of Edward Compton. The Comptons' remarkable story will be featured in the book, "The Mackenzies Called Compton". (*Nigel Warwick*)

Bart. In three Retford playbills now in the collection at Nottingham a Mr. Pero and a Mr. W. Pero are in the casts.

Pero and company were back at Northampton in 1790 announcing that their May-June season could last but three weeks because they had to move on to Stamford on June 22. Members were Messrs. Paulet, Sidney, O'Brien, Craneson, James, King, Peters, Mason, Spencer and Robertson, Mrs. Paulet, Mrs. Sisson, Mrs. O'Brien, Mrs. Craneson, Mrs. Mason and Mrs. Campbell (from the Theatre Royal, Bath). This was their last recorded visit to Northampton.

From Stamford in July, 1793, Mr. Pero reported on the theatre there to James Winston that before it they had played in barns and it was a "wonderfully grand theatre". "Lately we have much improved it by taking away the heavy pillars and putting in their place small cast iron ones." Business at the Races and the Fair was very good and principal performers were well rewarded at their benefits (the business done seems to have been in contrast to that at Northampton). The house held £60 when full. The Earl of Exeter had his private box with his arms under it. By August, 1794, the company was billed as "Taylor and Robertson (late Pero's)".

Back in Northampton, April, 1790, had seen the Riding School in use by Wilkinson's Company of dancers, vaulters, musical performers and horse riders from Astley's and Hughes Riding Schools, London. These were afternoon performances at 3 p.m. but in the evenings some of the company also appeared at the Woolpack Inn, where the attractions included "The Learned Dog, Learned Horse, Singing Dancing and several favourite tunes on the double set of musical glasses, which for beauty of tone exceed all instruments in the world". Other miscellaneous entertainments during the last decade of the eighteenth century included a show of wax figures at Balaam's Coffee House, in May, 1793, and a visit by a Spotted Indian Youth, also at the coffee house, in June, 1795. This living exhibit was said to have been sent to England in 1789, "born of black parents, his head is covered in white wool, his breast, arms, legs etc. of a delicate white equal to any European, spotted and intermixed with black, resembling a beautiful leopard".

Mr. Beynon, whose company was the next to take the boards at Northampton, had already appeared there as a member of the Nottingham and Derby. He was with the company under Mr. Pero until 1786. According to Tate Wilkinson he was "the son of an eminent ribbon weaver at Coventry". Wilkinson had seen him acting at the Glasgow Theatre in the summer of 1775 and engaged him when Mr. Fleetwood, a member of his company at York, fell ill the following February. Of Beynon, Wilkinson wrote : "He was of great service to me during my emergency . . . had a great share of spirit and did not want his own good opinion. I am told he has improved and is now a manager in Warwickshire."

With his wife Beynon was later with Jemmy Whitley's Company. During their first appearance with that troupe at Nottingham in 1778 he made an especially spectacular entry in The Institution of the Order of the Garter, described as "more comparable to a pageant than a play". Mr. Beynon, "in the person of the Genius of England, descended in a chariot, encircled with four transparent paintings representing Britannia presenting Magna Carta, The Star and Garter, The Emblematical Silver Anchor and The George and Dragon, supported by cherubim in the clouds". He was also supported by three married ladies in the company, Mrs. Sisson, Mrs. Carleton and Mrs. Mucklow who appeared as aerial spirits. This spectacle was stated "never to have been shown anywhere else but at the Theatre Royal, Drury Lane, where it had been requested by several hundred people of fashion who had missed seeing it at the late Installation at Windsor". Mr. Beynon appeared the same night as a stage jockey, riding Laburnum in a depiction of the Grand Subscription Race at Nottingham.

The Beynons were in the Whitley Company at Stamford in July that year and also the following year and at Nottingham in 1780, 1782, 1784 and 1786. They were probably with the company continuously over this period.

At some stage after 1786 Mr. Beynon formed his own company and in the summer of 1793 played a season in Daventry, Northamptonshire, including the day of the Fair when "the market place was extremely crowded, which afforded a favourable opportunity to some of the light-fingered tribe to ease an unfortunate butcher of his purse and 25 guineas". The company included Messrs. Skitt, Bristow, Rawling, Ingall, Smith, Hume, Wright, Black, Davies, Richardson, Miss Smith, Miss Norris, Mrs. Curtis, Mrs. Smith, and Mrs. Strickland.

When they performed *The Clandestine Marriage* by G. Coleman and D. Garrick on the King's Birthday "God Save the King" was sung by gentlemen of the town and neighbourhood and the much-admired song of "Rule Britannia" was given with full chorus by the same gentlemen "by whom the band will be assisted". On the last night but one, Sir George and Lady Shuckburgh commanded *The Suspicious Husband* and on the last night, Friday, June 14, *How to Grow Rich* was given by desire of the gentlemen of the Sheaf Bowling Green.

From Daventry the Beynons moved on to Northampton for a stay of extraordinary and perhaps illegal duration. Opening on June 17, they carried on until the following January, with a break from July 31 to September 19. That summer was a very hot one and just before the break a number of post-horses "expired on the road".

On the first night of the season *The School for Scandal* was teamed with the musical farce *The Waterman* a piece reflecting the ascendance of water transport at that time. Shakespeare was prominent with *Hamlet* on July 1, *King Lear and His Three Daughters* on Wednesday, July 17, *King Richard II* on Monday, July 29, and *Macbeth* on Monday, July 22, when gentlemen of the town and neighbourhood assisted in the chorus of the music added by Purcell.

Where did the company go in the interval at Northampton from Wednesday, July 31, and Thursday, September 19? One possible call would be at Warwick where the races usually took place early in September. There are no playbills or newspapers to confirm this (though there may be some elsewhere to deny it).

The re-opening play was *The London Merchant* or *George Barnwell,*

Another Shakespeare piece *The Merry Wives of Windsor* was described as "never acted here these 20 years" when it was produced on Monday, October 21 (did someone keep records?) and teamed with Sheridan's farce *The Scheming Lieutenant*. When Lady Wake commanded the comic opera *Inkle and Yarico* on Friday, November 1, Mr. Galot played a concerto on the violin before the following farce, *The Agreeable Surprise*.

The *Poor Soldier* had been such a success, reflecting the sympathy felt for troops abroad that John O'Keefe provided a sequel *Patrick in Prussia*, which the Beynons gave in October, the month in which the King granted a petition for a barracks to be built in the town, which was no doubt good for trade as well as signifying patriotic fervour. In November the international situation was further reflected by a "night free of every expense, the whole emoluments and receipts appropriated to the laudable purpose of purchasing warm cloathing for the use of the British troops on foreign service who in a cold climate are fighting for the protection of our laws and constitution". The aforementioned *The Poor Soldier* was a suitable choice for this evening.

The following month some of the audience may have been disappointed when Shield's *Peeping Tom of Coventry* was staged, for though Lady Godiva is often talked about in it she never appears, rather like Mrs. Grundy! That evening concluded with an address from an unexpected pen—"an address to the ladies and gentlemen of Northampton and its environs written by a clergyman of this town and spoken by Mr. Bristow".

A number of productions were under the eye of Mr. Stratton "from the Theatres Royal, London, York and Norwich where he had the sole direction and superintendence of all the pantomimes and dances produced at those theatres". It was he who directed "an entirely new pantomime entertainment called *Harlequin Gladiator* or *The Rites of Hecate* with new music, scenery, machinery and decorations". He also played Macheath in *The Beggar's Opera*.

One announcement said that "Tickets delivered by Messrs. Roberts, Buck and Childs will be admitted" (a form of benefit) and the last night was a triple benefit performance of *She Stoops to Conquer* for Mr. and Mrs. Fothergill and Mr. Swindall.

A single playbill at Stratford-upon-Avon (Page 170) shows that the Beynon Company were there in June, 1795. Although the playhouse was described as "the New Theatre" it must have been a fit-up because the first permanent theatre was not opened until 1827.

At Northampton a further Beynon season brought an interesting guest: at least I assume that "Mr. Palmer of the Theatre Royal, Drury Lane" was the celebrated Mr. Palmer who had vainly struggled with the law in London and who was to drop dead on stage at Liverpool while performing in *The Imaginary Illness*. Previously an actor at the Drury Lane and Haymarket theatres, John Palmer had been accidentally stabbed on stage at The Lane by an actress while appearing in *The Grecian Daughter*. The blade of a stage dagger had failed to retract and he was confined to his room for some time afterwards, meantime reading in the Press a number of accounts of his own death.

After his abortive attempts to open the Royalty Theatre in London (see the Interlude) he played a number of seasons in the provinces until his dramatic exit at Liverpool on August 2, 1798, where he had been distraught since hearing of the death of his second son. In the play *Le Malade Imaginaire* his lines called for a mention of his wife and children and "There is a better world", immediately after which he dropped dead, leaving eight children who, in the course of a few months, had lost father, mother, brother and uncle.

Only one advertisement refers to his 1796 appearance at Northampton. On December 17 the Mercury announced that for his second night Mr. Palmer would appear as Hamlet with Mr. Waldron, from the Theatre Royal, Haymarket, as Polonius and the gravedigger. Then there were to be comic sketches by Mr. Palmer and finally Samuel Foote's farce *The Lyar* with Mr. Palmer again in the title role. That was on Monday, December 19. The following Wednesday *The Dramatist* and *The Agreeable Surprise* were given, with Mr. and Mrs. Dyer "who have performed in some of the finest theatres in the kingdom".

The season was marred in January by the death of Master Theophilus Beynon, son of the manager. He died in the town on the 28th "after a severe and lingering illness which he bore with a stoic attitude seldom seen at his years, particularly under sad accumulated afflictions".

As the season continued into 1797 an element of monarchical and patriotic propaganda recurred when on January 23, the advertisement for *King Louis of France* spoke of "Republican cruelty" and "men who hide their villainies under the specious title of Reformist" adding that the useful lesson which might be deduced was "that a restricted monarchy preserves intire the chartered liberties of the meanest subject" :

May all Republicans with envy see
A monarch happy and his subjects free
May peace expand her olive-branching wings
And Freedom smile beneath the reign of Kings.

Rather than savouring these noble sentiments the audience were no doubt more interested to see "The King conducted to the scaffold by Petion, with a view of the guillotine, executioner and soldiers". Somewhat incongruously the evening concluded with *The Merry Mourners*.

February brought another monarch to his destruction on the Northampton stage. This time it was Charles I of England and there was a warning to "guard against that band of monsters who under the specious name of Freedom become the destroyers of true liberty and religion". Again there was propaganda in poetic form :

Rouse Britons nor let their artful plan
Threaten our coast and force us, thus, to arms
Let Edward's spirit, let great Henry's fire
Your bosoms warm and every nerve inspire
Drive back such wretches to their native den
Abhor their crimes and shine like Englishmen.

The same month, however, the Mercury reported on a trial at Bourne, Lincolnshire, when a blacksmith named Joseph Tye was sentenced to be taken immediately from the court to the castle at Lincoln and there kept in solitary confinement for twelve months, without seeing or speaking to anyone "except the person who takes him his victuals". What was the monstrous crime of this free-born Englishman? He had spoken these words : "Damnation to the King. The King is a rascal and all who belong to him. This government is a despotic government. Kings are of no use. They have no kings in France and neither will they ever have any."

There was no end to the depiction of Afflicted Royalty. At the end of the month the company staged *Maid of Normandy* telling how "A queen in a short time was hurled from the most splendid and exalted pinnacle of earthly greatness and plunged into the lowest gulph of misery and despair."

The establishment of the National Anthem in the early 1790s, and the insistence on its being sung in theatres, was due partly to concern for the King in his insanity and partly to fears that the series of treason trials

Mr. P A L M E R's Second Night,
From the THEATRE ROYAL, DRURY-LANE.
THEATRE, NORTHAMPTON.
By His Majesty's Servants.
On MONDAY Evening December 19, 1796, will be
presented, The T R A G E D Y of
H A M L E T.
HAMLET, Mr. P A L M E R.
POLONIUS & GRAVE-DIGGER, Mr. WALDRON
From the Theatre Royal, H.-Market.
Between the Play and Farce some Comic Sketches by
Mr. PALMER.
To which will be added, the admired Comedy of
The L Y A R.
Written by S. FOOTE, Esq.
Young Wilding the Lyar, Mr. P A L M E R.
To begin this Night at Seven o'Clock.
Boxes 3s.—Pit 2s.—Gallery 1s.
And on Wednesday Evening, the much-admired
COMEDY of
The D R A M A T I S T.
The Parts of Vapid and Mariane by Mr. and Mrs.
DYER; who have performed in some of the first
Theatres in the Kingdom. With the FARCE of
The AGREEABLE SURPRIZE.
COWSLIP, Mrs. DYER.
Mr. BEYNON, with due Deference, informs the
Nobility, Gentry, and the Public in General, that
every Effort shall be exerted to render the Entertain-
ments amusing and rational; and, from the Novelty
of fashionable Pieces and Performers which will be
produced, hopes it may premise that no Affiduity
will be wanting to attain their Patronage.
Constant Fires kept in the Theatre.

"CONSTANT FIRES kept in the Theatre" in December, 1796, with Mr. Palmer of Drury Lane making a guest appearance with the Beynon Company. (*Northampton Mercury*)

which took place heralded an English Revolution like the one on the other side of the English Channel. Those in the cheaper seats were often vociferous in their demands for it to be sung, preferably by the lined-up cast. Thus was the tradition of the National Anthem in houses of entertainment established.

The seeds of possible revolution can be found in the most innocuous places, once you start looking, as Senator McCarthy of the United States of America did in our day. In London in 1794 there was opposition to a play by Holcroft called *Love's Frailties*. The innocent-sounding title masked a play in which one character was made to say "I was bred to that useless and most worthless of professions, that of a gentleman". If the stage was a pulpit, the sermons were usually strictly orthodox.

Extra services were offered at Northampton by two members of the Beynon company, Mr. Dyer being ready to give fencing lessons to "any gentleman who may honour him with his commands" and Mr. Askew to tune a harpsichord for 5s., a pianoforte for the same sum and a spinet at the cut rate of 3s.

On Thursday, March 3, along with *The Road to Ruin*, the audience were treated to select pieces by the Band of the First Regiment of Fencible Dragoons, with a solo on the trumpet by Mr. Schmidt and another on the bugle horn by Mr. Pussell. The band played on several subsequent evenings, variety being added by trumpet trios and quartets. Nor was this the total of military co-operation. When the company performed *The Recruiting Officer* or *The Art of Enlisting* the part of Sergeant Kite was taken "for this night only" by Sergeant Major Gough, of the Fencible Dragoons. On another night he gave an epilogue and appeared as a drunken sailor in *The Jolly Tars*.

The Fencibles were a curious military formation formed to serve only in Great Britain and Northern Ireland. Three years earlier a 1,000-strong regiment of Fencible Infantry had been set up in Northampton, under the command of Major John Kerr. A member of the committee which organised it was Robert Abbey, who had been a Coroner of the town since February, 1782, and who was to initiate and see through the project to build Northampton's first permanent theatre in 1806. The unit he helped to form in Northampton was to have the thankless task of keeping the two factions of Irishmen apart, in days when all Ireland was under the British crown. The regiment was in Ireland at the time of the Irish Rebellion of 1798.

Two Fencible Dragoon officers, Major Webb and Captain Quist, bespoke performances during the 1797 Beynon season and others to do so were J. H. Thursby, Lt. Charles Isham, Cornet, and the Gentlemen of the Northampton Troop of Yeomanry.

The need to recruit more fighting men had been reflected in an advertisement early that year: "His Majesty's Forces, First or Chatham Division commanded by Major-General Innes. Recruits wanted. Ten guineas and a crown bounty. Two guineas to a bringer. Now is the time or never— Spanish War—Dollars—Grog—and Pretty Lasses." Who could resist? You had to apply to Captain Loddington, Sergeant Robert Dixon at the Lion and Lamb, Bridge Street, Northampton, or any of the party quartered in the neighbourhood.

All in all the Beynon Company appear to have integrated themselves with the town more than others. For a couple of years, in view of the time they spent here, they might well have honoured Northampton by assuming the title "The Northampton Company" so that the town might have been ranked theatrically with Bath, Cheltenham, Lincoln, Bristol, Nottingham and Derby, etc.

When they performed for a benefit night of Mr. Waldron, on Friday, March 17, the advertisement appeared to indicate that he was Town Crier of Northampton. But this seems open to doubt as immediately following the end of the Northampton season on Friday, April 7, 1797, we find Messrs. Smith and Waldron respectfully informing the ladies and gentlemen of Towcester and its environs that they were to appear at Messrs. Smith and Phipps, the Old White Horse, in that town to deliver a series of entertainments called *The School of Thespis* or *A Medley to Cure the Heartache*, including Stevens' Lecture on Heads, songs comic and serious, and duets accompanied by Mr. Hume, leader of the Band at the Northampton Theatre.

In February, 1798, there is a further reference to theatricals at Towcester when the performance of *The Rivals* was to be at "The Theatre, Towcester" and a Mr. Smith was in the cast along with Mr. Aiken and Mrs. Thornhill (late Miss Walton), on Friday, February 3, the last night.

The following December the Cheltenham Company managed by Messrs. Watson and Richards announced an eight-week season in Daventry, including *The Castle Spectre, Lover's Vows, The Stranger, Heir At Law* and *Shakespeare's Jubilee*, "got up with every necessary apparatus and as performed by the company at the Theatres Cheltenham, Gloucester, Coventry, Leicester etc." The season began early in the New Year and at Easter the company announced that they were due to open a new theatre at Cirencester. This company played at the Warwick theatre from November to January 31, 1800, and returned there in 1802 when they included "fireworks on the true philosophical principle, occasioning neither smoke nor smell".

ACT
THE
THIRD

CUPBOARD DRAMA

...recounting how the Lincoln Company came to Northampton and gave the last performances in the make-shift theatre and then opened the town's first "real" theatre, which appeared to be splendid at the time but was subsequently regarded as a Dingy Little Cupboard and was more recently described as a Theatre Un-Royal.

THE GRANTHAM THEATRE drawn for James Winston's publication The
Theatric Tourist. (*Lincolnshire County Library at Grantham*)

Scene One

ENTER THE LINCOLN

The final Northampton company of the era of make-shift theatres was that of the Lincoln Circuit, managed jointly by Mr. Thomas Shaftoe Robertson and Mr. Robert Henry Franklin, whose tour included Lincoln, Newark, Boston, Grantham, Wisbeach (as it was then spelled), Huntingdon, Peterborough and Spalding.

The company had been founded by Dr. Dennis (ninety-three half-pints a day) Herbert. After a spell as a butcher's apprentice his son Nathaniel turned to the stage and performed in the West Indies for several years until, hearing of his father's death, he returned in expectation of taking over. Instead control was passed by his crotchety and unpredictable mother to a son-in-law named Stevens. Stevens went off, however, to give an entertainment which he called simply "Heads" and passed his interest in the company to an actor named Dyer.

This information comes from a letter written by Thomas Shaftoe Robertson to James Winston, who was collecting theatre history for publication. When Nathaniel failed with an opposition company which he set up friends intervened and he was given control of his late father's company after making suitable financial arrangements with his mother. Not having much ready money himself, he entered into a partnership with Jemmy Whitley who appointed as his deputy for this purpose James Shaftoe Robertson, and later sold the share to him.

Robertson's family hailed originally from Perthshire, Scotland, but his father became a senior servant of Lord Clive or Lord Powis in the area of Ludlow, where James was born, probably in 1723. He went to Ludlow Grammar School but ran away at seventeen to go on the stage. While acting at Loughborough he married Miss Ann Fowler. The three children of the marriage were Thomas Shaftoe; James, who became a manager on the Nottingham and Derby Circuit; and George, who became a printer and stationer at Peterborough.

Three years after the death of James Shaftoe Robertson, Nathaniel Herbert decided it was time for another change and sold his share to Mr. Whitfield, formerly of Drury Lane, for £300 and became landlord of the White Horse Inn, Baldock. But by the time Robertson's widowed mother handed over her interest to him as a coming-of-age present the other manager, with a two-thirds share, was a Mr. Miller.

A few years after taking over, Thomas Shaftoe Robertson entered into a marriage which, as far as I know, was to prove childless. His bride was Miss Frances Ross, who was later described in the memoirs of the actor Fred Belton as a fine actress of the Siddonian school and who when asked why she preferred to remain in the provinces rather than act in London replied that she would rather "reign in Hell than serve in Heaven".

In a letter from Newark on December 1, 1803, her husband recalled that his partnership with Miller lasted a stormy ten or twelve years during which time "such frequent dissensions arose that it became necessary to separate". It was as a result of these rows that the company lost its seasons at Kings Lynn where they had performed for nearly forty years. The magistrates there decided to hand the licence instead to the Norwich Company. To fill the gap the Lincoln troupe began to visit Huntingdon.

Miller sold his two shares to Robertson for £1,200 and he sold a half of the property to Mr. Franklin for £900. The result was gratifying. "Robertson and Franklin" was a partnership noted for its unanimity and understanding, exactly the opposite to "Miller and Robertson".

As this information comes from T. S. Robertson himself there is little reason to doubt its accuracy. He also tells us that Franklin was the son of a Sheriff of County Limerick, Ireland, and a member of a landed family. He had been a classical student at Trinity College, Dublin, before feeling the call of the stage, on which he proved a capable and versatile performer.

Some of Franklin's previous history is given by Tate Wilkinson : "Mr. Franklin made his appearance at Hull in Sir Lucius O'Trigger. That gentleman, without any compliment, has a natural turn for the muses and has wrote many little pieces deserving of much approbation. His merit as a comedian appears to be in the lower comic Irish characters. His behaviour is that of a gentleman and his education, I believe, demands it from him as a just debt. He surprised all the hearts of the young ladies at Stamford (of Mr. Pero's Company) to such a degree, that he with his Dublin persuasive argument, most honourably has taken to wife a lady of very respectable connections and fortune and by his and her endeavours will, I hope, always make their pot boil."

Franklin's name first appears as co-manager of the Lincoln Company at Peterborough in July, 1796, where, announcing his benefit on Tuesday, July 19, he apologised for the fact that he had "not had the honour of appearing more frequently before them", explaining that this was "occasioned by the circumstance of his engagement with Messrs. Taylor and Robertson's Company not being yet concluded". Franklin's loyalty and honesty appear to be transparent. "He also begs leave to observe that the consideration of the many favours repeatedly conferred on him by his Stamford friends renders it impossible for him to quit his engagement on any account before its due expiration."

He was moving from an acting position with a company in which one Robertson, James, was a partner, to become the partner of another Robertson, Thomas Shaftoe. Apart from brotherly considerations, the latter

ROBERTSON AND FRANKLIN were joint
managers of the Lincoln Company in 1802
(left). Between then and 1804, the last season in
the make-shift theatre (above) Franklin had
died, leaving Robertson as sole manager. In
December that year Mr. Abbey, Coroner and
solicitor, advertised for support to build a new
theatre. (Northampton Mercury)

was not, in any case, the sort of man to persuade him to break his contract, whether written or not. "The Mogul", as he was nick-named, was an honourable man. Of him the actor and manager F. C. Wemyss wrote in his memoirs : "Mr. Robertson was regarded more like the father of a family than the director of a theatre; and were I asked to point out a strict and justly honest man, Mr. Thomas Robertson, the Lincoln manager, would be that man."

The first "Lincoln" season began at Northampton on Thursday, April 25, 1799, with *Everyone has his Fault* and *The Agreeable Surprize*. Later came *The Castle Spectre*, with which the company were to open a new theatre in the town seven years later, *The Stranger*, *Lover's Vows*, *Heir at Law*, *He's Much to Blame*, *Secrets worth Knowing*, *False and True*, *Laugh When You Can*, *The Jew and the Doctor*, *Botheration*, *The Secret*, *The Will*, *The Poor Soldier*, *The Way to Get Married* and *The Sultan*. The average reader may have heard of none of these plays : little of the drama then being written or produced has stood the test of time : it is as lost an era as if it never existed.

Only three advertisements illumine the season—there are no surviving playbills—plus the parting one : "The managers return their most sincere acknowledgments to the Ladies and Gentlemen of Northampton and the public at large not only for the support the theatre has been honoured with but for the politeness and candour they have so universally met with during the season and beg leave to add that it shall always continue to be equally as it is at present their unremitting study to merit the patronage of a public to whom they are bound by the warmest gratitude and most heartfelt respect." You had to know your place in those days and the actor's was way down the ladder.

The following year, 1800, the company were back in April for a further six-week season with a number of the same plays and others some of which at least you may not have heard of. There were *Pizzaro*, *Little Bob and Little Ben*, *The Birthday*, *The Neglected Daughter*, *Ways and Means*, *The Prize*, *The Deaf Lover*, *The Romp*, *Wives as They Were and Maids as They Are*, *The Irishman in London*, *The Wise Men of The East*, *No Song No Supper*, *Speed the Plough*, *Fortune's Frolicks*, *The School for Scandal*, *The Rivals* and *Macbeth*.

His first play for twenty years, Sheridan's *Pizzaro* was the talk of London when first produced at Drury Lane in April, 1799. He borrowed the plot from a weighty melodrama by a German author, Kotzebue. He had been very tardy, completing the last lines on the very morning of the first night. It included some music and words for some of the choruses were passed to the composer Kelly on scraps of paper and do not appear in the printed version, having presumably been mislaid.

During the first season only the managers had been named in the newspaper but during the second visit company members were identified— Messrs. Brown, Twiddy, Cooper, Wright, Rutley, Evans, Walcot, Messrs. Stanari and Tilliard (musicians), Mr. and Mrs. Tuthill, Mr. and Mrs. Elliott, Mrs. Kendall, Miss Chapman, Miss Bullen and, of course, Mrs. Robertson.

Robertson and Franklin were still managers for the Northampton season of 1802 (after a gap this time of two years) from April 26 to June 7, and one of the players was a Mr. J. Franklin, presumably a relative of the co-manager. Other players not mentioned two years earlier were Mrs. Brunton, Mr. and Mrs. Clarke, Mr. Stanley, Mr. and Mrs. Mason and Mr. and Mrs. Wilde. Performances were bespoken by Lady Isham (*The Rivals*), Mrs. Bouverie (*The School for Scandal*), Mrs Thornton (*The Poor Gentleman*), the Mayor and Corporation (*Speed the Plough*) and the officers of the Royal Regiment of Horse Guards (*The Rivals*).

Usually the last night was a managerial benefit or, when there were two, the senior manager. Thus it was usually Mr. Robertson's prerogative. But the last night of 1802, June 26—it was *The Winter's Tale* with Mr. Robertson as Leontes—was for Mr. Franklin. It was also to be his very last Northampton benefit because at Peterborough, aged but thirty-two, he "paid the debt of nature" as his partner picturesquely termed his decease.

In 1803 there was another blank at Northampton as far as theatre is concerned but an advertisement in June reveals that the Riding School was still in use for entertainment. Messrs. Davis and Bannister, as managers, announced that Jones Royal Circus Company of Equestrians would entertain first in the Riding School (also described as "The Amphitheatre") and then at Boughton Green Fair. Eight-year-old Master Davis performed on the tight-rope and on one and two horses. The last mention of entertainment at the Riding School that I have come across is of March, 1815, when Messrs. West and Woolford fitted it up as a circus and performed every evening except Good Friday including the celebrated Mr. Ducrow jumping "over garters, a board of lights, through a balloon etc. "There were boxes at 3s. (children 2s.), pit 1s. 6d. (children 1s.), and gallery 1s. (children half-price). There were Egyptian pyramids of "men piled upon men" and ladies and gentlemen were taught the polite art of riding".

In 1803 too there was a season at Wellingborough, at what was described as the New Theatre, by Mr. Lacy, from the Theatres Royal, London, lasting apparently from the beginning of May to mid-June; and also earlier in the year a season at Daventry, which came to an abrupt conclusion when the theatre, in a barn, was burned to the ground. A couple of years later there were some private theatricals near Northampton when *The Mayor of Garratt* was presented with a star amateur cast at Woburn Abbey, home of the Dukes of Bedford. They included the Duchess, the Marquess of Tavistock and his brother Lord Charles Russell. The theatre was "neatly fitted up and there were several changes of scenery".

At Northampton *John Bull or An Englishman's Fireside* was the opening attraction of 1804, with Mr. Robertson now sole manager. Tickets and places for the boxes for what was to be the last season at the old theatre were to be taken of Mr. Wright at Mr. Parbery's, upholsterer, in Abington Street. There were three Shakespearean choices: *As You Like It* was on May 7; *Hamlet* on June 1; and when *Romeo and Juliet* was given on June 9 the audience may not have realised that it was the very last play to be presented in the old theatre, for not until the following December was there an announcement in the Mercury seeking support for a project to build a new one.

On May 7, the proceeds of *As You Like It* and *Love Laughs at Locksmiths*, were given by Mr. Robertson to the Patriotic Fund at Lloyds "for those who suffer or merit in the defence of their King and Country".

Bespeaking performances during this season which marked the end of "fit-up" theatre in Northampton were Mrs. Armytage, Mrs. Bouverie, the Officers and Corps of Northampton Volunteer Infantry, and William Dolben and the Finedon Volunteers.

On the last but one night Robertson wrote a letter to James Winston, which has miraculously survived. Datelined "Theatre, Northampton, June 1804", it is revealing : "Northampton Theatre is so bad a building that a drawing of it would disgrace a publication. Next season I shall open a new theatre." The publication was James Winston's monthly The Theatric Tourist, which fizzled out after a few issues.

Now we know why Northampton needed a new theatre—the old one was a disgrace. The advertisement of December 8, 1804, stating that "complaints have long been made of the want of a proper theatre in the town," was put forward by Robert Abbey, who was connected with the old theatre in some way (as manager according to one account) and was a Coroner.

However long-felt the need, support was lukewarm : the £1,500 required, in sixty shares of £25, was so slow coming in that Abbey threatened to call the whole thing off.

In 1921 the Mercury published an article about the 1806 theatre mentioning a leather-bound volume called Register of Plays, by John Cole. Its 177 octavo pages of manuscript gave an account of performances during the first six years, up to 1812. The newspaper had purchased the book from Mr. Billingham's bookshop on the north side of Marefair, opposite the theatre. Details and incidents not elsewhere recorded were given in it. The theatre is described as "elegant, containing two tiers of boxes and pit and gallery. The pit has twelve rows of benches, covered with matting and well constructed. The colour of the boxes is green relieved with fancied embellishments in white, designed and executed by Mr. Merrick (and assistants) from the Theatre Royal, Drury Lane." It was said to be on the lines of the Haymarket Theatre, London. It all sounded quite grand but the statistic for the pit gives the game away. Imagine twelve park seats set close together and you have the distance from the orchestra to the centre boxes.

The site was incredibly small. Today it is difficult to envisage it since the Shakespeare Inn which stood alongside was demolished in 1974 as part of a plan to construct a dual-carriageway road. The theatre building itself had disappeared just over fifty years earlier in a previous road-widening. It stood on the corner of Marefair and Horseshoe Street (formerly Crow and Horseshoe Lane).

By turning the pages of the Stamford Mercury it is possible to fill in the entire year's movements of the Lincoln Company and in so doing it becomes apparent that Northampton's was not the only new theatre they opened in 1806. There were two others, at Boston and Lincoln. For some decades people had been getting tired of the old fit-ups and though the new buildings were often mean indeed by present-day standards—I have also coined the word "un-royal" for them—they were a great improvement on what they replaced.

The New Year had found the company in mid-season at Grantham where they had begun on Monday, December 23, 1805. The Grantham theatre story was outlined, with others, by Thomas Shaftoe Robertson in a letter to James Winston on December 1, 1803 : "In its first state was a rude temporary building of pit and gallery in Westgate. Thirty years back a more convenient one was built in the Market Place but with no boxes. Ten years back front boxes were added. In 1800 (?) the lease being out a handsome new theatre with circular upper and lower boxes was built by Joseph Lawrence. When full will contain about £50."

Some of the plays during the six-week run were *The Venetian Outlaw*, *The Follies of a Day*, *The Fashionable Lover* (by desire of Lady Welby), *The Deserted Daughter* (for the benefit of Mr. Cooper and Mr. Wright), *Of Age Tomorrow*, *The Prior Claim* (by desire of the Officers and Corps of Grantham Loyal Volunteer Infantry), *Hamlet*, *The Turnpike Gate*, *Matrimony*, *The Provok'd Husband* (by desire of Miss Cholmley and for the benefit of Master Brown and Miss Carlile), *Richard III* (for the benefit of Mr. and Mrs. Sharples), *The Soldier's Daughter* (for the benefit of Mr. Neville and Mr. Norman), *The Strangers* (for the benefit of Mr. Hitchener and Miss Spilsbury). *The Castle Spectre*, which was to be the opening play at Northampton, was performed at Grantham for the benefit of Mr. and Mrs. Brown while the manager and his wife had their benefit on the last night, Saturday, January 25.

Next came Boston where the new theatre was opened with *The Castle Spectre* and an appropriate address given by the manager on Wednesday, January 29. Boston had had a theatre some thirty years earlier, built by the Corporation within a few yards of a former temporary one in a granary in the Market Place. At the time, the new one had proved entirely satisfactory but the passing of three decades made it seem too small and a subscription was launched for a new one. The opening address was received, the Stamford Mercury records, "by a very large and elegant audience and with that flattering applause which could not fail being extremely gratifying to the feelings of the manager and the whole of the performers. We do not remember to have seen a better or more respectable company and from the elegance of the house and the general accommodation we doubt not but the theatre will be well attended the whole season."

Mrs. Brunton appears to have been a guest at Boston, perhaps to mark the inauguration, the last night of her appearing being Monday, February 7. As there was to be a General Fast on Wednesday, February 26, both the Market Day and the theatre performance were moved forward to the Tuesday. The perennial *The Provok'd Husband* was chosen by Messrs. Neville and Norman for their joint benefit. Mr. Neville's special contribution was "The Cries of London" while Mr. Adamson donated a song with a musichall style title, "What a Beauty I did Grow".

A mere forty-eight hours separated the last night at Boston, on Thursday, March 13, and the opening at Wisbeach, on Saturday, March 15, where the theatre, while not new, was announced as having "undergone considerable improvement and will be lighted up with a new and elegant chandelier". Here the theatre was, I believe, Mr. Robertson's own property, having been erected some fifteen years earlier in the centre of the town at the back of York Row, replacing a much less convenient one at the end of the town on the road to Spalding.

At Wisbeach the manager emerged each year in a Masonic light. This year's announcement was that "By desire of the Lodge of Strict Benevolence of the Ancient and Honourable Society of Free and Accepted Masons, held at the Vine Inn, Wisbeach" the new comedy of *The School for Friends* would be performed, with a Masonic epilogue by Brother and Sister Robertson. A melodrama, *The Tale of Mystery*, would follow. Tom Robertson appended a more fraternally phrased invitation: "Brother Robertson respectfully informs Brethren resident in and about the neighbourhood that should any make it convenient to confer upon him the favour of their company, places will be kept in the pit for their accommodation, together with a select number for the Brethren of the Lodge. Brother Robertson also informs visiting Brethren that it is the intention of the Lodge to meet at the Vine a few minutes previous to the time of beginning and from thence to proceed to the theatre." Whether the Lodge attended in Masonic garb is not clear : certainly they did at some other theatres.

The last night was on Wednesday, April 30, leaving the company five days to draw their wagon to Northampton and make sure everything was in order for the opening night of the new theatre in Marefair. Meantime the Boston New Theatre was opened for the three nights of the Boston Fair by one Signor Belzoni with a three-part entertainment consisting of : 1. Hydraulics (fire and water mixed together); 2. Phantasmagoria; 3. Feats of strength (Patagonian Sampson will carry five to ten men with ease).

At Northampton the Mercury was predictably warm about the opening night : "Our new theatre was opened on Monday night last with a very neat and appropriate address delivered by Mr. Robertson. The play of *The Castle Spectre* and the after-piece of *The Weathercock* were afterwards performed in a style that justly merited the spontaneous and reiterated plaudits of the audience which was numerous and genteel. The subscribers to his undertaking are deservedly entitled to the thanks of every liberal-minded person, as they have not only been the means of ornamenting the town with another public building but of combining rational amusement with its growing prosperity."

Shakespeare came first to the new theatre on Thursday, June 12, when *Romeo and Juliet* shared the bill with *The Hunter of The Alps*. Other titles of the first season were *The Stranger, The Follies of a Day, The Sultan, The Honey-Moon, Love Laughs at Locksmiths, The Prior Claim, The Soldier's Daughter, The Purse, Who Wants a Guinea?,* and *The Sleeping Beauty or Harlequin in Northampton.*

From Northampton the Lincoln Company moved on to Peterborough where a new theatre had emerged at the turn of the century, just behind

the parish church. Here again there was military sponsorship, a performance of an un-named play being by desire of the Peterborough Volunteer
Cavalry. Yet again *The Castle Spectre* was on the bill, for Saturday, July
26, but with an interesting difference : playing the part of Osmond "for this
night only" was Mr. Manly of the Stamford Theatre (he was by now joint
manager with Robertson) and also appearing was Miss Robertson, another
member of the Nottingham and Derby Company.

Huntingdon, the next port of call, keeps up the story of newish theatres.
For many years the scene of the drama had been a barn but about 1799
new premises were erected at the rear of the George Inn, planned by Mr.
Rowles, nephew to Mr. Holland, architect of the Theatre Royal, Drury
Lane. Huntingdon was not one of the most fruitful calls and was visited
for the Race Week and every second year.

By Saturday, August 16, the company were opening at Spalding and by
Wednesday, September 10, they were at Lincoln to complete the hat-trick
of new theatre openings. Performances in Lincoln had seemingly been
restricted to private houses until about 1731 when a small playhouse,
measuring about twenty-two yards by eight, was erected by Erasmus Audley
in a lane under the castle, later known as Drury Lane. Named after a
local businessman the lane was so narrow that carriages could not pass
into it and ladies were carried there in sedan chairs. In an episode rather
contrary to the theme of church v. drama it is on record that for a performance of *Romeo and Juliet* choirboys from the cathedral were allowed
to take part wearing their surplices. After the Thespians had moved away
to the lower city this playhouse was converted to two cottages. In 1764
came the first theatre in the King's Arm Yard, High Street, stated to be an
adapted building. The earliest surviving bill is of 1766. After a last performance on November 4, 1805, it was rebuilt.

The company had a long season at Lincoln and even then the last night
was postponed a week "because of the late election" and after that there
was an extra night on Monday, November 10, by desire of Col. Ellison,
M.P., presumably a celebration night.

The theatre which the Lincoln Company opened on September 10, 1806,
lasted until November 26, 1892, when it followed the fashion for theatre
funerals by being burnt down. A replacement theatre, on the same site, was
opened on December 18, 1893. The building which was the King's Arms
has for many years been a club and is now named the City Club.

It was presumably as an act of what we now call rationalisation that
Whitley had abandoned Newark, where the Lincoln had a Duchess in the
audience on their 1806 visit. The Duchess of Newcastle requested *The
Honeymoon* and *Love Laughs at Locksmiths* on November 28. Other
bespeaks were by the young ladies of Miss Winter's School, Collingham,
who saw *The School for Scandal* on Friday, December 12; and the Newark
Loyal Volunteer Infantry who selected *The Soldier's Daughter*.

An incident in the Newark Theatre in November, 1802, provided a
startling intimation that the audiences were not universally respectable and
genteel. To quote the Northampton Mercury : "A ruffian threw a half-pint
glass from the gallery which struck one of the performers, Mr. T. Robertson,

with great violence on the face. We are happy to say he was not materially hurt and that the offender is in custody." Dodging missiles was an occupational hazard. During a season at Portsmouth E. C. Everard reported : "Our situation on the stage from being rendered unpleasant was sometimes dangerous : apples and oranges we got pretty well used to from the frequency of their appearance but when our unthinking spectators would sometimes salute us with a potato or even a pint or quart bottle, it was above a joke."

Christmas Eve 1806, on a Wednesday, was the last night at Newark and then it was back to Grantham to begin the year's routine all over again.

Only for one more year, 1807, was Northampton to figure in that pattern however; either business at the new theatre was not up to scratch or "The Mogul" decided on rationalisation of his circuit, Northampton being out on a limb from his other calls.

ON THE LAST BUT ONE NIGHT of the performances in the make-shift theatre Thomas Shaftoe Robertson wrote the letter opposite to James Winston. In it he describes the old theatre as "so bad a building that a drawing of it would disgrace a publication." It is among a collection of his letters to Winston, publisher of "The Theatric Tourist", at Lincolnshire County Library at Lincoln.

Sir

Inclosed with this I have sent you Drawings of Huntingdon & Newark Theatres — I am ashamed that I have been so long a time in procuring them, but it is owing to the Negligence of the Draughtsmen — I sent them repeatedly Letters & at last I have received them — I was in hopes to have sent you at the same time a Drawing of Peterbro Theatre, but that is not yet done — I shall be there on Sunday — as we finish here Tomorrow & commence our Season at Peterbro on Tuesday — & being on the Spot I'll take care that it shall be completed — I have not order'd any more Numbers than that which you sent me at Wisbeach — therefore if you please to be so good to direct any of your Booksellers to send me the remainder of the Numbers that are out directed to me Theatre Peterbro Northampton I hope the Publication answers your Expectations & with my sincere wish for its success

I am Dr Sir
Yours
T. Robertson

Theatre Northampton

June 14th 1804

I am in a great bustle being the Close of our Campaign here —
Northampton Theatre is so bad a Building that a Drawing of it would disgrace a Publication — Next Season I shall open a new Theatre —

BY DESIRE OF

LADY BUCKINGHAMSHIRE.

THEATRE, LINCOLN,

This present SATURDAY EVENING OCTOBER 27th, 1798, will be prefented

A NEW PLAY, CALLED THE

CASTLE SPECTRE.

The CASTLE SPECTRE is univerfally allowed to be, without Exception, the moft interefting Piece that has been reprefented on the British Stage for many Years. The Incidents and Situations are all felected from the beft Romances extant, and are (in the moft impref-five and judicious manner) combined by the Author, fo as to form a Chain of dramatic Effect, not equalled by any modern Production. The Efcape of Percy—the Character of the African Misanthrope—their lovely Simplicity and Diftreffes of Angela; the grand and ftriking Apparition of her Mother's Spectre; the miraculous Difcovery of her Father, after having been for fixteen Years immured in the Caftle-Dungeon—the Dream, Remorfe, and Fall of the Tyrant Osmond, and confequent Felicity ever attendant on Innocence and Virtue—are pourtrayed in a Stile, which has given as much Delight to an English Audience, as any Theatrical Exhibition ever yet impreffed.

Reginald,	Mr. ROBERTSON,	Percy,	Mr. FRANKLIN,
Father Phillip,	Mr. TUTHILL,	Haffan,	Mr. HEMLEY,
Kenric,	Mr. ELLIOTT,	Motley,	Mr. WALDRON,
Saib,	Mr. VEHETSLEY,	Muley,	Mr. COOPER,
Edric,	Mr. BROWN,	Ofmond,	Mr. RACKHAM,
Spectre,	Mrs. TUTHILL,	Alice,	Mrs. ELLIOTT,
Angela,	Mrs. T. ROBERTSON.		

The principal Scenes difplayed in the Piece are ENTIRELY NEW, *and will appear in the following Order:*

In Act II.

The ARMOURY of EARL REGINALD's Ancestors,

REGINALD's STATUE, reprefented by PERCY,

The celebrated Glee of " Megan, oh!" from the Water beneath the Tower,

AND PERCY's ESCAPE FROM THE TOWER WINDOW.

In Act III.

The CASTLE MONASTERY,—the Portraits of REGINALD and EVELINA, and the
SLIDING PANNEL for ANGELA's ESCAPE.

In Act IV.

GRAND PERSPECTIVE VIEW of the INSIDE of the ORATORY, with
The APPEARANCE of the CASTLE SPECTRE.

In Act V.

THE CASTLE DUNGEON—REGINALD's PRISON.

ANGELA's firft INTERVIEW with her FATHER—PERCY's Attack on the CASTLE.
OSMOND's Difcovery, and Attempt to STAB his BROTHER,
ANGELA's HEROISM, final Triumph and Happinefs.

TO WHICH WILL BE ADDED A MUSICAL FARCE, CALLED

NETLEY ABBEY;

OR, The WOODEN WALLS of OLD ENGLAND.

Gunnel *(a Britifh Tar)*	Mr. FRANKLIN,	Old Oakland,	Mr. HEMLEY,
Captain Oakland,	Mr. RACKHAM,	Jeffery,	Mr. BROWN,
Sterling,	Mr. ELLIOTT,	Rapine,	Mr. CLARKE,
M'Scrape *(the Fiddling Barber)*	Mr. ROBERTSON.		
Catherine,	Mrs. CLARKE,	Lucy Oakland,	Mrs. ELLIOTT,
Ellen Woodbine,	Mifs VALENTINE.		

☞ Days of Playing next Week, *TUESDAY. WEDNESDAY, and FRIDAY.*

[BROOKE, PRINTER.]

LINCOLN gave its name to the circuit of the company which gave the last performance at Northampton in the make-shift theatre and the first in purpose-built premises. The opening production at the latter in 1806 was of "The Castle Spectre". Here is a bill of the same play when it was given by the company at Lincoln in 1798. (*Lincolnshire County Library at Lincoln*)

Scene Two

THEATRE UN-ROYAL

Let us finally turn back the calendar to look a little more closely at what went on in the Northampton theatre on that first night of May 5, 1806.

What of the play, *The Castle Spectre*? A Member of Parliament, Matthew Gregory Lewis, was its author. His nickname was "Monk" and although his play about a turreted ghost is now almost entirely forgotten his name does live on to the extent that his three-volume novel about a monk, which gave him his nick-name, was the basis for a horror film of 1974, called *The Monk*.

Monk Lewis (1775–1818) had plundered abroad for his sources while a diplomat. His play was an amalgam of bits and pieces from other works. The original of one character was thought to be Juliet's nurse.

Set in the Castle of Conway it had a prisoner in a dungeon; someone leaping from a tower into the river; and a scene in the oratory in which the heroine sees the spectre, her murdered mother ... "Her white and flowing garments spotted with blood; her veil is thrown back and discovers a pale and melancholy countenance; her eyes are lifted upwards, her arms extended towards heaven and a large wound appears upon her bosom ... the spectre waves her hand, bidding farewell, instantly the organ's swell is heard; a full chorus of voices chant Jubilate; a blaze of light flashes through the oratory and the folding doors close with a loud noise. Angela falls motionless to the floor."

It was like a Hammer Films production. And correspondingly it made what they now call a bomb when staged at Drury Lane. One account is that it took £100,000 there. And even though the music was scant, the piece above mentioned being the most memorable, it made the name of Michael Kelly who was described by a colleague as "an imposer rather than a composer". He used to hum his tunes to an Italian, Mazzanti, who wrote them down and harmonised and scored them.

Some of the scenes remained long in the minds of those who saw them. In his 1861 novel, Gryll Grange, Thomas Peacock put his own boyhood memories into the mouth of one of his characters, Miss Ilex: "In my young days ghosts were so popular that the first question asked about any new play was: is there a ghost in it? *The Castle Spectre* had set this fashion ... the opening of the folding doors disclosing the illuminated oratory; the extreme beauty of the actress who personated the ghost; the solemn music to which she moved slowly forward to give a silent blessing to her kneeling daughter and the chorus of female voices chanting Jubilate made an impression on me which no other scene of the kind ever made."

The Jubilate, which had so powerful an effect, was a mere four bars of unremarkable harmony : I suppose that today its composer would have made a fortune by selling it for a cigar or scent TV commercial, so great an impression did it make on the ear.

Yet the play had some merit. Into the mouth of a negro slave serving as a castle guard Lewis put these words : "My heart once was gentle; once was good; but sorrows have broken it, insults have made it hard. I have been dragged from my native land; from a wife who was everything to me, to whom I was everything. Twenty years have elapsed since these Christians tore me away . . . was I not free and am I not a slave?"

Lewis offered a wager to Sheridan with the stake as "all the money the play has brought to the box office". Sheridan replied that he could not afford so much but "I'll bet you all it's worth".

The play which set a vogue in castles, dungeons, bleeding ghosts and general blood, thunder and lightning was subsequently staged at the Mare-fair theatre in Northampton by Mr. Raymond's Company in August, 1827, and by the Bath Company in August, 1831.

What would an audience of 1975 think of it? Instead of being transfixed in their seats they might well fall about in mirth at the ludicrousness of it, like they do if shown an early silent horror film. This was what happened when the play was revived at London's Gaiety Theatre in the 1880s by John Hollingshead who included it in a series called "The Palmy Days". The cast did not ham the piece but played it in deadly earnest. Neverthe-less, as W. Macqueen-Pope recorded in his history of the Gaiety : "These relics had a curious effect on the public . . . they roared with laughter, louder and longer than they had roared at any Gaiety burlesque which was written to be funny. Their mirth was so violent that they even broke the stalls as a result of their uncontrollable laughter."

Even allowing for the exaggeration and elaboration with which W. Macqueen-Pope has been charged of late, there is sufficient evidence here to illustrate the point that the taste of audiences changes with the age and their degree of sophistication. Playwrights, apart from the avant garde ones, normally provide for what they believe to be the current taste of the audiences : as Northamptonshire's John Dryden put it in the prologue of his play *Rival Ladies* (writing of himself) :

> *He's bound to please, not to write well, and knows*
> *There is a mode in plays as well as clothes.*

And what did posterity have to say about the new theatre which was such an ornament to the town when it was opened in 1806? For some years there was no criticism of it, none that survives at least, not even from Charles Mathews who three times played there and who, when he visited Stratford-upon-Avon in December, 1814, wrote ". . . behold it was a barn ! A miserable barn."

But disenchantment increased with the passing years though in the Press it tended to be muted, possibly because the succession of managers were potential advertisers. It was left to an upstart new newspaper, the Northampton Albion, to make a spirited attack on it in 1875. It said that although the old theatre probably suited the requirements of the town of sixty years before it was now a disgrace to any respectable community, with an interior so poverty-stricken as to give rise to a feeling of disgust every time one entered it.

But when the last curtain had fallen and the theatre had become a warehouse for corn more overt comment was possible, more especially comparing it with its more ornate successor, the Theatre Royal and Opera House, opened in Guildhall Road in 1884.

There was some particularly outspoken comment nearly five years later when the time came to sum up on the first regime at that newer theatre, on the occasion of the departure of John Campbell Franklin, who had built it, and Isaac Tarry, the auctioneer and amateur actor who had managed it. The Mercury now stated that "the value of Mr. Tarry's work can only be judged by those who remember the DINGY LITTLE CUPBOARD in Marefair that formerly served as a Playhouse for the town, and the very inferior dramatic fare then provided".

A further reference was to the "queer cramped little place at the corner of Marefair now used as a corn house". It went on : "The drama was in very ill repute at that time in Northampton. There is a very fervent prayer in the theatrical profession : 'From Hell, Hull and Halifax, Lord Preserve Us.' These three well-known places being regarded as places to be avoided. We doubt not that had the spelling of Northampton begun with an aspirate it would be so distinguished for Hull and Halifax—we cannot speak of the other place—could scarcely be worse off in a theatrical sense than Northampton was in the old days." Thus, had Northampton retained its original Saxon name the word among the profession might well have been "From Hell, Hull and Hamtune, Lord Deliver Us".

It occurs to me too that in selecting Theatre Un-Royal for the title of my history of the Dingy Little Cupboard I chose better than I realised at the time, not having then read the files of 1889!

The parting presentation to Isaac Tarry took place in surroundings which by their nature bestowed honour upon him. It was in the Council Chamber in Northampton Town Hall, the chairman of the Testimonial Fund, Mr. C. C. Becke (son of a former secretary of the Marefair Theatre) occupying the Mayoral seat. Mr. Becke said that Mr. Tarry had raised the theatre life of the town from the lowest depths—"Only three or four years ago our theatre was little better than a barn and I am afraid the companies who came here were fitted for the place they had to act in."

If you have not already read the story of the Dingy Little Cupboard, may I mention that a few copies are still available.

On the other hand if you would like to hear more about the theatre which Franklin built and Tarry managed you may care to subscribe towards my next book, for it will embrace the 1884–1927 history of the Theatre Royal and Opera House, Guildhall Road, now known as Northampton Repertory Theatre or Royal Theatre.

NEW THEATRE, NORTHAMPTON.

MR. ROBERTSON most respectfully an-
nounces to the Town and Vicinity of Northampton, that he shall have the Honour of OPENING
the NEW THEATRE on MONDAY, MAY 5th, 1806,
with the Play of

The CASTLE SPECTRE.

Preceding the Play,
AN ADDRESS,
WRITTEN FOR THE OCCASION,
To be spoken by Mr. ROBERTSON.

To conclude with the new popular Farce of
The WEATHERCOCK.

☞ The last Night on Monday, June 16th.

*** Days of playing, Mondays, Wednesdays, Fridays,
and Saturdays.

N. B. The splendid Spectacles of CINDERELLA,
or the LITTLE GLASS SLIPPER, the LADY of the
ROCK, the HUNTER of the ALPS, VENETIAN
OUTLAW, with other new and popular Pieces, are
in Preparation, and will be brought forward as early
as possible.

Patrons

Sincere thanks are expressed to the Patrons listed below. By pre-paying (or pre-ordering in the case of libraries and some other organisations) it is they alone who have made the publication possible.

The very first subscription, on November 27, 1973, was from Mr. Harry Greatorex, Patron-in-Chief of the venture. The second supporter was Mrs. Jessie Knight who, oddly enough in view of the theme of the book, used to run a theatre in former stabling at her former home Harpole Hall, Northants. The third Patron was Sir Hereward Wake whose aunt, the late Miss Joan Wake, was of such immense help with Theatre Un-Royal.

While thanks are the due of all Patrons I am especially grateful to those who are appearing in "my little list" at the end of these Northampton Theatre History books for a second or third time i.e. those who were also Patrons of Death of a Theatre (1960) and Theatre Un-Royal (1974). And, indeed, quite a number of them have already subscribed to the fourth and final book in the series, of which details are given on a later page.

Here then is the list of those who turned the present book from an idea into text and pictures :

CAROLYN ADAMS
(Stony Stratford)
JOHN ADRIAN
(London)
HILARY R. ALFORD (Mrs.)
(Corby)
PROFESSOR ISKA ALTER
(New York, U.S.A.)
DONALD ANDERSON
(Great Hallingbury, Herts)
CHARLES APPLEYARD
(Highbury, London)
WILL ARNOLD
R. W. ASHBY
(Muscott)
CAPTAIN W. ASHBY
(Aynho)
GRAHAM ASHLEY
(London)
G. L. ATTERBURY (Mrs.)
(West Haddon)
MARY ATTERBURY (Mrs.)
(West Haddon)
ROBERT J. AYERS
(Stony Stratford)
DR. ROBERT AYLING
(Edmonton, Canada)

J.T.B.
BOB BAKER
(Market Harborough)
ANDRE BALDET
DEREK J. BARBER
KATHLEEN M. D. BARKER
(Wembley)

LT-COL. DENNIS BARRATT E.R.D.
(Great Billing)
WALLY BATEMAN
(Ashton, Roade)
GILBERT BATES
G. H. BELGION (Mrs.)
(Titchmarsh)
J. C. BENNETT
DIANA K. BERESFORD (Mrs.)
(Oundle)
N. J. BERRILL
(Clifton Reynes)
JOAN BETTS
HENRY BIRD
(Hardingstone)
GORDON BOSWELL
(Hardingstone)
TED BOTTLE
(Coalville, Leic.)
NORMAN BOWLES
(Aldwincle)
PETER BRINSON
(London)
J. FRANCIS BROWN, C.B.E.
(London)
LT-COL. K. C. BROWN
(Ashton)
DUKE OF BUCCLEUCH AND
QUEENSBERRY, V.R.D.
H. BULLARD
(Duston)
ALAN BURMAN
E. M. BURR
(Greens Norton)

I. D. BUTLIN (Mrs.)
(Kettering)
ROBIN BUTTERELL
(Wells, Somerset)
J. A. BYRNES
(Elizabeth, New Jersey, U.S.A.)

JEREMY H. CALDERWOOD
(Harpole)
J. A. CALLOW B. A. (Miss)
(Stratford-upon-Avon)
BRIAN R. CARTER
(Milton Malsor)
CANON J. L. CARTWRIGHT
(Peterborough)
I. M. CHAMBERLAIN (Mrs.)
R. J. CHAPMAN
(Towcester)
PHILIP CHARLETON
(Walton-on-Thames)
RICHARD C. CHATBURN
C. CHATBURN (Mrs.)
(Lincoln)
DAVID CHESHIRE
(London)
CYRIL A. CHOWN
DIANA CHUDLEY (Mrs.)
(Creaton)
MR. and MRS. W. V. CHURCH
MR. and MRS. F. A. CLARKE
(Chapel Brampton)
THOMAS J. CLARKE
(Hackleton)
MR. and MRS. S. E. CLAYSON
FRANK and PEGGY CLOWES
DR. R. B. COLES
H. A. VICTOR COLLIN
(Lubenham, Market Harborough)
DR. L. W. CONOLLY
(Edmonton, Canada)
E. H. COOPER
HORACE COPSON
JULIA COWARD (Miss)
BRIAN COX
(Higham Ferrers)
L. and A. B. CURTIS
(Boughton)

GLADYS DAVIES
(Little Brington)
C. M. DELANEY (Miss)
MR. and MRS. PETER DESBOROUGH
(Great Billing)
C. E. A. DEXTER
(Chapel Brampton)
CYRIL E. DIAMOND
(Thrapston)
PHILIP DICKENS
(Great Houghton)
W. A. DICKENS (Mrs.)
J. E. DOLBY
BRYAN J. DOUGLAS
PROFESSOR GEORGE BRENDAN
DOWELL
(Goucher College, Maryland, U.S.A.)

F. DRIVER (Mrs.)
(Rhyl)
MAURICE J. DUNMORE
(Hardingstone)
D. DURHAM

OLIVE ELLIOTT (Miss)
(Harpole)
JAMES ELLIS
(South Hadley, Mass., U.S.A.)
MARQUESS OF EXETER

REV. J. W. H. FAULKNER
(Bedford)
MR. and MRS. MICHAEL FIELD
(Hanging Houghton)
MRS. A. C. FINNIMORE
ARTHUR and ELLEN FISHER
(Girard, Ohio, U.S.A.)
THE EARL FITZWILLIAM
(Milton, Peterborough)
MARGARET FOOT (Mrs.)
(Pinner)
DEREK FORBES
(Hertford)
RICHARD FOULKES
(Nether Heyford)
WILFRED H. FOX
(Pattishall)
G. B. FREEMAN
(Horton)
SIR GEOFFREY DE FREITAS
K.C.M.G., M.P.
H. C. R. FROST

COUNC. JOHN JAMES GARDNER
and MRS. GARDNER
(Mayor and Mayoress of Northampton,
1975-6)
H. W. GEARY
(Kettering)
NORMAN E. GIBBS
(Harlestone)
MARGARET GLADYS GILBERT
L. J. GILES
CHRISTOPHER J. GLAZEBROOK
SIR GERALD GLOVER
(Pytchley)
F. J. GOODMAN
MADGE GOSLING
(Moulton)
JULIE GRAHAM
(Staverton)
DEREK GRAY
(Kettering)
HARRY GREATOREX
(Swanwick, Derbyshire)
D. M. GREEN
(Staverton)
LT.-COL. T. R. L. GREENHALGH
(Overstone)
PHILIP M. L. DE GROUCHY
(Southampton)
MR. and MRS. ROBIN GUINNESS
(Hardingstone)

PATRONS 209

BRIAN G. HALL
LIONEL HAMILTON
VINCENT S. HALTON
ALEX HANCOCK
SIR WILLIAM HART C.M.G.
(Turweston)
VICTOR A. HATLEY
ALFRED HAWTIN
ARTHUR HEATH
(Kettering)
IRIS HENSON
(Manchester)
LADY HESKETH
(Easton Neston)
LORD HESKETH
(Easton Neston)
P. M. HEYGATE (Mrs.)
(Litchborough)
PHILIP H. HIGHFILL Junior, Ph. D.
(Washington, U.S.A.)
BARRY HILLMAN
GEORGE HOARE
(Boughton)
MR. and MRS. J. HOCKENHULL
(Great Doddington)
NORMAN L. HODSON
(Desborough)
BRENDAN HUGHES
WINSTON HUGHES F.B.I.S.T. and
MRS. ELLEN HUGHES
MR. and MRS. S. G. H. HUMFREY

TONY IRESON
(Kettering)
SIR GYLES ISHAM, Bart.
(Lamport)

VERNON W. JACKSON
(Wellingborough)
MR. and MRS. A. JACKSON-STOPS
(Wood Burcote)
LOUIS JAMES
(Bridge, Kent)
ARTHUR JONES M.P.
(Pavenham, Beds)
PROFESSOR H. A. JONES
(Great Bowden)
MICHAEL JONES
LESLEY JOSEPH

GERALD KENDALL
(Scaldwell)
PAUL KERTI
(Kettering)
SYDNEY KILSBY
E. R. KNAPP
(Duston)
ELIZABETH L. KNIGHT
(Ecton)
JESSIE KNIGHT (Mrs.)
JOYCE and FRANK KNIGHT
(Portugal)

H. C. (BERT) LAWRENCE
MARGARET E. LEASK
(Lane Cove, Australia)

M. C. LEWIS (Miss)
(Moreton Pinkney)
SANDRA LEY
N. LINE
PROFESSOR W. B. LONG
(Bronx, New York, U.S.A.)

ANGUS MACKAY
(London)
DR. DONALD M. MACKAY
(London)
JOSEPH MACLEOD
(Perthshire)
CECIL MADDEN, M.B.E.
(Chelsea)
RAYMOND MANDER and JOE
MITCHENSON THEATRE
COLLECTION
(London)
PAUL MANN
(Sherington)
MONICA MARSON (Mrs.)
CYRIL MARSTON
(Milton Malsor)
A. C. MASON
(Deene Park)
MASAHIKO MASUMOTO
(Nagoya, Japan)
IAN MAYES
(Hardingstone)
RON MEARS
(Kettering)
DAVID O. MICHEL
(Milton Malsor)
W. E. MIDDLETON
M. MILLBURN, M.A., (Miss)
MR. and MRS. A. J. MINNEY
(Kettering)
W. ROWAN MITCHELL
(Brixworth)
DR. J. MOLONEY
J. A. J. MONRO
F. A. MOORE
(Kettering)
A. C. MUNKS (Mrs.)
(Rottingdean, Brighton)

HAROLD J. NASH
MARGARET V. NASH (Miss)
PETER NEWCOMBE
(Blisworth)
PROFESSOR ALLARDYCE NICOLL
(Colwall, Malvern)
FRANK NIGHTINGALE
KEN and JULIA NUTT

BRENDAN O'BRIEN
(Athlone, Ireland)
EVA ONLEY
(Wellingborough)

DR. B. W. PAINE
(Elmley Castle, Worc.)
W. E. PARKER
COUNCILLOR KENNETH R.
PEARSON M.B.E., A.E.

DR. ALICIA C. PERCIVAL
  (London)
A. DYAS PERKINS
A. E. PERKINS
W. E. PIGOTT
  (Eastbourne)
RAYMOND P. POOLE
J. A. H. PORCH
  (Maidwell)
DAVID POWELL
DAVID J. PRIOR
  (Thrapston)

GEORGE RALPH
  (Holland, Michigan, U.S.A.)
COUNCILLOR and MRS. JOHN
  RAWLINGS
  (Mayor and Mayoress of Northampton,
  1974-5)
JACK READING
  (London)
HYLDA REECE (Mrs.)
  (Grafton Regis)
JOHN RICHARDS
  (Cardiff)
K. H. RISDALE
JOHN ROAN
  (Wootton)
GRACE E. ROBERTS
OSBORNE ROBINSON, O.B.E.
MR. and MRS. REX ROBINSON
W. ROGERS
  (Nether Heyford)
SYBIL ROSENFELD
  (London)
P. E. L. ROUYER
  (Bordeaux, France)
MR. and MRS. J. E. ROWLATT
  (Wellingborough)

MOLLIE SANDS
  (London)
MARGARET SAULL (Miss)
  (Edgbaston)
C. B. SAVAGE
RICHARD SAVAGE
  (Western Australia)
PAUL SCOFIELD
  (Balcombe, Sussex)
ANN SHORE
  (Kettering)
SIR SACHEVERELL SITWELL, Bart.
  (Weston Hall, Towcester)
VIDA SLINN (Mrs. Eric Slinn)
MR. and MRS. JOHN F. SMITH
  (Towcester)
THE EARL SPENCER

HENRY G. SPOKES
  (Milton Malsor)
VICTORIA SQUIRES
  (Duston)
T. R. STAUGHTON
NINA STEANE
  (Kettering)
JOY STEWART
  (Moulton)
GRACE M. STURGIS (Mrs.)
  (Finedon)

D. NORMAN TAYLOR
WILFRID TEBBUTT
  (Kettering)
PHIL THOMAS
PROFESSOR PETER THOMSON
  (Exeter)
ANNE TIBBLE
  (Guilsborough)
ERIC TIMS
  (Wellingborough)
MEG TOYER (Miss)
VALERIE TRAVIS
BRIAN TRELIVING
KAY TREMBLAY
  (Flore)
FRED TUCKLEY

DR. F. F. WADDY
  (Great Brington)
SIR HEREWARD WAKE
  (Courteenhall)
PETER WAKE
  (Hambleton, Hunts)
DAVID A. WALMSLEY
OSWALD BARRETT WARD
PETER J. WARD
  (Enon, Ohio, U.S.A.)
GRETA WARWICK (Mrs.)
DR. JOHN WESTON, F.I.O.B.
MAURICE WHITING
  (Photography)
ETHEL WHITTINGHAM (Miss)
PETER A. WILCOX
HELEN WILKINSON
CARL WILLMOTT
  (Leeds)
LYNN WILSON
  (Holcot)
COUNCILLOR ROGER WINTER
PETER WOOD
  (Great Shelford, Cambs.)
JOSEPH E. WRIGHT
  (Nashville, Tennessee)

JOHN REGINALD YATES
  (Stourbridge)

LIBRARIES AND OTHER ORGANISATIONS

ABINGTON VALE MIDDLE SCHOOL, NORTHAMPTON
UNIVERSITY OF AUCKLAND, NEW ZEALAND
BEDFORDSHIRE COUNTY LIBRARY
BIRMINGHAM PUBLIC LIBRARIES
BRITISH LIBRARY, LENDING DIVISION (Boston Spa, Yorks)
BUCKS COUNTY LIBRARY
ROYAL LIBRARY OF COPENHAGEN
UNIVERSITY OF CHICAGO
CHRONICLE AND ECHO, NORTHAMPTON
DALHOUSIE UNIVERSITY LIBRARY (Halifax, Nova Scotia, Canada)
DERBYSHIRE COUNTY LIBRARY
UNIVERSITY OF DURHAM
EDINBURGH UNIVERSITY LIBRARY
UNIVERSITY OF ESSEX
MARC FITCH FUND
GARRICK CLUB (London)
GUILSBOROUGH GRANGE BIRD and PET PARK (Major and Mrs. Stuart Symington)
LANCASTER UNIVERSITY
LEICESTERSHIRE LIBRARIES
LINCOLNSHIRE LIBRARY SERVICE
THE LONDON LIBRARY
UNIVERSITY OF LONDON LIBRARY
UNIVERSITY LUND OF SWEDEN
UNIVERSITY OF LEICESTER
LEICESTER UNIVERSITY CENTRE, NORTHAMPTON
LIVERPOOL CITY LIBRARIES
MINNEAPOLIS PUBLIC LIBRARY
MUNSTER UNIVERSITY, WEST GERMANY
NENE COLLEGE, NORTHAMPTON
MERCURY AND HERALD, NORTHAMPTON
CITY OF NOTTINGHAM PUBLIC LIBRARY
READING UNIVERSITY
JOHN RYLANDS UNIVERSITY LIBRARY OF MANCHESTER
SAN DIEGO STATE UNIVERSITY, CALIFORNIA
SHAKESPEARE BIRTHPLACE TRUST (Stratford-upon-Avon)
SHAKESPEARE INSTITUTE, UNIVERSITY OF BIRMINGHAM
UNIVERSITY COLLEGE OF SWANSEA
MOTLEY BOOKS LTD. (Romsey, Hampshire)
NORTHAMPTON COLLEGE OF TECHNOLOGY (now part of Nene College)
NORTHAMPTON COLLEGE OF FURTHER EDUCATION
NORTHAMPTON SCHOOL FOR BOYS
NORTHAMPTON MERCURY COMPANY
NORTHAMPTONSHIRE LIBRARIES
NORTHAMPTONSHIRE RECORD SOCIETY
NORTHAMPTON AND COUNTY INDEPENDENT
NORTHAMPTON REPERTORY THEATRE
NORTHAMPTONSHIRE RECORD OFFICE
NORTHAMPTON THEATRE GUILD
UNIVERSITY OF NOTTINGHAM
PENNSYLVANIA STATE UNIVERSITIES LIBRARY
CORPS. H.O. ROYAL PIONEER CORPS (Simpson Barracks, Wootton)
OVERSTONE SCHOOL FOR GIRLS
SCOTT BADER COMMONWEALTH
UNIVERSITY OF ST. ANDREW'S, FIFE, SCOTLAND
ST. DAVID'S UNIVERSITY COLLEGE (Lampeter, Wales)
UNIVERSITY OF SHEFFIELD
SHEFFIELD CITY LIBRARIES
SMITH COLLEGE LIBRARY (Northampton, Massachusetts)
SOCIETY FOR THEATRE RESEARCH
SOUTHLANDS COLLEGE, WIMBLEDON
TRENT PARK COLLEGE OF EDUCATION
VICTORIA and ALBERT MUSEUM, LONDON
VICTORIA and ALBERT MUSEUM, LONDON (Theatre Section)
WESTMINSTER CITY LIBRARIES

PATRONS DECEASED

Patrons who have, to my knowledge, died since subscribing for this book are

THE EARL SPENCER

MR. S. H. G. HUMFREY

Patrons of Theatre Un-Royal who have died include Mrs. Dorothy S. Cook (Widow Turvey of radio's The Archers); Mrs. Sylvia Woodger; Mr. A. L. de Bruyne, of Edinburgh; Mr. M. Belgion, of Titchmarsh; Mr. C. T. Groom, of Overstone; Mr. H. L. Cheney, of Wellingborough; and Mr. W. J. A. Peck, of Rushden.

NEXT PRODUCTION

(AND POSITIVELY FINAL AND FAREWELL APPEARANCE)

For our next production and positively final and farewell appearance we shall present The Mackenzies Called Compton, incorporating the History of Northampton Theatre Royal and Opera House, 1884–1927. It will represent the first attempt to set down in its entirety the story of the Compton Comedy Company, the longest touring company in theatrical history. Just as Drama That Smelled covers the period (pre-1806) BEFORE that of Theatre Un-Royal (1806–1884) so the future book will carry on AFTER that period, from 1884 to 1927.

This time the venture does not have to start from scratch because a number of people have already subscribed or ordered copies—252 in fact. However, with costs rising as they have been and as they will continue to do—even if only the Governmental 10 per cent—this figure will be far from adequate; the estimate is that 500 will be required and this is the target. The subscription is again £5 but in view of the incredible rise in postal costs, for copies to be sent outside Northampton, the sum of 50p must be added for postage.

Subscriptions are earnestly sought, before costs escalate out of reach altogether. Names of all Patrons will again be listed. Send your £5 (plus 50p if outside Northampton) to Lou Warwick, 54 St. George's Avenue, Northampton. The money will be kept in a Trust Account and not spent pro tem on preliminary expenses. It will therefore be available for return in the event of the collapse of the venture or of the author.

Quite apart from the unthinkable possibility of failing to reach this target, L.W. recognises that he is mortal and just in case the book does not appear appends a synopsis of it :

You may have wondered why the sister of the late Compton Mackenzie, the novelist, is named Fay Compton. Well in fact the real name of the actress was Fay Mackenzie. Charles Mackenzie, their grandfather, took the alternative name (as Henry Compton) when he decided to go on the stage, so as not to shame his family, the profession of acting being well down the social scale in those days (in fact it "smelled"!)

The father of Fay Compton and her literary brother, Compton Mackenzie, was Edward Compton whose company was the first to appear at Northampton Theatre Royal and Opera House when it opened in May, 1884. On the opening night of the first Shakespeare Memorial Theatre at Stratford upon Avon, April 23, 1879, Edward Compton was Claudio in "Much Ado About Nothing". In 1881, soon after its inauguration, the Compton Comedy Company itself provided the 13 play repertory at the Stratford Festival and was again there in 1882.

The Compton Comedy Company had been founded with money left to Edward by his intended bride, the actress Adelaide Neilson, she having dropped dead during a trip to Paris to choose her trousseau. She would have been marrying for the second time, her first husband having been the son of a Northamptonshire clergyman. Had the bride-to-be lived, Fay Compton and Compton Mackenzie would never had been born, for they were the children of the subsequent marriage

14—TDTS * *

of Edward Compton to American-born Virginia Bateman, who was his leading lady on the opening night at Northampton in 1884, with the young Compton Mackenzie probably asleep in the dressing room, in his cradle.

Travelling all over England, Scotland and in many places in Wales and Ireland, the Compton Comedy Company was to have a remarkably long life. Started by Compton in 1881 at Southport it carried on even past his death in 1918, to become a repertory company in Nottingham from 1920–3, a venture which collapsed, after which it resumed touring before fading away.

For many years Edward Compton was joint owner of the Northampton Theatre with Milton Bode, a remarkable character operating from Reading who was soft-hearted enough in one respect as to be a pigeon fancier and have a bird bath in his Monte Carlo garden but hard-headed enough in business as to hold out for 23 weeks in 1909, when the Northampton pit orchestra went on strike for union rates of pay—and even then to refuse them recognition. Bode, who was born in Birmingham, operated theatres at various times in Leicester, Chester, Dalston, Huddersfield, Wolverhampton, Carlisle and Leamington, as well as at his home and base at Reading.

Apart from some mentions in Compton Mackenzie's Memoirs, no book has yet covered the fascinating life-in-a-suitcase existence of Edward Compton and his eternally touring company. So this book will be more than a local theatre book. But locally it will embrace the early years of Northampton Amateur Operatic Company, which was cradled at the theatre. Like the author's recent books, Theatre Un-Royal, and Drama That Smelled, it will also take in a good deal of local history and matters of general interest, so as to set the theatrical happenings meaningfully against the background of what else was going on in the 43 years covered.

The book will stop at 1927 because that is when the stage of the theatre was taken over by Northampton Repertory Company, who are still going strong there today. The Repertory years from 1927–48 are covered in Aubrey Dyas's coming-of-age volume, "Adventure in Repertory".

Patron-in-Chief: Professor Allardyce Nicoll.

Index

Abbey, Robert, 182, 189, 192
Aberdare, Lord, 136
Abingdon, 155
Abington, 81
Abington Abbey, 26, 81-4
Abington Church, 26, 78
Abington Park Museum, 82
Abington Street, 34, 40-1, 45-6, 61, 122, 149, 191
Accidents, 49, 154, 166
Adams, Mrs., 144, 149
Adamson, Mr., 193
Adcock, 162
Advertising, 50
Agnew, Mr., 37
Aiken, Mr., 183
Ailesbury, Marquess of, 136, 138
Aldwych Theatre, 134
Ale, 36
Alexander, George, 133
Alford, 154
All Saints Church, 83, 94-5, 105, 149
Althorp, 15-21, 24, 26-7, 29, 80, 84, 127
Althorp Hunt, 81
Althorp, Lord, 81
Ancaster, Dowager Duchess of, 146
Andrew, Sir Eusebius, 20
Angel Hotel, 54-5
Anglesey, Marquess of, 136
Anne of Denmark, 16-25, 29, 89
Armistead, Mr., 119
Armytage, Mrs. 192
Arnold, J., 93
Arts Council, 167
Arts Theatre Club, 43
Ascot, 154
Ashfield, Mr., 68
Askew, Mr., 182
Astleys and Hughes Riding School, 177
Aston, Tony, 111
Aufrere, Pearl, 121
Aylesbury, 89

Baines, Cecil Hamilton, 128
Baker, Mr., 150
Balaams Coffee House, 177
Baldock, 187
Baltimore, 126
Banbury, 38, 154
Bankruptcy, 120, 128, 138
Bannister, Mr., 116, 119
Bannister (Davis & Bannister), 191
Barker, Kathleen, 127-8

Barnard, see Bernard
Barns, 49
Barrett, Mr., 149
Barry, J., 97
Barton, 46
Bath, 21, 33, 37, 53, 55, 76, 90, 99, 112, 117, 123, 127, 145
Bath Company, 200
Bath & Bristol Company, 73
Bath, Marquess of, 136
Baynes, Adam, 24
Beatrice, Madamoiselle, 97
Becke, C. C., 201
Becket, Thomas à, 122
Bedford, 115, 122, 155, 163
Bedford, Duchess of, 191
Bedford, Duke of, 92, 155, 191
Bedford, Rev. Arthur, 92
Bedfordshire Militia, 60
Bell Inn, 122
Belzoni, Signor, 194
Benefits, 54
Benson, Frank, 39, 97
Benson, Mr., 54
Berkhamstead, 36
Berkshire, 158
Bernard, Lady Elizabeth, 78, 82-3
Bernard, Sir John, 78, 82-3
Berridge, Rachelle Estelle, 136
Berrill, H., 98
Berriman, Mr., 36
Berwick, 17
Bethnal Green, 94
Beynon's Company, 177-183
Beynon, Mr., 93, 170, 177
Beynon, Mrs., 170
Beynon, Theophilus, 180
Billingham, Mr., 192
Bilton, Belle, 136
Bingham, 153
Birmingham, 46, 102-3, 119
Black, Mr., 178
Black Boy Inn, 171
Black Lion Inn, 54, 149
Blackwell, Richard, 61
Blanchard, Lomas, 55
Blanchard, Mr., 55, 58-60
Blanchard, Mrs., 55, 58, 60
Blandford, 160
Bloom, Claire, 169
Bode Milton, 133
Booth, Mr., 120

Booth, Miss, 93
Boston, 154, 187, 193
Boughton Green, 91, 113, 191
Bourchier, Arthur, 121
Bourne, 181
Bouverie, Mr., 81
Bouverie, Mrs., 191–2
Bradlaugh, Charles, 63
Brecknock, 145
Brecon, 146
Brentford, 44
Brett, Hon., Maurice, 136
Bridge Street, 39, 103
Bridges, Mr., 60
Brigg, 46
Brighton, 77, 138
Bristol, 37, 73, 92, 100, 103, 107, 112, 117,
     120, 123
Bristow, Mr., 93, 170, 178–9
Brixton, 138
Brixworth, 67–9, 148
Brooke, Gustavus Vaughan, 137
Brown, Master, 193
Brown, Mr., 144, 148, 190, 193, 198
Brown, Mrs., 193
Brown, Pamela, 169
Bruce, Baron, 138
Bruce, Earl, 138
Bruce, Hon. Lyndhurst, 136
Brudenell, Baron, 138
Brunton, Mrs., 191, 193
Buck, Mr., 179
Buckhill, Mr. Justice, 135
Buckingham, 39, 155
Bull, Peter, 169
Bullen, Miss, 190
Bunn, J. C., 127
Burghley House, 17, 20, 164
Burton, Lord, 136
Burton, Richard, 169
Buszard, Dr., 97
Buxton, 155
Byron, H. J., 168
Byron, Miss, 172

Cairns, Earl, 135
Caistor, 46
Cambridge, 35, 47, 146, 163
Cambridge, Duke of, 136
Camden, Lord, 84
Campbell, Mrs., 177
Campion, S. S., 43, 97
Candles, 15, 36, 90
Canning, George, 119
Canterbury, Archbishop of, 97, 122
Cardiff, 34, 98
Cardigan, 36
Cardigan, Earl of, 132, 138

Cardigan, Countess of, 132
Carleton's Company, 74–7, 120
Carleton, J., 74–7, 120
Carleton, Mrs., 75, 77, 178
Carlile, Miss, 193
Carlino, Signior, 165
Carrighan, Andrew Joseph Gosli, 166
Carrington, Eva, 136
Castilian Street, 66
Castle, Northampton, 122
Castle Ashby, 134, 136
Castle and Falcon, 154
Catholic Amateur Minstrels, 98
Cathcart, Lord and Lady, 172
Cavendish, Lord Richard, 81
Cecil Hotel, 136
Chamberlain, Mr., 150, 170
Chambers, Mr., 147, 149
Chapman, Miss, 190
Charles I, 24, 29, 58, 105
Charles II, 33, 36, 71, 94–5, 107, 121
Cheltenham, 77, 119, 147, 158, 183
Chequer Inn, 49
Chester, 117
Chevalier, Albert, 99
Chichester, 90
Childs, Mr., 179
Chippendale, 155
Cholmly, Miss, 193
Christian IV, 16
Christy Minstrels, 93
Church Lane, 171
Churston, Lady, 137
Churston, Lord, 136
Cibber, Colley, 66
Cibber, Mrs., 58
Cibber, Theophilus, 115, 169
Cirencester, 183
Circus, 113
Clarendon, Mr., 57, 60
Clarges, Sir Thomas, 81
Clarke, Mr. and Mrs., 191, 198
Clavering, Mrs., 57
Clavering, Robert, 63
Cleveland, Duchess of, 121
Clifford, Lord de, 137
Clifford, Camille, 137
Clinton, Lord Thomas, 81
Cloncarty, Lord, 136
Clonmell, Earl of, 136
Clopton, Sir Hugh, 81
Coffee House, 177
Coffee Room, 150
Colchester, 119
Cole, John, 192
College St. Church, 97
Collier, Jeremy, 92
Collins, Mr., 112, 159

Colman, George, 44, 117
Colpi, Signior, 165
Combe Abbey, 17
Community of St. Mary the Virgin, Wantage, 100, 175
Compton Comedy Company, 55, 133
Compton, Earl, 134
Compton, Edward, 55, 104, 133
Compton, Mrs. Edward, 100
Compton, Henry, 133, 155, 174
Compton, Hon. Spencer, 57
Compton, Susannah, 133
Compton, William Bingham, 135
Compton, Wynyates, 134
Conway, 199
Cooke, George Frederick, 44, 154
Cooke, Mr., 162
Cooke, Mrs., 166
Cooper, Henry, 97
Copen, Mr. and Mrs., 37
Cork, 114, 125
Corn Exchange, 99
Coronation, 55, 148
County Gaol, 113, 121–2, 124, 126, 150
County Hall, 122
Court Theatre, London, 100
Courtneidge, Robert, 39
Covent Garden, 55, 67, 72, 91, 117, 119, 148, 166
Coventry, 46, 92, 122, 143, 146, 150, 177, 183
Cowey, Earl of, 121
Coysh, Mr., 34–5, 118
Craneson, Mr. and Mrs., 177
Cransley, 168
Craven, Mr., 156, 157, 159
Craven, Mrs., 156–7, 159
Cromwell, Oliver, 29
Cromwell, Sir Oliver, 20
Cross, Mr., 172
Crownhill, 136
Crow and Horseshoe Lane, 192
Cullen, Cardinal, 99
Cullen, Lady, 167–8
Cullen, Lord, 168
Cumberland, Mr., 150
Cumberland, Duke of, 46
Cumberland, Earl of, 20
Cunningham, Mr., 59
Curtis, Mr., 156–7, 159, 178
Curtis, Mrs., 159–60, 178
Curzon, Hon. Frederick, 136

Daly, Mr., 125
Dangan, Viscount, 121
Daniels, Samuel, 21
Dare, Zena, 137
Davenant, 24, 70

Daventry, 66, 120, 178, 183, 191
Davies, Mr., 112, 178
Davis, Master, 191
Davis & Bannister, 191
Davis, Mr., 150
Davis, Mrs., 150
Deacon, Mr., 61
Deane, Barbara, 134
Deene Park, 132
Delapre Abbey, 62
Denmark House, 24
Derby, 34, 46, 60, 66, 74, 103, 122, 163
Devizes, 160
Devonshire, Duke of, 84
Dicey, William, 35
Dickinson, Major, 57
Didier, Mr., 54
Dimond, William, 127
Dimond, William Wyatt, 127
Dingley Hall, 17
Dixey, Phyllis, 133
Dogs, Dancing, 171
Dog, Learned, 177
Dolben, William, 192
Don, Sir William, 120–1
Don, Lady Emily, 120–1
Donelly, Francis, 137
Dongworth's, Mr., 169
Donnell, Mr., 144, 148
Donnell, Mrs., 144, 148, 166
Donnelly, Christopher, 113
Dorchester, 160
Dormer, Mr., 156–7, 159
Dormer, Mrs., 156
Dorset Gardens, 36
Douai, 146
Drapery, The, 124
Dreadful Fire, 39, 43
Drewry, Patrick, 92, 99
Drink, The, 39, 59, 101–4, 154
Drogheda, Countess of, 121
Drucker, Adolphus, 63
Drury Lane, 35–6, 40, 45, 58–9, 66–7, 71–2, 76, 80–1, 84, 99, 113, 117, 119, 123, 130–1, 145, 178–9, 187, 190, 192, 199
Dryden, John, 33, 36, 70, 174, 200
Dryden, John (not dramatist), 39
Ducrow, Mr., 191
Dublin, 76, 99, 125, 163, 188
Dunn, Mr., 172
Dunn, Mrs., 168
Dunstable, 84
Duppa, Brian, 29
Durravan, James, 73
Durravan, J., 55, 57, 73
Durravan, M., 55, 73
Durravan, Mr., 55, 60
Durravan, Mrs., 55

Durravans' Company of Comedians, 49, 53–74, 143
Dyer, Mr., 180, 182
Dyer, Mrs., 180–1

Easton Neston, 20
Edinburgh, 15–16, 76, 171–2
Edwards, Master, 165
Effeminacy, 129
Eldred, Mr., 37
Elizabeth, Queen, 16–17, 21
Elizabeth, Princess, 16–17
Elliott, Mr. and Mrs., 190, 198
Elliston, 126
Elrington, 112
Elrington, Joe, 163
Ely, 83
Empire Palace of Varieties, 103
Equity, 155
Esher, Lord, 136
Euston, Countess of, 137
Euston, Earl of, 137–8
Evans, Mr., 146
Everard, E. C., 154, 195
Everard, Mr., 168
Exeter, 37
Exeter, Lord, 80, 177
Exeter, Marquis of, 164–5, 167

Farebrother, Louisa, 136
Fareham, 43
Fellowes, Alderman, 112
Fencible Dragoons, 182
Ferguson, Mr. and Mrs., 172
Fermor, Richard, 20
Fielding, Sir John, 117
Filden, Mrs., 150
Finedon Volunteers, 192
Fire of Northampton, 122
Fish Street, 123
Fitzherbert, Mrs., 116
Fitzroy, Hon. Henry James, 137
Fleetwood, Mr., 80, 177
Flynn, Errol, 128
Foote, Maria, 133
Foote, Samuel, 115
Fortescue, Miss, 135
Fotheringay, 16
Fothergill, Mr. and Mrs., 179
Fowler, Ann (Mrs. Robertson), 187
Franklin, James Campbell 201
Franklin, J., 191
Franklin, Robert Henry, 187–91, 198
Franklins Gardens, 98
Fraser, James, 93
Fraser, Mr., 119
Fraser, Lady Antonia, 17
French, Sir Frederick, 90

Froggatt, Mr., 54–5
Furguson, Mr., 156–7, 159

Gaiety Theatre, 103, 121, 136–7, 200
Galot, Mr., 179
Gamble, Mr., 149
Garmoyle, Viscount, 135
Garrick, David, 67, 72, 79–84, 90, 117, 123
Garwood, Mr., 93
Gas, 91
Gasquoine, Rev. T., 97
Gastrell, Rev. Francis, 81
Gates, Mr., 123
Gautrey, Rev. R. Moffatt, 98
Gay, John, 110
George II, 67, 79
George III, 55, 59
George IV, 59
George Inn, Huntingdon, 195
George Inn, Kettering, 167
George Inn, Northampton, 39, 47, 54–5, 171
George Inn, Stamford, 154
George Row, 123
Gibraltar, 160
Gielgud, John, 169
Giffard, 115
Gifford, Mr., 17, 19
Glasgow, 177
Glassington, Miss, 162
Glocester, Mr., 150
Glocester, Mrs., 69, 72
Gloucester, 183
Glover, Frederick, 114
Glover, Jimmy, 99
Gobion, Henry, 43
Gobion, Hugh, 43
Gobion, Richard, 43
Gobions, 42
Godwin, Mrs., 58, 60
Goodhall's Company, 165
Goodman's Field Theatre, 115
Gosberton, 46
Gosli, Mr., 166, 168, 172
Gosli, Mrs. (nee Whitley), 168, 172
Gough, Sgt. Major, 182
Grafton, Duke of, 37, 46, 79–80, 115, 137–8, 171
Grafton House, 20, 24
Grafton Hunt, 80
Grafton Regis, 80
Granby, Marquis of, 60
Grantham, 60, 153, 165, 187, 193
Grantham Loyal Volunteers, 193
Grayson, Larry, 168
Greatheed, Lady Mary, 146
Greatorex, Harry, 55
Greenhough, Thomas, 54, 123–4

Gregory, James, 102
Guildhall Road, 123, 201
Gunning, Sir Robert, 150
Guys Cliffe, 146

Halifax, 201
Halifax, Earl of, 63
Hall, Dr., 82
Hall, John, 126
Hall, Mr., 110
Hall, Susannah (nee Shakespeare), 82
Halliwell, James Orchard, 82
Hamilton, Lady, 55
Hamilton, Sir William, 81
Hampton on Thames, 80, 84
Hanbury, Ann, 83
Hanbury, Mr. William, 81, 149
Harlestone, 84
Harpole Hall, 41
Harrington, Countess of, 133
Harvey, John (John Harvey Thursby), 83
Haselwood, Sir Nicholas, 20
Haselwood, Sir William, 68, 122
Hasely, Dorothy (Dolly Tester), 138
Hatton, Major Edward Finch, 134
Hatton, Sir Christopher, 17
Haymarket, 44, 113, 150, 171–2, 179–80, 192
Haynes, Mr., 37
Headfort, Marquess of, 136
Headfort, Marchioness of, 137
Heaton, Virginia Lucie, 136
Heaton, Captain David Remington, 136
Helmsley, 106
Henley, Mr., 198
Henlowe's Company, 127
Henrietta, Maria, 24, 105
Henry, Prince, 16, 20
Herbert's Company, 34, 60, 166, 187
Herbert, Dennis, 127, 187
Herbert, Nathaniel, 166, 187
Herbert and Whitley's Company, 166
Hereford, 79
Herman, Mr., 171
Hertford, Marquess of, 121
Hickman, Mr., 54–5
Hicks, Seymour, 134
Hillyard, Mr., 63
Hinchinbroke Castle, 47
Hinchinbrook Priory, 20
Hind Inn, 36–8
Hitchcock, Mr., 156
Hitchener, Mr., 193
Hobart Town, 121
Hogarth, 44
Holdenby, 17, 24, 29, 81
Holland, Mr., 195
Hollingshead, John, 103, 200

Holmes, Mr., 156
Holy Sepulchre Church, 94, 171
Holy Week, 99
Holywell House, 80
Horncastle, 46
Hornsby, Mr., 37
Horse Guards, 61, 191
Horse, Learned, 177
Horseshoe Street, 100, 192
Horsey, Miss de, 132
Horton, 39
Houghton, Lord, 132
Howard, John, 122–3
Howe, Lord, 136
Howell, Mr. and Mrs., 37
Howes, Mr., 82
Hudson, Mr., 156
Hudson, Mrs., 90
Hughes, Mr., 123
Hull, 93, 117, 188, 201
Hull, Canon R. B., 94–7
Hull, Rev. John, 94
Hume, Mr., 178, 183
Huntingdon, 47, 155, 187–8, 195
Huntingdonshire, 158
Hussey, Rebecca, 126
Hussey, Mr., 117

Ingall, Mr., 178
Inverness, 96
Irving, Henry (Sir), 104, 120, 132–3
Isham, Lt. Charles, 182
Isham, Sir Euseby, 29
Isham, Sir Gyles, 29
Isham, John, 29, 68
Isham, Justinian, 29, 68
Isham, Thomas, 29, 68
Isle of Wight, 130, 160
Isteds, Mrs., 57
Italy, 80

Jackman Company, 39, 143
Jackman, Isaac, 81, 130–1
Jackman and Morgan Company, 59
Jackson's Company, 43, 67
Jackson, James, 94
Jackson, William Francis, 128
James, Mr., 172, 177
James II, 36, 121
James VI (James I), 16–24, 89
Jefferson, Thomas, 29
Jefferys, Ellis, 136
Jersey, 160
Johnson, Mr., 150
Johnson, Samuel, 79, 116
Jones, Charles, 44–5
Jones Company, 41, 44

Jones Royal Circus Company of Equestrians, 191
Jonson, Ben, 17, 21, 127
Jordan, Mrs., 130

Kane, Mr., 166
Karno, Fred, 123, 154
Kean, Edmund, 91, 130
Keating, Dr., 98
Kelly, Michael, 199
Kelmarsh, 81, 149
Kemble Company, 59, 124, 167, 174
Kemble, Anne, 144, 147
Kemble, Elizabeth, 144-5, 150
Kemble, Fanny, 71
Kemble, Frances, 144-5
Kemble, Henry, 144
Kemble, John Philip, 93, 119, 121, 144-6
Kemble, Mrs., 144-5, 148-50
Kemble, Roger, 125, 143-50
Kemble, Sarah (Siddons), 144, 146-7
Kemble, Stephen, 144-5, 150
Kendal, Dame Madge, 61, 155
Kendall, Mrs., 190
Kennedy, Mr., 120
Kent, 33
Kerr, Major John, 182
Kerr, William, 84
Kettering, 46, 68, 98, 167-8
Kew, 46
Kilsby, 24
King, Mr., 90
King, Mr., 177
Kings Lynn, 188
King's Men, 21, 105
Knapp, Rev., 172
Knight, Mrs. Jessie, 41, 43
Knightley, Sir Valentine, 20

Lacy, James, 80
Lacy, Mr., 55, 191
Lacy, Mr., bookseller, 172
Lamport, 29, 68
Lancaster, 120
Lavoisier, 90
Lawrence, Joseph, 193
Ledwith, Mr., 144, 148
Lee, Henry, 47, 73, 89, 90, 116-17, 153, 160
Lee, Richard, 43
Leeds, 24, 163
Leicester, 17, 55-6, 73-4, 83, 103, 122, 143, 155, 183
Leigh, Lord, 37
Leighton Buzzard, 69
Leister, Mr., 168
Lennox, Lord Wm. Pitt, 90
Lent, 99
Leominster, 144, 146

Lewes, Charles Lee, 146, 154
Lewis, Matthew Gregory, 199
Leyton, Mr., 66
Lichfield, 60, 74, 79, 93, 143
Light, Mr. and Mrs., 166
Limerick, 125, 188
Lincoln, 122, 127, 162, 187, 195, 198
Lincoln Company, 61, 143, 154, 166, 187-201
Litchfield, Rev. F., 126
Little Billing, 39, 83
Liverpool, 103, 117, 119, 179
Loder, Lt. Basil, 134
Loder, Sir Robert, 134
London, 15-16, 67, 79, 92-3, 97, 117, 154, 179, 191
London, Bishop of, 94
London County Council, 94
London, Great Fire, 43
London, Guildhall, 46
London, S.S., 137
Longueville, George, 39
Lord Chamberlain, 45, 79, 115
Loughborough, 187
Lucan, Lady, 126
Lucas, Dr., 91
Ludlow, 61, 187
Lyceum, 120
Lymington, 160

MacCabe, Cardinal, 99
Mackenzie, Henry (Compton), 133
Macklin, Charles, 81
Macnaghten, Frank, 103
Macqueen Pope, W., 200
Macready, William Charles, 88, 119
MacTavish, J., 96
Maddocks, Mr. and Mrs., 162, 166
Maidstone, 90
Maidwell Hall, 134
Makeham, Eliot, 169
Malmesbury, 36
Malvern, 176
Manchester, 112, 117, 120, 134, 154, 163-5
Manchester, Bishop of, 93
Manchester, Princes Theatre, 93
Manchester, Theatre Royal, 93
Manly, Mr., 167, 195
Mapples, Mr., 172
March, Earl of, 80
Mardlin, F. H., 103
Marefair, 192
Margate, 77
Market Harborough, 50
Market Hill, 55, 60, 113, 149
Market Place, 55
Market Square, 39, 55, 113
Markham, Daisy, 135-6

Marks, Mr., 170
Marriott, Mr., 156–7, 159, 172
Martin, Betty, 112
Mary, Queen, 36
Mary, Queen of Scots, 16–17
Mason, Mr. and Mrs., 172, 177, 191
Masterman, Mr. and Mrs., 150
Mathews, Charles, 93, 119–20
Mathews, Mrs., 93
Matthews Brothers Christy Minstrels, 93
Maunsell, Col., 167
Maxwell, Mr., 170
May, Olive, 137
M'Cready, 119
McGibbon, Mr., 154
Mears Ashby, 56
Melton Mowbray, 49
Merrick, Mr., 192
Methodism, 61, 112
Metropolitan Tabernacle, 94
Mexborough, Lord, 115
Miller, Mr., 188
Missiles, 195–6
Monk, Mrs., 166
Montague, Captain, 47
Montague, Emmeline, 133
Montague, Lord, 122
Montague, Sir Charles, 20
Moore, Mr., 68, 166
Moot Hall, 66, 120
Morgan, Frederick, 59
Morgan, Mrs. (nee Jackman), 59
Morris, Mr., 144
Moss, Harold, 135
Mossop, Mr., 127
Mucklow, Mrs., 178
Mudie's Company, 154
Music, 36, 55, 59, 66, 116, 149, 178–9, 182–3, 190

Nag's Head, Stamford, 165
Napleton, Rev. John, 100
Naseby, 24
Nash, Elizabeth (nee Hall), 82
Nash, Thomas, 82
Nashe, Thomas, 127
Nason, Capt. and Mrs., 170
Nells, Miss V. E., 171
Nepecker, Mr., 58, 60
Neville, Mr., 193
Newark, 163, 166, 187–8, 195–6
Newark Loyal Volunteer Infantry, 195
Newcastle, 114, 117, 145
Newcastle, Duchess of, 195
Newcastle, Duke of, 136
Newgate Prison, 123
Newport, Mr., 172
Newport, Isle of Wight, 160

Newport Pagnell, 68, 80, 155, 158
Newsome, S. H., 129
New Theatre, 104, 129, 133, 169, 174
Newtondon, 120
New York, 63, 121
Nicoll, Allardyce, 176
Nicholson, Nora, 169
Noel, Lady Mary, 165
Nollekens, Joseph, 80
Northampton Amateur Dramatic Club, 131–2
Northampton Association for Prosecution of Felons, 81
Northampton Club, 122
Northampton, Earl of, 53, 63, 66
Northampton Hunt, 150
Northampton Lunatic Asylum, 123
Northampton, Marquess of, 134–8
Northampton Public Library, 62, 158
Northampton Repertory Company, 128
Northampton, Roman Catholic Bishop of, 98
Northampton Theatre Guild, 28, 111
Northampton Town Council, 97
Northampton Volunteer Infantry, 192
Northampton Wesley Guilds, 98
Northamptonshire Philharmonic Society, 34
Northamptonshire Record Office, 62
Norris, Mrs., 170
Norris, Miss, 170, 178
Norwich, 33, 35, 37, 117, 119, 172, 179
Norwich Company, 188
Nottingham, 17, 34, 46, 76–7, 98, 112, 120–1, 123, 153, 163, 166, 178
Nottingham and Derby Company, 76, 143, 172, 177, 187, 195
Nottingham Derby and Stamford Company, 168, 172

Oakham, 34
O'Bryan (O'Brien) John Anderson, 166–9, 171, 177
O'Bryan (O'Brien) Mrs., 166–7, 177
Old White Horse, 183
Orkney, Countess of, 137
Orme, Denise, 136
Ormerod House, 83
Osborne, Mrs., 144
Ossory, Lord, 84
Oundle, 46–7, 68–9
Overstone, 83
Overstone, Lord, 83
Oxford, 122, 146, 154

Paganini, 119
Paget, Lord Victor, 136
Palace of Varieties, 103
Palestine, 84

Palmer, John, 113, 179–81
Palmer, Mrs., 55
Palmerston, Lord, 84
Parbery, Mr., 191
Paris, 127, 171
Parr, Sir William, 39
Pasham, Mrs., 55
Pasham, Mrs. Boarding School, 69
Pattishall, 91
Paulet, Mr. and Mrs., 177
Peacock Hotel, 39, 47, 54–5, 74
Peacock, Thomas, 199
Peel, Lady Delia, 27
Penn, Mr., 120
Peover, Mr., 156–7, 159
Peover, Mrs., 159
Pepys, 70
Percy, Esme, 169
Perthshire, 187
Pero, Mr., 169, 177, 188
Pero, Mrs., 73
Pero, William, 172
Peterborough, 39, 166, 187–8, 191, 194–5
Peterborough, Bishop of, 98
Peterborough Volunteer Cavalry, 195
Peters, Mr., 168, 177
Philadelphia, 126
Phillips, Mr., 150
Phipps, C. J., 103
Phipps, Mr., 36
Phipps, Pickering, 98
Pickering, Sir Gilbert, 40
Pittsburgh, 126
Play House, 62–4, 66
Plough Variety Hall, 103
Poitier, Miss, 67
Pollard, Rev. F. W., 98
Pope Pius, 99
Portsmouth, 103
Potterspury, 46, 80
Poulett, Countess, 137
Poulett, Earl, 136
Poulton-le-Fylde, 94
Powell, Miss, 150
Powell, Mr., 46
Power, Jacobella, 37
Powers Company, 37, 92, 107–8, 171
Preston, 44–5, 120
Price, Edward, 38
Prince of Wales, 45–6, 58, 60, 92
Prince of Wales Musichall, 100
Prynne, William, 105
Puffing, 154
Punch and Judy, 68
Pussell, Mr., 182
Pytchley Arms, 43
Pytchley Hall, 29
Pytchley Hunt, 81

Queensberry, Marquess of, 80
Queens Road Chapel, 98
Quelch, Mr., 47
Quelch, Mrs., 54–5
Quist, Captain, 182

Racecourse, 61
Races, 96–7
Rackham, Mr., 198
Radnor, Lord, 117
Raikes, Robert, 35
Rate Book, 62
Rawling, Mr., 178
Raymond, Francis, 127, 200
Raymond, Mrs., 127
Raymond, Patrick, 114
Rayner, Widow, 45
Raynsford, Mrs., 69, 148
Raynsford, Mr., 81
Rea, John, 74
Read, Mr., 170
Read, Mrs., 162, 166
Red Lion Inn, 39, 40, 47, 54–5
Reeves, Harvey, 104
Reformatory, 126
Retford, 172
Richard, Prince, 46
Richards, Mr., 183
Richardson, Mr., 168, 170, 178
Richardson, Mrs., 168, 170
Richmond, 38, 106
Richmond Hill, 115
Richmond-Watson, Mr. and Mrs. R. N., 80
Riding House, 41–4, 90–1
Riding School, 61–2, 123, 177, 191
Riding School Yard, 54, 63
Riding, The, 61–2
Riding Yard, 61
Rippingale, 46
Robert Bros., Circus, 169
Roberts, Mr., 179
Robertson, Mr., 61, 166, 177
Robertson, Miss, 195
Robertson, George, 187
Robertson, James, 187–8
Robertson, James Shaftoe, 61, 166, 187
Robertson, Thomas Shaftoe, 187–197
Robertson, T. W., 61, 131, 134–5, 168
Robertson, William, 155
Robinson, Lady, 167–8
Robinson, John, 167
Robinson, Sir George, 168
Robinson, Mr. and Mrs., 168
Romilly, Lt.-Col. F. W., 134
Rose and Crown Inn, 102
Rosenfeld, Sybil, 33–5, 127
Ross, Frances, 188
Rous, Lady, 55

Rous, Mr. and Mrs., 37
Rowles, Mr., 195
Roxburghe Club, 79
Royal Cheshire Militia, 57
Royal Academy of Dramatic Art, 92
Royal Scots Guards, 134
Royalty Theatre, 113, 180
Rugg, Mr., 165
Russell, Lord Charles, 191
Russia, 99
Rutley, Mr., 190
Ryde, 130
Ryley, S. W., 114

Sadler's Wells, 74, 171
Salford, 41
Salisbury, 73, 107, 112, 160
Salisbury, Roger, 39
Salvation Army, 101
Samwell, Sir Thomas, 66
Saracen's Head, 46, 54
Saunders, Mr., 68, 149, 170–1
Saunders, Emily (Lady Don), 120
Savernake, 138
Scaliogni, Signior, 171
Scarborough, 46
Schmidt, Mr., 182
Scofield, John, 61–3, 123–4
Scott, Captain, 61
Scott, Clement, 131
Seabrook, Mr., 68
Sedgerley Park School, 146
Senlis, Simon de, 171
Services in theatres, 100–1
Shakespeare, William, 21, 69–71, 78, 81–2,
    84, 105, 116
Shakespeare Hotel, 66
Shakespeare Inn, 103, 192
Shakespeare, Susannah, 82
Sharing system, 158
Sharples, Mr. and Mrs., 193
Shatford, James, 73, 153–60
Shatford, Mrs., 90, 153–60
Sheaf Bowling Green, 178
Sheep Street, 40
Sheffield, 172
Sheridan, 81, 119, 200
Shuckburgh, Lt. Basil, 84
Shuckburgh, Lady, 84, 178
Shuckburgh, Sir George, 178
Siddons, Henry, 147
Siddons, Mrs. Sarah (nee Kemble), 84, 93,
    125, 144–7, 154, 163
Siddons, William, 145–6
Sidmouth, Lord, 119
Sidney, Mr., 144, 149, 177
Sidney, Mrs., 144, 149
Simpson, Robert, 128

Sinnet, Mr., 170
Sisson, Mrs., 177–8
Skitt, Mr., 178
Smells, 89–91
Smith, George Manby, 137
Smith, Mr., 144, 148–50, 170, 178, 183
Smith, Mrs., 144, 178
Smith, Miss, 170, 178
Smith, Master, 144, 149
Smith, Dr. Richard, 36
Smith and Phipps, 183
Smock Alley Theatre, 163
Snagg, Thomas, 114
Society for Suppression of Races, 96
Society for Theatre Research, 54
Somerset House, 24
Southampton, 103
Southgate, Mr., 150, 168, 172
Southport, 133
Southwark, 103
Spalding, 34, 166, 187, 195
Spencer, 15, 29, 63, 84
Spencer, Countess, 27, 79–81, 84
Spencer, Earl, The, 79–80, 84
Spencer, Gabriel, 127
Spencer, John, 19, 20, 53
Spencer, Mr., 177
Spencer, Sir Robert, 18, 20
Spiller, James, 119
Spilsby, 46
Spilsbury, Miss, 193
Spotted Indian Youth, 177
Spread Eagle, 54
Squire, William, 89
St. Albans, 80
St. Andrew's Hospital, 123
St. Giles, 62
St. Giles Square, 147, 149
St. Giles Street, 45, 62–3
St. Gregory on the Green, 96
St. Ives, 35, 155
St. James Palace, 79
St. James Theatre, 133
St. John's Church, Stamford, 166
St. Matthew's Church, 98
St. Michael's Church, 98
Stafford, 93
Stamford, 20, 34, 46, 77, 83, 153, 163–7,
    173, 177, 188, 192, 195
Stamford Arts Centre, 167
Stamford Theatre, 163–7, 177
Stamford Chess Billiards and News Club,
    167
Stanari, Mr., 190
Stanford, Mrs., 164
Stanley, Mr., 191
Stanton, Mr., 57, 60
Stanton, Mrs., 57

Steele, John, 36
Stevens, Mr., 74, 187
Stevenson, Joshua, 171
Stilton, 69
Stockwood, Rev. John, 92
Stony Stratford, 69
Strand, 84
Stratford-upon-Avon, 29, 66, 71–2, 81, 97, 105, 170, 179, 200
Stratton, Mr., 179
Strickland, Mrs., 178
Strolling, 154–5
Sun Music Hall, 100
Sutton, Miss, 73
Swan Inn, 39
Swan Inn, Newport Pagnell, 155
Swan Inn, Wellingborough, 157–9
Swan and Castle, 39
Swan and Helmet, 38
Swan and Talbot, 46
Swindall, Mr., 179

Talbot Inn, 36, 38
Tankerville, Mr., 162
Tarry, Isaac, 201
Tate, William, 20
Tattershall, 46
Tasmania, 121
Tavistock, Marquess of, 60, 191
Taylor, Mr., 124, 150
Taylor, Mrs., 159
Taylor and Robertson Company, 177, 188
Teeton, Mr., 171
Terriss, Ellaline, 134
Terry, Ellen, 39
Tester, Dolly, 136, 138
Thaw, Alice, 121
Theatre, Marefair, 34, 84, 91, 97, 100, 122–3, 126, 131, 201
Theatre Royal and Opera House, 44, 55, 97, 99, 100, 103–4, 123, 133, 175, 201
Thespian Dictionary, 163
Thomas, William, 74
Thomson, Mr., 150
Thompson, Mr., 171
Thompson, Samuel, 61
Thornton, Mr., 162
Thursby, Ann, 79, 81, 83
Thursby, John Harvey, 83
Thursby, Mr. and Mrs., 81
Thursby, Mrs., 66
Thursby, Neville, 84
Thursby, Sir George, 84
Thursby, Rev. William, 83
Tilliard, Mr., 190
Titchmarsh, 40
Tollers Company, 36
Towcester, 156, 158–60, 183

Town Council, 97, 104
Town Crier, 183
Town Gaol, 62–3, 122–4, 150
Town Hall, 34, 93, 96, 99, 114, 118, 201
Trasler, Mr., 62–3
Trent Bridge, 153
Truwhitt, Miss, 150
Tuthill, Mr. and Mrs., 190, 198
Tye, Joseph, 181
Tyers, Mr., 124
Twiddy, Mr., 190
Twiss, Francis, 145

Upper Ossory, Earl of, 155

Valentine, Miss, 198
Vaughan, Miss, 150
Vehetsley, Mr., 198
Ventnor, 130
Vernsberg, Mrs., 170
Vestris, Madame, 119–20
Victoria Hall, Kettering, 98
Victoria, Queen, 120, 132
Vine Inn, Wisbeach (Wisbech), 194
Virginia, U.S.A., 29

Wake, Lady, 179
Wake, Sir William, 69
Wakefield, 163
Wakefield Lawn, 46, 80, 137
Waldron, Mr., 180–1, 183, 198
Wallaker, Mr., 170
Walpole, 79, 80, 108, 110
Walsh, Katie, 137
Walsall, 103, 145
Walton, Miss, 183
Wantage, 100, 175
Wantage, Lady, 33
Ward, Mr., 54
Ward, John, 145, 154
Ware, R. Redding, 130
Warner, Mr., 150
Warwick, 38, 46, 77, 119, 178, 183
Warwick Company, 47–9
Warwickshire, 113, 177
Watson, Mr., 77, 119, 158, 183
Watson, Mrs., 162
Watson, Sir Edward, 20
Waylett, Mr., 171
Webb, Major, 182
Weldon, 134
Welby, Lady, 193
Welcombe, 82
Wellingborough, 39, 46, 68, 157–9, 191
Wemyss, F. C., 126, 190
Wesley, John, 61
Wessex, 159–60
Westminster Abbey, 84

West and Woolford, 191
Weston Favell, 81, 83
Whipping, 106, 112–13
Whitaker, Mr., 41
White, Mr., 150
White, Mrs., 150, 172
White Hart, 167
White Horse Inn, Baldock, 187
White, Sir Thomas Wollaston, 172
White, Stanford, 121
Whitehouse, Mrs., 133
Whitfield, Mr., 166, 187
Whiting, George S., 98
Whitley, Elizabeth, 166
Whitley, James Augustus (Jemmy), 57, 66, 112, 120, 128, 144, 153, 163–72, 177–8, 187
Whitley, Mrs. Cassandra, 164, 166
Whitley and Herbert's Company, 162
Whitley, Judith, 166
Whittlebury, 134
Whitworth, Henry Billington, 122–3
Wightman, Mr., 119
Wilde, George De, 63
Wiehe, Dagmar, 134
Wiehe, Col. F. G. A., 134
Wilkinson, Tate, 58, 90, 93, 171–2, 177, 188
Wilkinson's Company, 177
William III, 67
William IV, 130
Williams, Harcourt, 169

Williams, Bransby, 39
Williams, Mr., 41
Williamson, J., 98
Winchester, 107
Winchilsea, Earl of, 134
Windsor, 20, 178
Windsor Lodge, 46
Wingfield, Sir Robert, 20
Winston, James, 177, 186–7, 192–3
Winteringham, 46
Winter's School, Miss, 195
Wisbeach (Wisbech), 35, 187, 194
Woburn, 155, 191
Wolverhampton, 147, 163
Wood Hill, 34
Woodward, Goodwin, 103
Woolford (West and Woolford), 191
Woolley's Boarding School, 69
Woolpack Inn, 177
Worcester, 33–4, 73, 115, 119, 137, 145–6, 163
Worksop, 17
Wright, Mr., 178, 190–1, 193
Wycherley, 121
Wymington, 100

Yarde-Buller, Hon. J. B., 136
Yardley Gobion, 43
Yeomanry, 182
Yohe, May, 136
York, 17, 29, 33, 35, 46, 93, 171, 177, 179